D0496501

Building a Portfolio

Early Years Care and Education S/NVQ Level

Townsend

LEVEL TWO

Units C1, C4, C8, C9, E1, E2, M3 and P1

Illustrated by Cathy Hughes

About the author

Mary Townsend started her career as a nursery nurse working in day nurseries. While her family were young she worked as a childminder and ran a playgroup for five years. She then trained as an infant teacher and worked in infant schools for 14 years. She went on to lecture in a college of further education on the NNEB and ADCE courses. She became co-ordinator of the NVQ assessment centre at the college, and an internal and external verifier for NVQ. She is now an independent training consultant, working with national organisations to support colleges and training providers in improving the quality of their training. She is deeply committed to raising standards in the early years sector and firmly believes that where they are being well delivered and assessed NVQs are making a significant contribution to achieving high quality care and education for our children.

While we have made every effort to contact people whose articles are featured in this book, we apologise if any authors have not been notified.

Published by Step Forward Publishing Limited
25 Cross Street, Leamington Spa CV32 4PX   Tel: 01926 420046   www.practicalpreschool.com
© Step Forward Publishing Limited 2003
Building a Portfolio for Early Years Care and Education S/NVQ Level 2   ISBN: 1-902438-87-6

Contents

Chapter 4: C8 Implement planned activities for sensory and intellectual development

Element C8.1 Provide activities, equipment and materials for creative play

Element C8.2 Play games with children

Element C8.3 Assist children with cooking activities

Element C8.4 Provide opportunities and equipment for manipulative play

Element C8.5 Examine objects of interest with children

contents

Note: Most articles have been published previously in *Practical Pre-School.*

Chapter 1

Introduction

You've decided you want to work with children. That's good! It's a rewarding career but it's also very hard work. You need lots of patience and there's a lot to learn. You've made a good start by deciding to do a National Vocational Qualification (NVQ) Level 2 in Early Years Care and Education.

You will have registered with an assessment centre – in other words a college or training provider which has been approved to deliver NVQs. They will find you a placement, or you may be lucky enough to have a job already. You can also work towards an NVQ as a volunteer, or combine a part-time job with voluntary work to get more experience. You will spend most of your time working with children and learning on the job. The great thing about an NVQ is that it's based on the work you do every day. You will normally spend one day a week at the training centre, where you will gain the knowledge you need to help you work with children.

This qualification will help you to gain a better understanding of children's needs - it will help you to learn about why you do certain things with children and for children.

When you have finished your training, you will have a nationally recognised qualification which means you can work as a nursery assistant in an early years setting. You will have the chance to go on to do more training at Level 3 and beyond if you want to. Early years provision is growing fast in the UK, and many more qualified early years workers are needed.

What are NVQs?

NVQs are based on the National Occupational Standards which have been agreed by experts working in a range of early years settings. They cover all the things an early years worker is expected to be able to do. There are three levels - Level 2 for people working under supervision, as an assistant or voluntary worker; Level 3 for people working under their own initiative as supervisors; and Level 4 for people in a managerial role, or very experienced practitioners.

NVQs are not like other qualifications. Instead of doing a course at college, you gather your own evidence that you can do all of the things you need to do to keep children safe and

happy, and help them to develop. A lot of your evidence will come from what you are doing with the children every day. You will put all your evidence into a folder, or portfolio.

For Level 2 there are eight mandatory units - that means ones which you have to do - and you choose two optional units to suit your own job role and interests. What you choose will depend on which kind of setting you work in, or which area of work you are most interested in. You should by now have been given a copy of your candidate handbook with full details of the units. Don't be put off by your first look through it. It looks complicated, but once you have worked through one unit, it gets easier! You don't have to start at the beginning and work through the units in a particular order. You can start with the unit you feel most confident about.

> *'I didn't really think about why I did things before, but now I think much more about how it is going to help the children.'*
>
> NVQ candidate

You may already have had an introductory session at your centre when the staff will have explained what NVQs are all about, and how the centre operates. Each centre works differently, although they all use the same early years standards. The centre will choose an assessor who will usually work with you throughout your NVQ. Your assessor may be working in your setting and be able to see you often, or she may just visit you once a month. You will get to know your assessor really well, and you will work closely with her or him. She will help you to plan what sort of evidence you will need to provide and watch you working with the children.

That means she will watch you doing activities with the children, such as painting, singing or playing a game, or helping children during routines, such as going to the toilet, washing their hands and eating their dinner. She does this to make sure you can do it competently. She will sit nearby, so that she can see and hear what's going on, but she won't join in. She will try not to make it obvious to the children that she's watching. She will write a record of what she observes, for you to keep in your portfolio as evidence. The only time she would interfere is if the children's safety was at risk. Being watched will seem a bit strange at first, but your assessor will put you at ease before you start by talking to you about what you'll be doing, and helping you to feel more relaxed. You'll quickly get used to being observed.

The aim of this book is to help you to gather your evidence from the things you do every day with the children, rather than working through set tasks and assignments which don't always suit your situation. That means it will be very individual and meaningful to you, which is what NVQ is all about. We will look at the different ways you can gather the evidence and give you some useful forms to use. We will also give you some resources to help you with your planning. This book covers the eight mandatory units but not the optional ones. Throughout the book, we will be referring to your candidate handbook. This is the book which contains the Early Years National Occupational Standards, which you will have been given when you registered. You will always need that with you.

You need to bear in mind that your centre may want you to work in a particular way, and in that case you may not have the freedom to gather the evidence in the way we recommend, but you will still find the book very useful.

'I understand a lot more now. I can put it into practice straight away because I'm working with the children every day.'
NVQ candidate

How do NVQs work?

NVQ Level 2 is made up of eight mandatory units and two optional units. Each unit covers a particular area of early years work. The mandatory units are:

C1: Support children's physical development needs

C4: Support children's social and emotional development

C8: Implement planned activities for sensory and intellectual development

C9: Implement planned activities for the development of language and communication skills

E1: Maintain an attractive, stimulating and reassuring environment for children

E2: Maintain the safety and security of children

M3: Contribute to the achievement of organisational requirements

P1: Relate to parents

Each unit is broken down into elements, which list all the things you need to be able to do, to show you are competent in that area of work.

Let's take an example - Unit C8. The title of the unit is 'Implement planned activities for sensory and intellectual development'.

That means, plan some activities to do with the children to help them develop their senses - sight, hearing, taste, smell and feel - and to help them learn. These are things you do every day with the children. Find the unit in your candidate handbook. Read the list of elements at the beginning of the unit. Don't worry about all the other reading at the beginning of the unit yet. We will go back to that.

These are the elements:

C8.1 Provide activities, equipment and materials for creative play

C8.2 Play games with children

C8.3 Assist children with cooking activities

C8.4 Provide opportunities and equipment for manipulative play

C8.5 Examine objects of interest with children

Many of the activities you carry out every day with the children will provide the evidence you will need. We will show you later how to gather your evidence. If you're not sure what some of them mean, the 'Notes on this element' will help you by giving examples. You will find these in each element in the handbook.

You will notice that each element has two main parts - performance criteria and range. The **performance criteria** (we will refer to these as PCs) are all the things you need to show you can do for that element. Sometimes they are written in a way that's difficult to understand so you need to break them into bits - for example, in C8.1, the first PC states 'Activities, equipment and materials selected are consistent with the curriculum plan and the children's developmental levels'. That sounds complicated, but you can break the statement down. 'Activities, equipment and materials selected ...': these are all the things you choose to do with the children, and the equipment and materials you use to do them. The next bit is: 'are consistent with the curriculum plan'. The glossary at the back of the handbook, which explains some of the words you may not understand, describes curriculum as 'all the activities and experiences which enable children to learn' and curriculum plans as 'what is to be done in the long, medium and short term so that children will achieve the learning outcomes'.

Most early years settings plan all the activities they are going to do with the children. They may make long-term plans for the whole year to make sure that they are covering all the areas of learning to help children learn and develop. Then they may have medium-term plans, such as a plan for a topic like 'Colours' or 'Ourselves' which could last a week, or a month. Lastly, they may have short-term plans - for a day, or even just for one activity. These are the ones you are most likely to be asked to do. For example, you might plan a painting activity, which fits in with a medium-term plan on the topic of 'Colours', or a number game, which fits in with the long-term plan to help children to develop an understanding of numbers. This is what the PC means when it says 'consistent with the curriculum plan'.

Learning outcomes, or Early Learning Goals as they are now called, are what we would expect children to manage to do during the Foundation Stage - that is, from the age of three to the end of Reception class. They are described in the *Curriculum Guidance for the Foundation Stage*, which is a document produced by the Department for Education and Skills (DfES) setting out what most children should be able to do by the end of their Reception year at school. Your setting should have a copy.

Now the last bit: 'and (consistent with) the children's developmental levels'. It's important that the activities you provide are right for the child's stage of development. For instance, you wouldn't give a baby Lego to play with because they put everything in their mouth, and could choke on the little pieces, but a four-year-old would enjoy building with it, and it would help to develop their manipulative skills.

Useful tip

Some performance criteria can seem very complicated. If you break them down into bits, as we have shown you, it will help to make them clearer. It will also stop you missing vital bits.

Now look at the **range**. This means all the different situations you may have to work in. For example, in C8.1 you need to show that you can organise all the different ways children play creatively, like painting and drawing, sand, modelling with dough, and so on. You need to think about what protective covering and clothing you might need, or any special equipment for children with disabilities such as limited vision. You also need to give children experiences outside as well as inside. The range will be different for each element, but by the time you have finished all the units, you will have covered every aspect of child care and development you are likely to come across.

This does not mean that you have done all of these things in your setting. Sometimes, you will not be able to show that you have actually carried out all of the range, but you will need to show evidence that you could do it if you had to.

Your assessor will want to observe as many of the performance criteria and range as possible, and she will plan with you when and how she will do that. She will also plan with you how you can provide the rest of the evidence you need. We will look at the different sorts of evidence you can use later. If you need any help with ideas or activities to provide for the element or unit you are working on, you will find some useful resources in each chapter. For example, if you need ideas about creative play, have a look at pages 98-101.

There are two other important sections in each unit which you need to know about. At the front of your candidate handbook you will find a section called the 'Statement of underlying principles'. They include:

◆ the welfare of the child

◆ keeping children safe

◆ working in partnership with parents/families

◆ children's learning and development

◆ equality of opportunity

◆ anti-discrimination

◆ celebrating diversity

◆ confidentiality

◆ working with other professionals

◆ the reflective practitioner

These are the principles which you must always work for if you are committed to giving children the best possible care and education in their early years. They have taken into account the United Nations Convention on the Rights of the Child and the Children Act 1989. You may have had them explained to you in your induction, but if not, you need to go back to the front of your candidate handbook to find a full explanation of what each one means. If you can, talk them through with your assessor. It would be also be useful to discuss them with your colleagues in your work setting.

When you're gathering your evidence for each unit, you **must always** think about the underlying principles. To help you do this, there is a grid at the beginning of each unit which shows which underlying principles, or values, you need to show evidence of in each element. (Throughout this book, we will refer to them as values, for short.)

Go back to the beginning of Unit C8 and look for the grid called 'Values statement' under the heading 'Principles of good practice'. Under each element it shows you which PCs refer to some aspect of the principles, or values. Try using the grid now to find the relevant element and PC, and think about how you might show that you know about the values. If you have any problems with this, go through it with your assessor.

Here's an example:

Go to the column headed **Element 3.** Look down the grid until you come to number 8. This means **performance criteria 8** in Element 3.

Look across to the left to see which value it covers. You will find **celebrating diversity.**

Now go to Element 3 in your handbook (headed C8.3 Assist children with cooking activities) and look at PC8. It says 'Aspects of the activity reflect children's own culture and extend their knowledge of other cultures'.

How would you cover this? You might do a cold cooking activity with the children, such as making sandwiches. This is a good opportunity to talk to the children about what they like in their sandwiches, and what other sort of bread they eat at home (remember to check whether any children have allergies). You can also use it as an opportunity to look at and taste different sorts of bread from other cultures, such as chapattis, pitta bread, and so on, to make children more aware and positive about differences.

Remember!
Celebrating diversity is not just about celebrating festivals like Diwali or Chinese New Year. It's about building it into everything you do so that it becomes a natural part of the children's experience, not something strange and different.

Knowledge evidence

Last of all, we need to look at the **description of knowledge, understanding and skills.** You will find this at the end of each unit, after the last element. This is where you need to provide evidence that you have the knowledge and understanding to show that you know **why** you do the things you do with the children in your care. This section looks a bit daunting, but don't panic! You will be able to cover a lot of it through the evidence you will be collecting for each element. If you're doing a modern apprenticeship, you will cover the knowledge through a technical certificate, which is a course approved by the awarding body.

This section is divided under four main headings:

- Development

- Curriculum practice

- Equipment, materials, environment

- Relationships

However, you will find that there is quite a lot of overlap from one section to another, and we will show you how you can cut down on the work by taking several points together. To help you, we have included the reference numbers of the relevant statements in each of the elements in the chapters, and explained briefly what you need to show that you understand. Some of the statements are relevant for more than one element. Where this is the case, we have put the statement in the first element it appears in, and put the other relevant elements in brackets. Talk about this with your assessor if you don't understand.

Most assessment centres will provide teaching sessions in the daytime for Level 2 learners who are not employed, which your placement supervisor must allow you to attend. If you are employed that may be more difficult, but you are entitled to time for study. You may be released in the day, or you may be able to go to evening sessions. Many centres have learning packs which you can use at home, and will usually recommend some textbooks. You will get a lot out of the sessions, and from sharing your ideas with other candidates, especially if you don't have much experience of childcare.

Your local Early Years Development and Childcare Partnership (EYDCP) will probably also have courses you can go on. Your setting should be sent information about these. Your manager will probably be able to tell you about them. If not, ring your local children's information service or education authority and ask what is available. It's important that you do training on first aid, food hygiene and child protection with experts in these fields. Although it is not a requirement for NVQ to take a recognised course in these areas, all early years practitioners should know about them really well.

The resources in this book will help you with your underpinning knowledge. There are some good practical ideas as well as some articles which will help you to think about your own practice and improve it. We have placed each article in the unit it's most relevant for but many of the articles are relevant for more than one unit.

Try to include as much knowledge evidence as you can into your work-based evidence. We will explain how you can do this in the next few pages. If there are still gaps in your evidence, you can write paragraphs on each relevant point. You should aim to make this short, clear and to the point, and wherever possible, use examples from your own work practice. Don't copy chunks from books, and don't include photocopied pages.

If you are not very confident about writing, ask your assessor if you can answer more questions orally (that is, tell her the answers) and she can write them down, or include an audio-tape of your answers as evidence. Your centre will normally be able to give you extra support to improve your writing skills if you need it.

> **note:**
> This book does not aim to give you all of the underpinning knowledge you will need for your NVQ. It is a resource book and guide, to help you to gather your evidence for each unit.

Gathering evidence

NVQ is different to other qualifications in that, instead of taking an examination, you show that you are competent by collecting evidence of what you do in your day-to-day work with the children. Your assessor will decide whether your evidence proves that you are competent.

Your candidate handbook has an explanation of the different sorts of evidence you can use. You will find this in the section at the beginning called 'The assessment process'.

There are two main types of evidence:

- Performance evidence - what you can do

- Knowledge evidence - what you know and understand

At the beginning of each unit there is a description of the different ways you can collect your evidence. It's not the same for every unit, but it will always be from the following approved methods listed in your candidate handbook:

- Direct observation by a qualified assessor

- Questioning

- Witness testimony

- Work plans

- Inspection of the setting by a qualified assessor

- Reflective accounts

- Log books, diaries and notes

- Work products

- Case studies, assignments or projects

- Child observations

- Simulation, role play or skills rehearsals

- Skills transferable from other performance

- Past achievements

- Formal written or oral tests/extended questioning

To make it easier for you to collect the evidence, we will look at some useful forms you can use. Your assessment centre may have their own forms, so check with them first. Evidence does **not** have to be written. If you are worried about doing a lot of writing, you can record your evidence onto a tape recorder, for example, or use a word processor.

Your assessor will ask you oral questions. You may be able to arrange with her to do extra questioning. This will depend on the amount of time she is allowed for assessment because, of course, it will be more time-consuming for her. If you think that you may be eligible for extra support, talk to your assessor. Many centres are able to get extra funding to help candidates with additional needs. Some assessment centres have access to a range of specialised equipment available for people with disabilities.

The following pages show you what sort of evidence you can collect. We have given examples to show you how to use the forms. There are also some blank forms which you can photocopy.

Types of evidence you can use

Direct observation

The most important type of evidence is direct observation by a qualified assessor, when your assessor watches you working. You will see in the section on performance evidence in your candidate handbook that there are some PCs (performance criteria) which must be observed. Your assessor will also have to observe at least one aspect of each range category. For the rest of the range, PCs and knowledge, you need to provide other types of evidence from the list above. Your assessor will write down what she observes on an **observation record** which is provided by the assessment centre. She will give you this to keep in your portfolio. She will cross reference it to the PCs, range and knowledge evidence. An example of what it might look like is given below:

Date	OBSERVATION RECORD	PCs/ Range	Knowledge evidence
20.10.02	I observed Lucy setting out a painting activity for children in the Reception class (4- to 5-year-olds). She set up 4 easels in the messy area, which had a wipeable floor and was away from the main play area. She had 4 aprons ready, and paint of various colours, including several shades of skin colour she had mixed, and several colours of paper. She talked to the children first about what she wanted them to paint - a picture of their friend. She got them to look at each other and talked about colour of eyes, skin, hair and clothes. Then she asked the children to put on their aprons, giving help where necessary. The children chose the paper and the colours they wanted. Lucy gave them freedom to paint their picture in their own way, giving encouragement as they worked. As each child finished she praised their efforts, and asked them about their picture. She wrote down what they said, ready to label them later for the display she was doing. She supervised them as they washed their hands, making sure they did it properly. She got them to hang their aprons up. **Note:** The knowledge evidence is not necessarily fully covered, but will contribute to the evidence required.	C8.1.2,3,R3 C8.1.5,7 C9.2.2,7 C4.3.1,6,8 C8.1.6 C4.3,R3,5 C8.1.9	C8 KE8,21 C8 KE8 C8 KE14 C9KE5,10,19 C4 KE7,12 C8 KE11,20,27 C4 KE26 C9 KE5,10

Signed .... (assessor) *A N Other* .... (candidate) L Smith

Questioning

Your assessor will often ask you questions about what she has observed, to check your understanding. She will write down answers to any questions she asks you. She will give you these to keep in your portfolio. The question sheet may be a similar format to the one below:

Date	ORAL QUESTION RECORD	PCs/ Range	Knowledge evidence
20.10.02	**Why did you choose this activity?** Because we're doing a theme on 'Ourselves' this term and I'm going to put a display of the children's pictures up on the wall.	C8.1.1	C8 KE7
	I notice you mixed several skin colours. Why was that? Because we have children from a variety of cultures here, and it's important that they can paint their skin the right colour. We encourage the children to be very positive about differences.		C8 KE20,27 C4 KE7,12
	What did the children gain from the activity? They learned to look at each other more carefully and think about everyone being different. They're being creative and learning their colours. They're developing fine motor skills.		C8 KE1,3,7,8 C8 KE12,14,23
	How did you make sure the children were safe and protected? I made sure the easels were fastened properly. We're in the messy area, which I can wipe down easily if there are any spills. The paint pots have non-spill lids. I made sure the children had aprons on to keep their clothes clean.	C8.1.3,8	C8 KE21
	How would you help a child with a visual impairment to enjoy painting? I'd do finger and hand painting with her so that she could feel the paint. If she had some sight I would use contrasting colours that she could see more easily.		C8 KE28

Signed..........*A N Other*.......................................(assessor)   L Smith ....(candidate)

Witness testimony

For things which your assessor is not able to observe easily, or to cover areas of the range, you can ask other people you work with to write a witness testimony. If you're a childminder you can ask parents and other professionals who visit you to write a witness testimony. You may need to explain the National Occupational Standards to them, so that what they write is relevant. You will need to have a list of people who have supplied witness testimonies in your portfolio, with a note of their job role or status. An example is given below.

Date	WITNESS TESTIMONY	PCs/ Range	Knowledge evidence
8.12.02	Elliot has been working with the one- to two-year-olds for the past month. He plays with them really well, and is very good at telling the parents what the children have been doing in the nursery. He is friendly with the parents and always greets them and their children cheerfully when they arrive. He remembers to ask them about anything we need to know, and records it carefully in the home-nursery diary. He takes account of this when caring for the children. If there is any information he needs to pass on, he does so. One day a parent asked him about a child's medicine. He knew that this was outside of his responsibility so he referred the parent on to his supervisor.

The parents think he's great! | P1.1.1,3,6 P1.1, R1,5, 7,8

P1.1.2

P1.2.1,3

P1.1.4 P1.2.4 | P1 KE7

P1 KE6

P1 KE1,2 |

Signed...S Kaur...........................witness   ....E Harding..(candidate)

Status of witness........................Nursery Manager..

Work plans

If you're involved in planning the routine and curriculum in your setting, you can use your plans as evidence. If you do this, you will need to write a brief explanation of how you were involved in the planning. It would be useful extra evidence to say how the plans were put into practice, and to evaluate their effectiveness - what the children gained from them, whether you would change them next time and so on.

If you're not involved in the planning, you will need to produce some evidence that you are able to plan. The activity plan format below (blank form on pages 28-29) will help you to do this. If you answer the questions thoroughly, this activity plan will cover much of the knowledge evidence you will need.

ACTIVITY PLAN

NAME: *Jasmine Tate* **DATE:** *15.01.03* **ACTIVITY:** *Display books to encourage children to use them*
AGE OF CHILDREN: *3 - 4yrs*

Before the activity:

Describe the activity you are planning. Describe how it fulfils the values statements for the element or unit you are working on.

I'm going to the library to choose books, then I will set them out in the book corner. I want to include dual language books, books with different sorts of pictures, traditional stories, books which show men and women in non-traditional roles, and books with people from a variety of cultures and people with a disability as the main character.

Why have you chosen this activity? What do you think the children will gain from it? *(Think about areas of development - physical, intellectual, language, emotional and social.)*

I chose it because it will help the children's intellectual development - learning about the world through books. Language - because I'll tell some stories and talk to the children about the books. They'll see different sorts of language and print.
Social - the children will share the books, and they'll learn about respecting differences in people.

Which children will be involved? Why? *(Will it be free choice? Have you targeted children who need particular help with, for instance, colour recognition?)*

All of the children will get a chance to see the books. I'll take groups of children in and look at the books with them, but they can choose to look at them at other times, too.

What equipment/resources/preparation do you need?

Get the books from the library. Tidy up the book corner. Put away the usual books to make room for the new ones. Display them nicely so that the children will be encouraged to look at them.

What will you do during the activity? *(Language you will use, help you will give, etc.)*

I'll encourage the children to be careful with the books. I'll sit in the book corner and talk about the books while the children look at them, and read the stories if they want me to.

After the activity:

Did the activity go well? Why? If not, why not?

The children enjoyed looking at the books and we read a few of them to the whole group at story time. I got a good variety which covered most of the things I wanted to. Some of them were a bit too old for the children. I didn't manage to find a book with a person with a disability.

Would you change it next time? If so, how and why?

I'd perhaps ring the library in advance next time, and tell them what I was looking for. I'd spend more time choosing the books. But the activity itself went really well and the children got a lot out of it. I'd like to take the children to the library, too.

ACTIVITY PLAN continued

How would you adapt the activity for older/younger children? For children with additional needs or disabilities?
I'd have to choose the books for the different age of children. For a child with poor sight I'd choose books with textures and sounds. For a child with poor hearing, bright colours, pop-up and lift-the-flap books. Children with poor muscle control would need board books or cloth books.

What did the children gain from the activity? Was it what you thought they would?
The children got a lot of enjoyment from looking at the books. They learned about different people and languages. They talked to each other a lot about the stories and listened to stories. They shared the books well.

What did you learn from it?
How important it is to choose the right books for the age of the children, and a good variety. That the library is a good place to get books. That you need to encourage some children to look at books, otherwise they never do.

Which PCs/range/knowledge evidence does it cover?
C9.4.1,2,3,4,5,8 R1,2,3,4,5,6,7,8,9,10 KE 7,15,20,21,22

Signed ......K.Sandhu................. (candidate)

If anyone observed you, ask them to sign that this a true record, and to comment if possible.

Signed ...M. Wright................... **Role:** ...Supervisor...............

Comment:
Kuldeep chose a good range of books, and set them up attractively. She interacted well with the children while they were using the books. The children gained a great deal from the experience.

Inspection of the setting

For some units, such as E2 which covers health and safety, your assessor will need to inspect your setting. She will ask you questions about how far you are responsible for health and safety in your setting, and whether you understand the reasons for things being the way they are. She will usually record this on the direct observation and oral question records.

Reflective accounts

These are a really useful way of writing (or talking) about things you have done which your assessor was not able to see. Perhaps something unexpected happened in the nursery, or you dealt with an accident, or a query from a parent. It could cover areas of the range. It's useful to try and identify which elements or units it will be relevant for, then you can make sure you cover the relevant details. There is no need to use a special format, you can write on ordinary A4 paper. (Alternatively, you can put your reflective account onto audiotape.) When you write your account, try to explain why you dealt with the incident the way you did and what you learned from it. Don't forget to refer to the knowledge evidence section, and cover any relevant points. The NVQ aims to make early years workers into reflective practitioners who are always thinking about the way they do things, so that they can improve. None of us ever stop learning, no matter how experienced we are.

Log books, diaries and notes

These can be used to record your day-to-day work with the children. You can, if you want to, keep a daily diary, but they can become repetitive. It's useful to have a sample of your routine, but once you have written that for perhaps a week, think more carefully about what you write.

You may find it helpful to carry a notebook around with you to record things which happen during the day. You can then write anything relevant in more detail in quiet times during the day, or when you get home. Try to pick out the main events rather than list all the routine things you do day after day. To record these events you can use the free description format of a reflective account, or keep your notes in a diary or notebook, or you may find the example of a candidate diary below helpful because it's a bit more structured.

CANDIDATE DIARY

NAME: Sonya Winters

DATE: 10.12.02   **INCIDENT:** Minor conflict between two children

What happened? Who was involved?
(Don't use names - number of staff/children/parents)

My supervisor and I were supervising free play with a group of eight children aged 3 to 4 years . Two children were building with the wooden bricks. Julie started throwing bricks at Sanjeet's building. Sanjeet pushed Julie away and shouted at her.

How did you react? What did you do?

I said to Julie that it was unkind to break Sanjeet's building, because he had worked hard to build it. I said 'Let's help him to build it back up again, and then I'll help you to build something yourself'. Julie happily helped with the building, and then went on to another activity.

Why did you do it this way?

Because I wanted Julie to see that it was unkind to spoil someone else's game, but I didn't want to make a big thing of it. I thought it would be better if I said we'd both help because it would calm the situation.

Did it work? If not, why not?

Yes, everyone calmed down

What have you learned from it? What would you do differently next time?
(Think about the values statements)

I learned that it's better to explain things to children and get them to think about their actions, and then to do something positive to put it right. And to be calm.

Which PCs/range/knowledge does this relate to?

C4.2.1,3,4,5,7 R3,7 C4.5.4 R1,3

If anyone observed you, ask them to sign that this is an accurate record
and to make a comment.

Witness...C.Black.....................

Status ...Supervisor.....................

Witness comment (if applicable)
Sonya handled this situation calmly and quickly settled the argument

Work products

You can use things like:

- policies and procedures of your setting - you must write a short note to show either how you have been involved in preparing them or how you use them in your daily work.

- curriculum plans - write a note to say how you were involved in planning and carrying out the activities, and what the children gained from them.

- examples of activities you have done with the children - only if you feel they are needed to support the evidence. Don't include a lot of children's work.

- menus, charts, details of outings and special events - explain how you were involved in preparing these.

- letters to parents, children's records, child observations and anything else you feel is a relevant piece of evidence - you **must** get permission from your supervisor or employer, and **always** remove names and check that the child or adult will not be recognised from anything in the piece of evidence, to keep it confidential.

- photographs of yourself working with the children, with a caption saying what the activity is, and how you are involved. Some centres don't let you take photographs, or only of the backs of children, so that they cannot be recognised.

Remember!
Whatever evidence you use from your workplace, do check with your employer that you can use it first.

Case studies, assignments or projects

This covers a range of other evidence, such as:

- assignments and projects set by your centre:

  - your centre may ask you at the beginning of the NVQ programme to carry out a project to cover all aspects of child development, because several of the units ask you to show your knowledge of this, and it's easier to cover it all together.

  - your centre may ask you to do assignments or answer questions to show your knowledge in each of the units.

- written work to cover areas of the underpinning knowledge and range which you have not covered with other, work-based evidence, perhaps because it is outside your experience or you needed to do some reading or research.

- a case study of a particular child, carried out over a period of time.

Child observations

You do not have to do child observation for Level 2, but you do need to get into the habit of observing children, because it's an important skill. You may be involved in filling in children's development records in your setting, so you need to be able to observe carefully. Observations help you learn a lot about child development, and individual children's needs, and they help you to plan appropriate activities for your children. They can also be used as evidence for some of the units. You need to gain permission from the parents before you include observations in your portfolio. Some employers ask for parents' permission for this when their child joins the setting, so check what the position is in your setting. A helpful format for you to use when you record your observations is shown (see right):

The observation

Joshua and Claire are both pouring dry sand into the sand wheel. They each use a spade to pick up the sand and pour it in, and laugh as the wheel goes round. Claire puts her hand under the wheel to feel the sand as it pours out. Joshua says 'I'm going to pour lots in. Let's fill the buckets'. He starts to fill a bucket, using the spade. Claire does the same, but then says 'I'm going to make a sandcastle'. Joshua fills his bucket and pours it into the wheel. 'Look how fast it's going!' Claire fills her bucket, pats it with the spade and turns it over, but the sand all falls out. 'Oh!' Claire said. Joshua says, 'You can't make sandcastles it's too dry. Try the wet sand over there'. (pointing) Claire takes her bucket and spade to the wet sand tray. This time she fills her bucket, pats it down and tips it over and makes a good sandcastle. 'Look Joshua!' she says, smiling. Joshua smiles and runs off.

Evaluation

Joshua and Claire played well together. They talked to each other and shared the sand wheel. Joshua showed more understanding about the different properties of wet and dry sand. I would expect this, as he is older than Claire. He helped Claire by explaining that she needed wet sand to make sandcastles.

Evidence covered
C8.1.2,6 R1,6 C4.1,2,3,7

CHILD OBSERVATION

Candidate's name *Nasreen Ashrag*	**Date** *21.01.03*

Title of observation:

Playing in the sand

Aim of observation: *(Which aspect of child development/behaviour are you aiming to observe?)*

To observe how children relate to each other and what they learn

First name of child: *(or fictitious name)* *Joshua*   **Age:** *(yrs & mths)* *3 yrs 8 mths*
           Claire   *3 yrs 4 months*

Description of setting: *(where observation is taking place, number of staff, children, equipment available, etc.)*

Sand tray in wet area. 2 children playing in the sand, 12 others playing with other activities. 3 adults supervising and me observing

The observation: Write this on a separate piece of paper, or other format you have chosen. Write what you actually observed in detail, using present tense (see left).

Evaluation: Comment on what you learned from the observation - link this to your aims.
Evaluate what the child's needs are, and make recommendations for future planning.

Signatures: Sign your observation and ask someone who witnessed the observation to sign it if possible.

Signed.............*S. Bright*.............(candidate)   **Signed**............*Anne Other*............(witness)

Simulation, role play, skills rehearsal

If you're not able to show a particular competence in your workplace - for instance, if you don't have the opportunity to bath babies or make feeds - you could be observed doing these things in a classroom situation. Or if you wanted to show your ability to handle a difficult situation with a parent which it would be inappropriate to observe, you could be observed in a role play. These are only used in exceptional circumstances.

Skills transferable from other performance

This can be used when it would be inappropriate to carry out direct observation, such as in the case of a child's disclosure of abuse. Some of the skills you would need in this situation may be observed in other work situations, such as how you

support a distressed child, how you communicate or how you handle difficult situations.

Remember!
It is absolutely vital that you keep all of your evidence together in your portfolio, with your assessment plans, and keep it in a safe place. Your centre will show you how they want the portfolio organised. It's usually best to divide the evidence unit by unit, and to number the pages.

Past achievements

You may have some past experience or other relevant qualifications when you start on your NVQ. You may be able to use some of this as evidence for your portfolio. Your centre will normally be able to advise you on this, and may take you through a process called accreditation of prior learning (APL) or accreditation of prior achievement (APA). In order to include any evidence from the past, you will need to prove that it is your own work, and that the information is not out of date. For instance, the work needs to show an awareness of equal opportunities and anti-discriminatory practice; information relating to child safety and protection must take account of the Children Act; and curriculum practice must take account of the Early Learning Goals or the National Curriculum. Evidence from the past cannot take the place of direct observation, but it can be used to cover parts of the range and knowledge evidence.

Formal written or oral tests/extended questioning

It is not usual to use tests as evidence for NVQ, because it is a qualification based on assessment of your competence in the workplace. However, there is a possibility that it may be used in the future for some aspects of assessment.

Personal skills review

Unit C8, Implement planned activities for sensory and intellectual development, is a good unit to start with, but it depends on your experience, the age of the children you work with and which areas you feel most confident about.

The personal skills review below will help you to identify the areas of your work you are confident about, and areas where you need to take some action to improve your competence. Read through the summary of units and elements and use the skills review first of all to help you to decide which unit to start with. You can photocopy and use the blank review sheet (Personal skills profile) below. You will need your candidate handbook to help you. Your assessor will be able to advise you about the best unit to start with.

When you have chosen a unit, do another personal skills review, this time based on the unit. You may find it easier to do this element by element at first.

◆ Go through the PCs and range for the element you are working on and fill in the appropriate boxes 1 - 5 on the review sheet.

◆ Go to the knowledge evidence section at the end of the unit and pick out the statements which are relevant to the element you are working on. Note which you need some help with in section 6 on the review sheet.

◆ Decide which activities you can arrange for your assessor to observe (box 7), and what other types of evidence you can use.

Note: As you become more confident, use this format to look at the whole unit rather than just one element.

The personal skills review will help you to be prepared for when you and your assessor plan your assessment. If you have done other units already and you feel confident to go straight into planning, you can leave this section out.

Action you may need to take:

If you have worked out which areas you may have difficulty with you will need to discuss with your assessor what you are going to do to put these right. For instance:

Section 2 You may simply need to practise an activity until you feel more confident. Ask your assessor or colleagues for help if necessary. If you need ideas for activities you will find the resources in this book helpful.

Section 3 You may need to ask your employer to give you the chance to move to a different age group, or to allow you to do things not normally within your role. You don't have to work with every age group to get an NVQ but if there are serious gaps, you may need to spend some time in another setting. For instance, if you work in a creche where you never have the same children for more than an hour, or you only work with children under two years old, or children aged seven to eight, you do need to consider getting wider experience.

Section 6 When you fill in this section, remember to check the knowledge evidence. We have identified the relevant knowledge evidence for each element in each of the chapters. You will normally need to do some training, as well as some reading and research to improve your understanding. Your centre will usually run training sessions, and/or provide learning materials and give individual support.

Section 4 If you want to use something from the past as evidence, your assessor will have to make sure that it is enough, takes account of current legislation, local regulations and best practice, and that it is authentic and reliable - that is, that it's your own work. Past experience cannot take the place of direct observation.

PERSONAL SKILLS PROFILE

I. Things I feel confident I can do

2. Things I don't feel confident about doing

3. Things I don't have the opportunity to do

4. Things I have done in the past

5. Areas of the range my assessor can observe

6. Things I don't understand (check knowledge evidence)

7. Possible activities my assessor could observe

8. Other types of evidence I could provide

Assessment planning

At this stage you will need to arrange a meeting with your assessor so that you can start planning your assessment. If this is your first unit, we would recommend that you plan together, but once you are confident, you can plan on your own if you want to. You will find a chapter on each of the mandatory units in this book, to help you with your planning. Your centre will have an assessment plan format, but here is an example (blank form to photocopy, page 32).

ASSESSMENT PLAN

Description of evidence/activity	To cover PCs/ Range	To cover Knowledge evidence	Date due
Choose a variety of books and display them in the book corner. Check the range for C9.4 to see what you need to include. Assessor will inspect the books and observe you using the books with the children. *Write an activity plan to prepare for the activity and evaluate afterwards. Write a list of the books you have chosen with reasons for your choice.* *Choose one book to use for a story with the whole group, and a few rhymes to finish off with. Assessor will observe you telling the story and singing the rhymes. If possible, use a visual aid with the story.* *Oral questions about care of the books and book corner; how you would enable a child with a disability or special need to take part; why it's important to provide positive images of different cultural groups and people with disabilities; length of times you would expect a 2-, 3- and 4-year-old to listen to a story* *(You may need to write a reflective account or use evidence from your diary to cover any areas not covered by the evidence above - to be discussed once you have completed the other evidence.)*	*C9.4.1-8 R1-11* *C9.5 1-9 R1-15*	*C9 KE1, 4, 6, 7, 8, 9, 11, 15, 16, 20, 21, 22*	*10.02.03*

Signed.............*K Sandhu*...............(candidate)   ....*M Wright*.............(assessor)

Date.............*12.01.03*.............   **Date**.............*12.01.03*.............

There are two ways of planning your assessment:

◆ You can take each element separately and plan an activity which your assessor will observe and other evidence you need for that element, **or:**

◆ Plan a whole session which will cover a range of activities and provide evidence for more than one element or unit - we sometimes call this **holistic assessment**. We recommend this way because it is a better use of your own and your assessor's time. We will explain this more fully in the section on cross referencing below.

Start by choosing an activity for your assessor to observe which will cover as many of the PCs and the range as possible. Remember to check which PCs must be observed, and remember too that at least one aspect of each area of the range must be observed. Look at which values statements you need to cover, too. It's a good idea to plan the activity using the activity plan format we suggested earlier in the chapter, or the one your centre uses. This will help you to be well prepared, and will also show your assessor that you have a good knowledge and understanding of the element or unit.

Decide how you will provide the other evidence you need. You will find suggestions about the most appropriate types of evidence at the beginning of the unit. Don't forget to include any work plans from your normal work practice, with a note to say how you were involved in preparing and carrying them out.

Cross referencing

The NVQ process encourages working across elements and units - we call this **holistic assessment**. This means that you can use one piece of evidence in several units. Because every page of evidence is numbered, you simply cross reference to the relevant page, regardless of which unit it is in. For instance, your assessor may have observed you playing a colour matching game with a group of children, which you planned for Element 2 in C8 (we usually write this as C8.2). She will probably have noted how you encouraged children to relate to each other and take turns (C4.2) and how you encouraged and praised children (C4.3). You were probably developing language skills (C9.2). If your assessor planned to spend some extra time observing tidying up and getting ready for dinner, she would also see evidence for C4.3 - helping children to develop self-reliance; for E2.1 - maintaining a safe environment; and for C1.1 - contributing to children's personal hygiene. In the same way you can cross reference for areas of the range. You can also do this for any of your written evidence. Some candidates find this difficult at first, and you may need time to get used to it. As you become more familiar with your handbook, you will find it easier to cross reference.

You will probably find it easier to concentrate on one unit at a time, but be aware of when evidence can be cross referenced to other units. To help you to do this, we have given you a simple format (see page 24). Put a copy at the beginning of each unit, and as you find evidence which you think will fit, list it on the sheet, with the page reference. At this stage, you don't need to worry about exactly which PCs, range or knowledge evidence it fits, as long as you know where to find it. When you start working on that unit, you can go back to the evidence and cross reference it into the appropriate place.

Note to assessors

If you're a new assessor, you will find this book invaluable in helping you to plan with your candidates. Hopefully, it will also be useful for experienced assessors, because it enables candidates to take more control of their assessment. We hope you will find the comments below helpful when using the book.

■ This book aims to help NVQ candidates to gather evidence based on their own work practice rather than working through questions and assignments. We have constantly encouraged candidates to refer to their candidate handbook so that they are fully aware of the standards they are working towards. This method of evidence gathering is more in tune with the philosophy of work-based training, but it does require careful guidance and support until candidates are confident about using the standards. They have been advised throughout the book to seek the guidance of their assessor.

■ The book does not aim to provide all of the underpinning knowledge that candidates need. They will find the key issues section and the resources in each chapter useful, but they will need to attend training sessions and do further reading.

■ We have provided suggested formats for evidence gathering, which may be photocopied, but we have explained to candidates that many centres will have their own formats, and these will be made available to them at induction.

■ We have suggested that it would be useful for the candidates to complete an assignment on all aspects of child development, in preparation for the development units (C1, C4, C8 and C9). This would provide the evidence for the first knowledge evidence statement of each of these units, and also help them to appreciate how closely linked all areas of development are. However, we have explained that this may not be the way their centre works, and that this is only a suggestion.

■ We have explained to candidates that they can work through the units in any order, as appropriate to their work experience, the order of the training sessions and the guidance given by their centre.

■ We have summarised and simplified the knowledge evidence required for each element, as this is often the section candidates find most difficult. Where a statement covers more than one element we have included it in the first element it appears in, and put the other relevant elements in brackets. Candidates may need you to explain this to them.

CROSS REFERENCING SHEET

Unit	
Description of evidence	**Unit/page reference**

Date	OBSERVATION RECORD	PCs/ Range	Knowledge evidence

Signed...(assessor)   ....(candidate)

Date	ORAL QUESTION RECORD	PCs/ Range	Knowledge evidence

Signed...(assessor)   ....(candidate)

Date	WITNESS TESTIMONY	PCs/ Range	Knowledge evidence

Signed...witness ....(candidate)

Status of witness...

ACTIVITY PLAN

NAME: **DATE:**   **ACTIVITY:**   **AGE OF CHILDREN:**

Before the activity:
Describe the activity you are planning. Describe how it fulfils the values statements for the element or unit you are working on.

Why have you chosen this activity? What do you think the children will gain from it?*(Think about areas of development.)*

Which children will be involved? Why? *(Will it be free choice? Have you targeted children who need particular help with, for instance, colour recognition?)*

What equipment/resources/preparation do you need?

What will you do during the activity? *(Language you will use, help you will give, etc.)*

Building a Portfolio Level 2 •
Photocopiable

After the activity:
Did the activity go well? Why? If not, why not?

Would you change it next time? If so, how and why?

How would you adapt the activity for older/younger children? For children with additional needs or disabilities?

What did the children gain from the activity? Was it what you thought they would?

What did you learn from it?

Signed .... (candidate)   If anyone observed you ask them to sign that this is a true record, and to comment if possible.

Signed ....   Role: ....

Comment:

CANDIDATE DIARY

NAME: **DATE:**   **INCIDENT:**

What happened? Who was involved? *(Don't use names - number of staff/children/parents)*

How did you react? What did you do?

Why did you do it this way?

Did it work? If not, why not?

What have you learned from it? What would you do differently next time?
(Think about the values statements)

Which PCs/range/knowledge does this relate to?

If anyone observed you ask them to sign that this is an accurate record and to make a comment.

Witness...   **Status** ....

Witness comment (if applicable)

CHILD OBSERVATION

Candidate's name	Date

Title of observation:

Type of observation: *(eg target child, free description, developmental check-list)*

Aim of observation: *(Which aspect of child development/behaviour are you aiming to observe?)*

First name of child: *(or fictitious name)*   **Age:** *(yrs & mths)*

Description of setting: *(where observation is taking place, number of staff, children, equipment available, etc.)*

The observation: Write this on a separate piece of paper, or other format you have chosen. Write what you actually observed in detail, using present tense.

Evaluation: Comment on what you learned from the observation - link this to your aims. Evaluate what the child's needs are, and make recommendations for future planning.

Signatures: Sign your observation and ask someone who witnessed the observation to sign it if possible.

Signed......................................(candidate)   **Signed**......................................(witness)

ASSESSMENT PLAN

Description of evidence/activity	To cover PCs/ Range	To cover Knowledge evidence	Date due

Signed..(assessor) ....(candidate)

Date... Date...

Chapter 2

Unit C1: Support children's physical development needs

About this unit

This unit is all about how you will support the physical needs of children from birth to eight years. That means helping children when going to the toilet and washing their hands, when they are eating and drinking, and helping to provide opportunities for exercise, rest and sleep.

All children are different, and have different needs. Your supervisor will have discussed any particular needs with each child's parent, so ask her if there is anything you need to know about. For instance, babies and young children usually have their own sleep times at home, so you need to stick to these in the setting as far as possible. Very young children have different needs to older children, so it will be useful if you can get experience with different age groups. If you work in a day nursery, it's easy to move from room to room, and if the nursery has an out-of-school club, that's even better, because you work with the full age range of children. If you work in a school, it's not so easy to complete this unit, but some centres give learners the chance to go to a nursery in the summer holidays to work with babies and children under school age. Ask if you can do this.

Remember!
You don't have to start with this unit. If you are more confident about another unit, you can start with that.

Links with other units

You will probably find it easier to do one element on its own to start with, but try to look at whole units together as soon as you are able, and also look at other units that are linked. There are some links between this unit and E2, Maintain the safety and security of children. Your assessor may help you to see where you can use some of the same evidence for both units. Talk to her about it. Have a look at E2 and see if you can spot some links. For instance, when you are helping children with eating and drinking, you are also making sure that the eating area is hygienic, that you and the children have washed your hands and the food has been safely stored and cooked. If you find any links, write them down on the cross referencing sheet we showed you in the introduction.

Values

Go back to the beginning of your candidate handbook and read through the 'Statement of underlying principles' again. Then have a look at the values statements for this unit. They are in a grid at the beginning of each unit. Your centre will normally make sure that you have a good understanding of the values during induction, and will come back to them throughout your training. If you feel that there is anything that you don't understand, talk it through with your assessor, because the values are at the core of everything you do.

For every unit you will need to think about the first two values - **the welfare of the child** and **keeping children safe** - because in all your work with children, these are the most important things to remember.

Let's look at the other values. It's important to work in **partnership with parents**. In this unit it means finding out from the parents all the information you need to keep children safe and healthy. Ask your supervisor what information the setting gives to parents about your routines, and what information they get from the parents, such as their child's likes and dislikes, any allergies, any foods they don't want them to eat, and so on. You will not usually be responsible for gathering this information, but you need to know about it. If you work in a day nursery you will probably talk to parents on a daily basis about how their child has been during the day, and what they have done, and they may give you information about things their child has done at home. Some nurseries keep a daily diary which parents can read, and add things they want the nursery to know.

note:
If a parent gives you important information you must pass it on to your supervisor. If a parent starts talking about things which are outside your responsibility, you must refer them on to your supervisor.

Nearly all of the things you do with children will have an effect on their **learning and development**. In this unit, it's important to help children to understand how important it is to keep clean and eat healthily, and to have enough exercise and rest. You also need to encourage them to become more self-reliant, that is, to carry out tasks like eating, dressing and washing themselves as soon as they are able.

The next three values - **equality of opportunity, anti-discrimination** and **celebrating diversity** - are closely linked. You need to be aware of how to give all children equal access to opportunities to learn and develop, whether they are boys or girls, able-bodied or have a disability, whatever their individual learning needs, their family, social or cultural group. You need to show that you respect all children and their families and challenge any form of discrimination, and that you help all children to enjoy and learn about the diversity of the world they live in, and accept difference as a positive thing. Children develop attitudes from an early age, so you have a crucial role to play in making those attitudes positive ones. In this unit, you need to know about the different cultural practices in relation to hygiene and diet. Remember, too, that different families have their own preferred ways of bringing up their children, and it's important that you try to follow their preferences.

Confidentiality is absolutely essential in your work with children. You must **never** share information about the children and their families with others outside of the setting. Even within the setting, you should only discuss things with the staff who need to know. Make sure you know what your setting's policy is on confidentiality. For instance, how are the children's records kept safe? Who is allowed to look at them? How is important information passed on? You also need to know whether you're allowed to take photographs of the children, or write observations of children, to use as evidence in your portfolio. Some settings ask for parents' permission for this. You should never include any children's records with names or information which could lead to a child being identified.

You will be **working with other professionals** all the time in your work. This may be the other members of staff in your workplace, or it may be visiting experts, such as health visitors, speech therapists or people from a visual or hearing impairment unit. Although at this stage in your career you may be the least experienced member of staff, you will still be able to contribute useful information if you have been working closely with individual children.

You will also find that you need to think about the last value statement - **the reflective practitioner** - in every unit. This is because, as a childcare practitioner - someone who works with children - you always need to think about what you are doing with the children, and why you are doing it. What will they gain from doing this activity? How will this experience help them to learn and develop? Is what I'm doing helping them to feel secure and happy? Is what I'm doing keeping them safe and healthy? Think about these last questions as you begin to look at the rest of the unit.

Getting started

In this unit you will need to show that you can:

◆ help children to toilet and wash hands

◆ help children when eating and drinking

◆ support opportunities for children's exercise

◆ support children's quiet periods

Have a look through the elements and use the personal skills profile, in Chapter 1 (page 21), to help you decide which areas you feel most confident to start with, and where you think you need more experience or training. Talk to your supervisor about this, so that she can make sure you get the experience you need, and the opportunity to practise your skills where you feel less confident. It will be helpful, too, to discuss with your assessor which units you will be covering at the centre when you go in for your training sessions. You will probably find it helpful to work through the units in the same order as you are doing the training at the centre. Your setting will also receive information about courses organised by the local Early Years Development and Childcare Partnership (EYDCP). Many of these are free, and well worth attending.

Remember!
It will be useful for this unit to get experience with as wide an age range of children as possible, so that you get a feel for their needs at different ages.

Once you have decided where to start, you need to agree an **assessment plan** with your assessor. She will help you to decide what evidence you need to collect, and write it down on an assessment plan, so that you both have a record of what you have agreed. In each chapter you will find some helpful guidance about the best way of collecting evidence from the things you do every day with the children. Your centre may have a set of assignments for you to work through, but your evidence should be based as far as possible on what you do in your work with the children, so always try to use examples. Ask yourself: How do I do this with the children? Why? Does it work? Could I do it better?

Element C1.1 Help children to toilet and wash hands

Key issues

For this element, you need to follow your setting's health and safety procedures for toileting and changing children. It's vital that you are meticulous about your personal hygiene and your hygiene routines with the children, because infection can quickly spread if you're not. Here are some key questions to ask yourself, or to find out from colleagues:

◆ Does your setting use disposable gloves when changing children?

◆ How do you deal with wet or soiled clothing?

◆ How do you deal sensitively with toileting accidents? (Some children will be upset, and need reassurance)

◆ If you work with babies, how do you make sure that the changing area is hygienic, and you don't spread infection?

◆ Do the children have their own flannels, towels and toothbrushes?

◆ How do you encourage the children to become self-reliant – to do things for themselves? How do you respect children's privacy? (This is important as they get older, and is particularly important for children from some cultural groups.)

◆ Are there any children who need special help with toileting?

◆ How do you make children aware of the importance of washing their hands properly?

◆ What signs and symptoms do you need to watch for? (Signs that might suggest an infection or abuse)

The **knowledge evidence** statements for this element are 1, 8, 13, 14 and 20. You will find these at the end of the unit. You will need to show that you understand:

◆ physical development and how it's linked to other areas of development (also C1.2, C1.3, C1.4)

◆ how you can help children to become self-reliant but ensure that they're safe

◆ how to recognise signs of infection, injury or abuse

◆ basic health, safety and hygiene when caring for children, and your setting's policies and procedures (also C1.2, C1.3, C1.4)

◆ the importance of children following the cultural practices of their families, and of respecting others' practices (also C1.2, C1.3)

> You may find it helpful to do an assignment to cover all the areas of development - physical, intellectual, language, social and emotional - which you can then use as evidence in all of the development units (C1, C4, C8, C9).

Your training sessions should cover all of the knowledge you will need for each unit. There are some useful articles at the end of this chapter, and your centre will be able to suggest some further reading to help you. Your assessor may give you a set of **questions** or **assignments** to complete, to show evidence of your knowledge, but if you collect the evidence we suggest below, you will have covered some of the knowledge evidence already. Your assessor will tell you which evidence you have already covered, and where you need to add some more information.

> **note**
> This book will not give you all the knowledge you need for your NVQ. It is a resource book and guide.

Which type of evidence?

Your assessor will talk to you about which evidence you need to gather and write it on an assessment plan. She will need to **observe** five PCs, but she may be able to see more than that. She will also need to observe at least one aspect of each range category. So she may see you working with children without infection (range 1), and with a child who asked you for help (range 2). For the other PCs and range statements, you will have to provide other evidence.

Your assessor will want to **inspect** the toileting areas, and ask you **questions** to check your understanding of your setting's procedures. She may ask you to include a copy of your setting's **health and safety procedures**, but if you do, you should explain them to her, or write a note, to say how you make sure you follow them.

You could ask your supervisor to write a **witness testimony** to say you have competently and sensitively changed a child who had an accident.

You might like to keep a **diary** or notebook to make a note of things as they happen. Describe what you did, why, and whether it was successful. You can use the format on page 30 if you find it helpful.

Remember!
You don't have to produce all of these sorts of evidence. You just need enough evidence for each PC and range statement. One piece of evidence can cover more than one PC or range.

Element C1.2 Help children when eating and drinking

Key issues

For this element you need an understanding of which foods are necessary to give children a balanced diet. There are concerns about the amount of junk food, which contains high levels of fat or sugar or both, that children eat, so it is important to make sure that they have a good, balanced diet in the nursery. You need to be aware of what special diets children may need, either because of their family preferences, cultural or religious beliefs, or because of particular medical conditions or allergies.

When giving children food, **always** check with your supervisor whether any children have an allergy or are not allowed particular foods or drinks. Some allergies, such as peanut allergies, can have very serious, life-threatening effects. You should avoid peanuts altogether for young children. Remember to check what is in foods before you give them, because it's not always obvious.

You also need to know what sort of food and eating equipment is appropriate for different ages, and for children with disabilities who may need special equipment. For instance, babies of six months will need their food liquidised, and in small portions. They are more likely to use plastic spoons which are softer on their mouth. Toddlers of 18 months will be able to eat food cut up small, and will be able to feed themselves with help. Five-year-olds may be able to use a knife and fork and cut up their own food (although in some cultures, food is eaten with the fingers), and be able to eat larger portions. Of course, all children are individuals, and some will have bigger appetites than others. Encourage children to feed themselves as soon as they are able, and involve them in setting the table, pouring out drinks, passing things and so on, as they become more capable. These are important social skills for them to learn. There will be spillages sometimes, but just deal with these calmly.

Hygiene is absolutely paramount when dealing with food. You need to make sure that tables are cleaned thoroughly before meals, that children and staff wash their hands before eating or handling food, and that food is stored safely. You will need to provide protective clothing such as bibs or aprons for younger children, and preferably, have special aprons or tabards for yourself. If you're not directly involved in preparing food, it would be useful experience for you to spend a few sessions in the kitchen if possible.

It's important to make the meals look attractive, to encourage children to eat. Don't make the portions too large. It's better to give more if they want it than too much for them to manage. Try to have a relaxed atmosphere for mealtimes and, if possible, a member of staff should sit with a small group of children, to reinforce positive behaviour, make the meal a sociable event and give help and encouragement where necessary. Never let mealtimes become a battleground and never force children to eat. Children have their likes and dislikes, just as adults do, so respect that.

The **knowledge evidence** statements for this element are 2, 3, 4, 9 and 14. You need to show that you understand:

◆ children's needs at different stages of development

◆ the basic dietary requirements for good health

◆ a basic knowledge of common food allergies

◆ food not allowed for the main religious faiths and for vegetarians and vegans

◆ how illness might affect a child's appetite

◆ the importance of social interaction at mealtimes

◆ a basic knowledge of hygiene and safety in relation to food

You will be able to show evidence for some of these points in your evidence for the PCs and range. For instance, if your assessor sees you talking with the children during the mealtime, that shows that you understand the importance of social interaction. Your menus should show a knowledge of the basic dietary requirements for good health, if you explain how they give the children a balanced diet.

Your training will help you to gain the knowledge and understanding you need. We strongly recommend that you

If you're not confident about writing, ask your assessor about other ways of gathering evidence. She may be able to ask more oral questions, or arrange some extra support.

take a food hygiene course. Most centres give you the opportunity to do this, and it gives you an extra qualification too. There are also some useful articles later in the chapter on healthy eating and food hygiene.

Which type of evidence?

Your assessor will need to **observe** all but two of the PCs, and one aspect of each range category. She will want to observe a mealtime, and inspect the arrangements for serving food. She will ask you **questions** to check your understanding. If your setting doesn't provide meals for children, you will need to use snack time and a cooking activity as evidence. You can include **menus** from your setting, but you will need to write a comment to show that you understand how they provide the necessary foods to give children a balanced diet, or you can make up your own menus. Include a copy of your food hygiene **certificate** to show that you have a good knowledge of food hygiene. You may like to cut out some **pictures** of different sorts of eating equipment - for babies, for children learning to feed themselves and for children with disabilities. You can find these in educational catalogues and baby magazines. Write a note to explain why they are used.

Element C1.3 Support opportunities for children's exercise

Key issues

This element is all about how you help to give children the opportunity for physical exercise and play. There are concerns that children today are not getting enough exercise, and are becoming unfit. Some of the possible reasons for this are that:

◆ children spend more time in front of the television or computer

◆ more families own cars so children don't walk as much

◆ parents are afraid to allow their children to play outside because of increased traffic and other dangers

So it's important that children have lots of time for physical play while they are with you, both indoors and outdoors. Some settings don't have a lot of space indoors for larger or wheeled equipment, so it's best to encourage children to play outside as much as possible. As long as children have suitable clothing, they can play outside in most weather. If your setting doesn't have a safe outdoor space, take advantage of the local park or playground.

Children need a variety of physical play and exercise to help their all-round development. This includes free play and more

structured sessions. Children need large equipment to help them to use their arms and legs to climb, ride, balance and so on, and small equipment like bats, balls, beanbags and hoops to develop throwing and catching, kicking and control skills. Singing games and music and movement will help them practise controlling their movements.

If you work with older children in a school, their exercise will be mostly through PE lessons planned by the teacher, so you may only be able to play a small part, perhaps working with a group. But you will be able to encourage the children to play playground games such as hopscotch, the farmer's in his den, and so on, at playtime. If you work with younger children, there will be times during the day when you can just have a quick singing game, or some activity like jumping and marching, to finish off a session or fill in a few minutes before dinner.

You need to be aware of safety when you're providing physical play for children, because it often involves large equipment for climbing, and moveable equipment. As a nursery assistant, you won't be left alone in charge of a group, but you need to know what the safety procedures are in your setting. Check with your supervisor what you need to know, such as how many are allowed on the climbing frame at one time, where children are allowed to ride the wheeled toys, and so on. If play is indoors, make sure that you give as much space as possible for physical activity, or have a set time when you clear furniture away to make a big space. Outdoors, you must make sure that gates are locked, and that there are no hazards such as glass thrown over a wall during the night, or animal excrement.

The **knowledge evidence** statements for this element are 5, 6, 10, 11, 12, 16, 17, 18, 19 and 20. You need to show that you understand:

- children's physical development, and how exercise helps growth - so that you can provide the appropriate range of activities for each age and stage of development

- how physical activity develops children's confidence

- how to provide non-stereotypical exercise and play (for instance, not skipping for girls, football for boys)

- your setting's health and safety procedures and the importance of adequate supervision

- the limitations of your setting in relation to physical play - for instance, the lack of space indoors, no safe space outdoors, particular hazards - and how to make best use of the space available

- the importance of respecting the cultural practices of families - for instance, some Muslim children are not allowed to undress in public, or bare their arms and legs.

Which type of evidence?

Your assessor will need to **observe** eight of the PCs and one aspect of each range category. She may ask **questions** about how you ensure that children are safe, and what the setting's health and safety procedures are, for instance for checking for damaged or unsafe equipment, and about how you make sure that boys and girls are given equal opportunity to use all equipment.

Plan an activity to cover as many of the PCs and range as possible. You could set out all the equipment for either indoor or outdoor play, and your assessor will watch you supervising and helping the children. Check with your supervisor that what you are planning is appropriate, and that another member of staff will be supervising, too.

Keep a record in your **diary** or write a **reflective account** of other activities you have done with the children, to cover some of the range. For instance, if your assessor observed outdoor play, you might write about an indoor session where you did some singing games with the children - this would cover 'without equipment' and 'indoors'. You will need to find out what sort of equipment is available for children with disabilities, and how you could adapt your setting to allow access to physical play for children with disabilities. You could use **pictures** to illustrate this.

Element C1.4 Support children's quiet periods

Key issues
It's important for all children, whatever their age, to have quiet

periods during the day. This may mean a sleep, especially for younger children, or it may just be a quiet time when children do quiet activities, or have a story. Some children spend a long time at the nursery each day, and need some rest. Where you have some children who need a sleep and some who don't, you need to provide quiet activities for those who are awake - so that they don't disturb the sleeping children, but also to give them a chance to relax and rest. Try to spend this time relaxing with the children, rather than rushing around getting jobs done. This will help the children see the value of quiet times, and cut down the disturbance for the sleeping children.

Babies and younger children usually have their own sleep pattern, so it's important that this is discussed with parents. Some parents don't want their children to sleep during the day, because then they don't sleep at night. You may need to come to a compromise about this, if you find that a child really needs a sleep. It will normally be your supervisor who discusses this with the parent, but you need to follow what has been agreed.

The **knowledge evidence** statements for this element are 1, 7, 14, 19 and 21. You need to show that you understand:

- how children's need for rest and sleep changes as they develop

- the importance of rest and sleep as part of the daily routine

- safety and hygiene, and effective use of space, when children are resting and sleeping

- how you ensure that sleep and rest routines reflect those of the home.

Don't forget to cover as much as you can in your evidence. Your assessor will give you some questions or assignments to fill any gaps.

Which type of evidence?

Your assessor will need to **observe** all but two of the PCs and one aspect of the range. Plan an appropriate time with her. She may ask to fit this in with the mealtime, and the toileting and handwashing routine - this would mean only one observation to cover three elements! She will probably ask you **questions** about how you take account of parents' wishes, and how you ensure that children are comfortable during rest times.

You could write a **reflective account** or **diary** about times when you have encouraged children to rest. You might like to write a **child observation** to show different children's sleep patterns or need for rest times.

Most children believe that if their hands look clean then they are clean. They need help to learn how to wash them properly

Children and handwashing

Hands are one of the main ways in which bacteria is transferred to food, causing illness in the form of food poisoning. Hands are also responsible for spreading viruses amongst children. Bacteria transmitted to towels are transferred to other hands using that towel.

Many infections are passed to children from animals, especially pets. A large number of dogs and cats carry the salmonella and campylobacter bacteria in their gut and because of their cleaning habits these bacteria are also present in their mouths. That is why children should be discouraged from allowing animals to lick them and to make sure they wash their hands after stroking or handling pets.

The problem children have with handwashing is that bacteria and viruses cannot be seen with the naked eye. They believe that if their hands look clean then they are clean.

When to wash hands
- after going to the toilet
- before touching and eating food
- if they look or feel dirty
- after playing with pets
- after coughing, sneezing or blowing your nose
- during and after farm visits

How to wash
- make sure the bowl/basin is at child height
- use soap and warm water
- rub the soap over both sides of your hands
- between every finger and around nails
- rinse off with clean warm water
- dry hands properly - with a clean towel or paper towel

So how can we help children to understand about germs, when they should wash their hands and how to wash them properly?

Understanding about germs
Explain that germs:
- are all around us
- most are good, only some are bad and can make us ill
- that you can't see them with your eyes
- that washing hands gets rid of the germs

What conditions do germs like? You can carry out an experiment to show this. Take some slices of bread and ask the children to touch half with dirty hands. (Their hands do not have to be obviously dirty - maybe they have not washed their hands after playing outside.) Next, place a clean and a dirty piece of bread in different conditions - dry/moist, warm/cold, dark/light. Leave the bread for a few days to encourage good mould growth.

Talk about how the 'cleaner' bread in dry/cold conditions has less mould growth than the dirty bread in moist/warm conditions, remembering that bacteria need food, moisture, warmth and time to grow.

> Salmonella and campylobacter are the main causes of food poisoning in the UK.

The yes/no game
This should be carried out after some group discussion on germs and handwashing. Have all the children sitting on the mat. Ask simple questions such as:

- Can you see germs with your eyes?
- Should you wash your hands after going to the toilet?
- Should you wash your hands before eating your lunch?
- Does your cat's coat have germs on it?
- If your hands look clean might they have germs on them?

The children should reply yes or no to every question. This game can also be played by raising hands for yes or by standing up for yes, staying sitting for no.

Painting hands
This can be carried out at a wash basin or by using bowls of warm water on a stand or table, preferably on a one-to-one basis.

- Each child puts on a protective shirt or apron.
- Put washable paint on their hands which they rub in, especially between the fingers and around the thumbs and wrists.
- The child washes their own hands with warm water and soap (running water is preferable) to remove the paint.
- After washing talk about how well they washed their hands and whether any paint is left. Discuss the importance of rubbing the soap well into the whole of the hand - front and back and of rinsing properly.
- The hands are dried well with paper towels or a clean hand towel.

Nancy Singleton, health improvement manager

What are the issues related to providing food for pre-school children? Beverley Spicer looks at the relevant guidelines and explains who you can turn to for more help

Feeding pre-school children: guidelines and good practice

New guidelines for school caterers were introduced in 2001. Although the legislation in these doesn't apply to private nurseries or childminders, they contain practical and useful guidance which can be used by anyone catering for the pre-school age group.

Healthy School Lunches: Guidance for School Caterers on Implementing National Nutritional Standards became compulsory from 1 April 2001. Separate guidelines were produced for nursery schools/units, primary schools and secondary schools.

The guidance for nursery schools/units applies to maintained schools in England. However, the document gives good practice guidance which would be helpful to any caterer or cook wishing to ensure healthy meal provision.

The document takes a practical and common sense approach. When asking, 'What is a healthy diet?' it states: 'There are no healthy or unhealthy foods, only healthy or unhealthy diets. For children aged five and under a healthy diet means broadly:

- A balanced diet with plenty of variety
- A diet which provides enough energy for satisfactory growth and development
- Plenty of fruit and vegetables
- Plenty of iron rich foods
- Plenty of calcium rich foods
- Not having sugary foods and drinks too often.'

National nutritional standards

There are national nutritional standards that apply to all lunches provided for children during term time, whether they are free or lunches which children pay for. There is no obligation to provide a paid meals service for part-time children in nursery schools and units. However, part-time children whose parents receive income support or income based jobseeker's allowance are entitled to a free lunch. Children cannot spend their entitlement on other school food such as breakfast or break-time snacks.

What are the compulsory standards?

The standards say that for lunches for children in nursery schools or units, at least **one** item from each of the following food groups

- MENU -
vegetable risotto
strawberry sponge
and custard

Healthy School Lunches for Pupils in Nursery Schools/Units: Guidance for School Caterers on Implementing National Nutritional Standards is published by the DfES and available from:
DfES Publications
PO Box 5050
Sherwood Park
Annesley
Nottingham NG15 0DJ
Telephone: 0845 602 2260
The reference that you need to quote is:
DfEE 314/2000
The publication is also available on
www.dfes.gov.uk/schoollunches

must be available every day:

- Starchy foods such as bread, potatoes, rice and pasta;
- Fruit and vegetables;
- Milk and dairy foods;
- Meat, fish and other non-dairy sources of protein.

The document points out that these are minimum standards. Some local education authorities may have higher standards and those should continue.

There are also some additional recommendations. Although these are not in the regulations, the Secretary of State:

- Expects that drinking water should be available to all children every day, free of charge;
- Strongly recommends that schools should offer some hot food, particularly in the winter months. A school lunch does not have to be a hot meal. However, a hot meal can be a useful morale-booster during the colder months. Parents often

prefer to buy a hot meal for their children and see it as offering added value; and

- Strongly recommends that drinking milk is available as an option every day.

Good practice

The guidelines include a chapter on 'Good catering practice', which includes useful and practical advice on meeting the standards and planning menus. For example, within the 'Bread, other cereals and potato' section it gives the following advice:

Points worth remembering when frying potatoes:

- Large pieces of potato, thick or straight cut chips, absorb less fat than thin or crinkle-cut chips
- Try to use a frying fat or oil which contains not more than 20 per cent saturated fat
- Have the oil at the correct temperature, change it regularly and drain it off well.

Similar practical advice is given within each food group. For example:

Meat and fish

Try to select the leanest cuts of meat you can afford and trim off any visible fat and take the skins off chicken. Drain or skim the fat from casseroles and mince wherever possible.

It is strongly recommended that servings of fish should include oily fish, such as sardines and mackerel which contain a type of fat beneficial to health.

Milk and dairy products

Milk and dairy products are an excellent source of calcium, which is important for good bone development. Skimmed milk is not suitable as a main drink for the under-fives. Whole or semi-skimmed milk should be used for this age group.

Do not rely too much on cheese as the main protein, for example for vegetarians. Try not to serve it more than once a week as the only vegetarian option.

Foods containing fat and sugar

Aim to keep the proportion of foods in this group to no more than about one tenth of the total food on offer over the course of a week. Try not to offer more than one fried item a day.

> ### Rich sources of folic acid
> - fresh raw or cooked brussels sprouts, asparagus, spinach, cooked black eye beans
> - breakfast cereals (fortified with folic acid)
> - liver
> ### Other good sources
> - fresh, raw, frozen and cooked broccoli, spring greens, cabbage, green beans, cauliflower, peas, bean sprouts, okra, cooked soya beans, iceberg lettuce, parsnips, chick peas
> - kidneys, yeast and beef extract

> ### Good sources of iron which are well absorbed
> - canned sardines, pilchards, mackerel, tuna, shrimps, crab
> - liver pate and sausage, kidney, heart
> - lean beef, lamb, pork: roast, mince, burgers, liver
> - chicken or turkey, especially dark meat, liver
> - sausages, grilled
> - fish paste

> ### Good sources of zinc
> - lean beef, lamb, pork: roast, mince, burgers, liver
> - chicken or turkey, especially dark meat, liver
> - sausages
> - hard cheeses
> - eggs
> - tinned pilchards, sardines, tuna
> - brown and wholemeal bread
> - whole grain breakfast cereals
> - red kidney beans, chick peas, lentils, nuts

> ### Good sources of calcium
> - hard cheeses, cheese spread, soya cheese
> - canned sardines or salmon, drained and mashed up with the bones, fish paste
> - tofu (soya bean) steamed or spread
> - milk and yoghurt
> - soya drink with added calcium
> - soya mince
> - ice cream
> - egg yolk
> - bread (except wholemeal), crumpets, muffins, plain and cheese scones
> - beans, lentils, chick peas
> - ready to eat or stewed figs

Use monounsaturated and polyunsaturated fats wherever possible for cooking, spreading and in dressings. Saturated fats include hard margarines, lard, suet and coconut oil. Monounsaturated and polyunsaturated fats include maize, corn, safflower, sunflower, soya, rapeseed, olive oils and spreads made from these oils.

Ice cream can be high in fat. Try not to serve ice cream as a dessert too often. Try non-dairy ice cream as an alternative.

Fresh, tinned and dried fruit can be incorporated into puddings. Dried fruit provides extra fibre.

Fruit and vegetables

Fruit and vegetables can be fresh, frozen, dried, canned or in juice form. Dried fruit is a good source of iron.

Steaming or cooking vegetables with minimal amounts of water, and serving as soon after cooking as possible, helps to retain nutrients. Long cooking times and keeping vegetables warm for long periods before serving will lead to heavy loss of some nutrients.

It is good to see the following statement within the 'Vegetables' section: 'Spaghetti hoops and other canned pasta in tomato sauce should not be served as a vegetable, but counted as part of the starchy food group'. This change alone will result in an improved Vitamin C and folic acid intake. This in turn may well result in an improved absorption of iron. It also teaches children that spaghetti is part of the starchy food group and not a vegetable.

The document also covers:
- Monitoring nutritional standards
- Improving the service – this section looks at pricing and promoting uptake of meals.
- Special dietary requirements – considers religious and ethnic groups, vegetarians and allergies.

The Government recommends that school caterers keep records of the food provided:
- to check that they are meeting national nutritional standards every day
- to see what items are being eaten. For example, are some foods running out too early? Are some dishes always left over? What foods are not being eaten?
- as a record of whether they are implementing healthier catering practices

Help yourself to water.

Reliable sources of information

So, who might you turn to if you are interested in taking an in-depth look at your menus or want some ideas for promoting a healthy diet? State registered dieticians (SRDs) hold the only legally recognised graduate qualification in nutrition and dietetics. State registration is an indication that a dietician is bound by an ethical code of conduct which the public can trust. Furthermore, SRDs are competent to practise and have professional indemnity insurance. Unfortunately, they are something of a rare breed with about 5,000 registered with the British Dietetic Association.

State registered dieticians are qualified to translate the science of nutrition into practical advice. They can be found working in a variety of areas. About half are employed by the National Health Service. The remaining 50 per cent work in education, industry, research or as freelance consultants. Of those employed by the NHS a wide variety of roles are undertaken. Some specialise in clinical settings, working on children's wards or with patients with kidney or liver failure. Others work in the community, sometimes with GPs or

promoting health of the general population, with the aim of disease prevention.

Community or health promotion dieticians would generally be the ones who work with teachers and care staff and you may well have access to one locally. Some dieticians may have a specific remit to work with schools, others may have more difficulty finding time to advise you.

To discover what dietetic services are available in your area, you can contact your local hospital and ask to speak to the dietetic department. Ask them if there is a community or health promotion dietician.

Local authority health promotion departments sometimes have an officer allocated specifically for schools and if they don't they will certainly have a resources officer. To contact your nearest health promotion department or service try looking in your local phone book. Alternatively, you can phone your local health authority or health trust, who should be able to give you the number.

Beverley Spicer, community paediatric dietician.

Building a Portfolio Level 2 • • •

Healthy eating guidelines for adults - which have been the same for more than 20 years - are clear. But are they appropriate for children and at what age do they start to apply?

Promoting healthy eating

The Government guidelines on healthy eating were drawn up as a direct result of disease patterns within the population. Too many of us are suffering from heart disease, diabetes, cancer, high blood pressure, strokes and obesity. Many of these diseases are on the increase.

'The balance of good health' is a visual representation - a picture of a plate of food - used by the Food Standards Agency to show the recommended proportions of foods that we should be eating, not necessarily on a daily basis, but over a period of time. The message is clear that we need to make fruit and vegetables and starchy foods, which include bread, potatoes, pasta, rice and other cereals, the main part of our diet. The high fat, high sugar section at the bottom of the plate is a clear acknowledgement that these foods are a part of everybody's diet. That the portion is small clearly demonstrates that they need to be kept to a minimum.

The healthy eating guidelines for adults are:
- Enjoy your food and eat a good variety;
- Eat plenty of starchy foods;
- Eat plenty of fruit and vegetables;
- Don't eat too many foods that contain a lot of fat;
- Don't have sugary foods and drinks too often;
- If you drink alcohol do it in moderation;
- Try not to eat too many salty foods and don't add too much salt to your cooking;
- Eat the right amount to be a healthy weight.

But does all of this apply to children and at what age do the guidelines start to apply? Growing children need plenty of energy (calories) and nutrients to ensure that they grow and develop well. A good appetite will usually mean that they get enough energy from the food that they eat.

There is, however, increasing evidence of poor diet in children. A national survey in 1995 showed that children's diets are too high in sugar (17 per cent of children aged 18 months to four and a half years have some form of tooth decay).

Obesity, and a particular type of diabetes related to obesity, is increasing in children. Children are less active than in previous generations, spending more time watching television and playing outside less, so they have lower energy requirements.

Clearly there are significant nutritional challenges facing children and their carers, but the balance of good health still applies to this group and you can use it as a basis for encouraging children to eat a varied diet. They should eat foods from four main food groups every day.

These food groups are:
- bread, other cereals and potatoes
- fruits and vegetables
- milk and dairy foods
- meat, fish, eggs and alternatives such as beans, lentils and soya

Bread, other cereals and potatoes

Whether it is bread, breakfast cereals, maize, potatoes, yams, rice, couscous, pasta or chapattis, most children don't need much encouragement to eat one or more of the foods from this group. A portion at each meal will provide energy, various nutrients

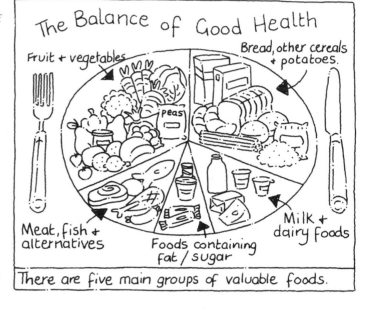

and some fibre. Ideally, children should try lots of different varieties of starchy foods, such as wholemeal bread as well as white.

Potatoes are a useful source of Vitamin C. Boil or mash them – or occasionally try chips. Thick straight cut chips have less fat or choose lower fat oven chips. Limit fried potato to once or twice a week.

Starchy foods are important in everyone's diet but they can be filling. This is especially true of wholemeal varieties. Be careful not to use too many wholemeal foods until the child is five. For fussy eaters, children with small appetites and children who are thin or slow growers use wholemeal varieties with caution after this age also. Of course, the reverse is true for children who are overweight, the wholemeal varieties are then very useful.

Toast, cereals and teacakes make useful snacks. They are more nutritious than biscuits and crisps and can often work out cheaper, too.

Fruit and vegetables

Fruit and vegetables contain vitamins, minerals and fibre and they liven up meals with colour, textures and flavours. Try to introduce lots of them from an early age, whether fresh, frozen, canned or dried.

The adult recommendation is to eat five portions from this group each day, one portion being an apple, a banana, a tablespoon of carrots, one or two florets of broccoli, and so on. Children should also aim for about five portions, but clearly not the same portion size. Try to give children a taste of five different fruits and vegetables each day. The amount that they will eat of each will vary from child to child depending on appetite, age preference, and so on.

When children flatly refuse vegetables, keep offering them but also offer more fruit. Make sure you show that you like eating them. It's counter productive to make a big fuss if children refuse, but remember, between the ages of one and five, all children should receive vitamin drops unless a wide variety of food is being eaten. Vitamin drops provide Vitamins A and D. They are available at minimal cost or are free to those on income support or an income-based job seeker's allowance, from health visitors' clinics.

Try some of the following:

- For snacks, try sticks of carrot, cucumber and celery; sliced apple, banana or pear; cherry tomatoes, sugar snaps or mangetout. Some children also like sliced raw mushroom or raw baby sweetcorn.

- Children's cooking sessions often generate interest in food so try to base these on healthy options. Get them to pile vegetables or pineapple onto pizza bases. They're much more likely to eat them if they've had a hand in the preparation.

- Try out some fruit art, making smiley faces with fruit and vegetables.

- Use a colourful display of fruit and vegetables as inspiration for paintings.

Milk and dairy foods

Milk is important for young children. At least half a pint of milk each day will provide energy for growth and calcium for bones and teeth. Semi-skimmed milk can be introduced from two years of age. However, fussy eaters, children who are thin or those who have a large intake of milk and seem to be dependant on it for a large proportion of their calories are best left on whole milk until they are older. Skimmed milk is not suitable for children under five. Some families and carers will also be eligible for free milk (seven pints per week).

If a child doesn't like drinking milk every day, they need at least two servings of milk-based dishes such as cheese, yoghurt, fromage frais, custard, milk puddings and cheese sauce. Contrary to popular belief, eggs don't fall into this category; they are not a rich source of calcium.

For children who are allergic to milk or for vegan children (not taking any animal products at all) it is important that they are getting enough calcium as well as some other important nutrients provided by milk. Doctors or health visitors will be able to advise on infant soya milks. Some children

may be referred by their doctor to a dietician who will be able to do a thorough check that the child's diet is adequate.

Meat, fish, eggs and alternatives

Young children need protein to grow and develop. Meat, fish, eggs, nuts, pulses

(beans, lentils, peas), foods made from pulses (tofu, hummus, soya mince) and Quorn are an excellent source of protein. Children need at least one portion from this group each day.

For children who are vegetarian or vegan two portions of vegetable proteins (pulses) or nuts daily will ensure enough protein. Whole nuts should not be given to children under five years, as there is a risk of choking. Allergy to nuts appears to be on the increase. If you suspect an allergy, avoid that food and check with the parent or main carer.

The fifth main food group covers foods that are high in fat and/or sugar.

Fat: Foods such as crisps, chips, biscuits, chocolate, cakes and fried foods are high in fat. They provide relatively little else in terms of useful nutrients. They are often popular with children - as well as adults! All of these foods need to be limited. Have a look at the balance of good health and remember they can be a part of a healthy diet, as long as they are only a small part.

Sugar: Breast milk is quite sweet and children continue to like sweet tastes. The total amount of sugar needs to be limited in children's diets, but even more important is how often they are taking sugar, sugary foods and drinks. When teeth are in frequent contact with sugary foods and drinks they will decay. To reduce the amount of sugar in a child's diet, try setting a precedent and only serve milk and water. This will reduce the total amount of sugar in a child's diet and reduce the frequency of sugar intake. Alternatively, only serve flavoured drinks at meal times; this limits the damage done.

Finally, keep a balance on food. Remember, there are no healthy or unhealthy foods just healthy and unhealthy diets. Food is there to be enjoyed, in as much variety as possible by children and adults alike.

Beverley Spicer, community paediatric dietician.

Children enjoy energetic, physical and free play. As they play they become aware of what they can do and begin to show an awareness of space, of themselves and of others. As they move they are also learning the language of movement – the speed, direction and position of their movements

Learning **words** for **actions**

Useful words
fast/slow
up/down
in/out
over/under
to the right/to the left
forwards/backwards
inside/outside
on/in
under/over
top/bottom
high/low

Fine days

When children are outside, encourage their movements by suggesting the following:

■ In a large open space encourage free movement – how fast or slow can they move? Can they move backwards and sideways as well as forwards? Can they change position – up and down as they move?

■ When using large play apparatus encourage them to describe their position – are they at the top or the bottom of the slide? Can they crawl under or over the bars?

Wet days

■ Although space is limited inside don't let the weather deter you! Think of action songs – 'The Grand Old Duke of York', 'Jack and Jill', 'The Hokey Cokey'. All these encourage children to move in certain ways and help them to understand the language used to describe movements.

■ Play a copying game – 'Follow my Leader' or 'Simon Says'. When your child is ready, let them take the lead and you do the copying!

All join in

'The wheels on the bus' has the ideal ingredients for an action song - simple, recognisable actions and lots of repetition. Even the youngest children will be able to join in with a simple action, long before they are able to speak clearly. If you tire of the same old lyrics, add your own verses.

Other good action songs:
'Here we go round the mulberry bush'
'Wind the bobbin'
'If you're happy and you know it'
'Brown girl in the ring'
'The bear went over the mountain'

The Grand Old Duke of York

Oh the grand old Duke of York

He had ten thousand men

He marched them up to the top of the hill

And he marched them down again.

And when they were up, they were up

And when they were down they were down

And when they were only half-way up

They were neither up nor down.

How can you give children the chance to do physical exercise and let off steam in a confined indoor space? Sara Stocks comes up with an activity to save the day

Make an indoor obstacle course

With careful planning you can design an indoor obstacle course that will cover most of the Physical Development ELGs. First, list the goals and consider how you can meet them in your environment. Then think about the major muscle groups that need exercising and the gross motor movements that help children to exercise those muscles. Discuss your plans with the children. They will surprise you with their understanding of what is required, so use their suggestions. Make a list of all the movements that you can think of and, using the equipment you have put together, a list of required movements.

Equipment

You may have indoor climbing frames or slides which you can use. If you do, then think about the approach to the equipment - encourage the children to skip or hop or jump to the base of the ladder. Think also about adding a new dimension, set it up differently, add a new idea or just move its position. Climbing up and down is best

restricted to those groups who have safe ladders and appropriate flooring.

If you don't have this sort of equipment, look at what you do have. You will have chairs and tables, mats and cushions and space. Clear the room as much as possible. You can arrange the chairs as a slalom, put them together as a tunnel to crawl under or mark a course that the children are to travel along (in different ways, hopping, jumping, crawling and so on). You can climb over a table, wriggle under it, run around it. Use mats to mark out star jumping areas, standing on one leg areas, roly poly areas. Set up hoops flat on the floor to walk through, stepping only in the circle.

Warming up

Always warm up muscles before doing any exercise. Strenuous stretches are not appropriate for this flexible and supple age group but you might like to have a fun run around the area you have cleared for the course or spend a few minutes dancing to a favourite song. (Some ideas for warming up are given on page 47.)

Setting off

Do a practice run, at a walk, with an older, sensible child to show what to do. Stagger the children as they set off and once they have started, keep them moving.

On the way around

Encourage children to have more than one go at an activity they find hard but then move them on. This is supposed to be fun! If there are children who are not managing much then make a note and practise again another day. Check that they have attended their milestone meetings with the health visitor.

Check how the children are moving from one activity to another. Don't waste opportunities – it is more fun to walk backwards (carefully!) than it is to walk forwards. If there is a queue they might hop or star jump or twist while they wait. Have a helper at each activity, monitoring safety and keeping the children motivated and mobile. Have an emergency stop signal (a loud whistle, for example) in case of an injury or to quieten down over-enthusiastic shouting! Encourage the children to encourage each other and to work as teams or partners where appropriate.

The finishing line

Have a collapsing area, ideally on a soft rug. Encourage the children to see how their bodies have reacted to the course. Feel for pulses, listen to each other's hearts and look at the rosy cheeks! Talk about the feeling of breathlessness (your body needs a lot of air to work so hard) and heat (your muscles are warmed up now aren't they!) When the children have finished, have a drink of water ready to replace the fluid they have lost and enjoy a group debriefing - What was your favourite thing? What was hard? What was easy? What would you change next time?

Sara Stocks

What to include

- ▪ Jumping
- ▪ Hopping (don't expect too much from your under fours here!)
- ▪ Skipping
- ▪ Stretching arms wide
- ▪ Stretching legs wide
- ▪ Crouching
- ▪ Crawling
- ▪ Twisting
- ▪ Climbing up and down (if you have safe equipment indoors)
- ▪ Running
- ▪ Balancing (on a line on the floor – a chalk mark is perfect or a rope if your flooring is not that sturdy)
- ▪ Placing feet carefully (stepping between hoops)

Vocabulary: skip, hop, climb, crawl, obstacle, under/over/around, pulse, heartbeat.

Here are some ideas for warming up before any kind of physical activity. This is strictly for fun - the children are too young for formal muscle stretches so make it a light-hearted game

Warm-up time

Toes: sleeping toes and wide awake toes - legs out in front, point toes away and then up

Calves: bending trees - feet firmly planted, lean forward, sideways and backwards

Knees: frog jumping - crouch down and jump from crouched position

Thighs: Jack in the box - curl up small and then jump up with arms above head

Hips: wriggly worms - feet firmly planted, slightly apart, hands on hips and wriggle!

Backs: bowing low - stretch up tall then curl up small

Stomachs: parachute falling - lie on tummies and hold arms and legs out

Hands: spider crawling - stretch hands out and wriggle fingers

Arms: windmill turns - stretch arms out and make circles with each one

Shoulders: do your ears hang low? - shrug as high as you can and relax

Neck: robot heads - stand perfectly still and just turn head from side to side

Face: growling lions - open mouth and eyes wide and growl!

Whole body: jump, run, stretch, dance and play

Sara Stocks

Children learn through being active, so channel their energy into some structured games. Here are a few ideas using a skipping rope and some bean bags. They can be done indoors or outdoors

Physical games

Most young children are nimble, flexible, robust, resourceful, creative and athletic. They have a lot to offer and we should be planning activities that are enjoyable, imaginative, challenging, promote confidence and, most importantly, build upon what a child can already do.

Activities should have a clear structure and time must be allowed for children to practise, improve and master new skills.
Children's safety is paramount at all times and simple ground rules should be set at the start of any physical activity. Adults working with the children should be alert and ready to intervene at any stage. They need to give support and encouragement, extending and challenging the children.

It is sensible to have a short, simple warm-up that the children are familiar with and will respond to, setting the tone for the lesson. Try playing 'Follow the leader' or using a tambourine to tap out rhythms for different actions such as walking, marching, walking on tip-toes, skipping, hopping, jumping, running, shaking, creeping and taking giant steps. If you use the tambourine it won't be long before the children are responding without any verbal instructions from you - great for developing listening skills!

Using a long skipping rope

Early Learning Goals: Move with confidence, imagination and in safety; Move with control and coordination.
Resources: Long rope, two adults.
■ Children stand in a line with toes to the rope (on the floor)

<u>XXXXXXXXXXXX</u>

On the instruction 'jump' the children jump two by two over the rope. Repeat several times.
(Teaching points: bend knees, swing arms.)
■ Introduce jumping backwards (much harder!) Line children up with heels to the rope and on the instruction 'jump' they jump backwards over the rope. Repeat lots of times!

■ Move children away from the rope. Wiggle the rope on the floor. Call children out individually and they have to run and jump over the moving rope.

■ Raise the rope and wiggle in the air. Call children's names individually to run and duck under the rope. (Be very careful of the height of the rope.)

Using bean bags

Early Learning Goal: Use a range of small equipment with increasing skill and confidence.
Resources: Bean bags.
■ Sit children in pairs facing each other and get them to throw the bean bag across to each other. Increase the space between them as they become more proficient.
■ Sit children cross-legged on the floor with a bean bag each. Get them to throw the bean bag past their nose into the air then catch it. Use the instructions - 'Ready, throw, catch, stop'. This keeps the control over the throwing and catching and you can see easily which children are having problems and need help and those that are proficient. Stress that the throw is not too high - to the top of their heads is fine.
■ Children sit on the floor and put a bean bag on their heads. On the instruction 'catch', they tilt their heads forward and let the bean bags drop into their hands.
■ Extend the above activity by getting the children to place the bean bag on their heads when standing then walk around balancing the bean bag on their heads - they can use hands outstretched at the side of their body to help them balance. On the instructions 'stop and catch' the children tilt their heads and catch the bean bag.

Pam Taylor

Introducing the language of movement to children alongside their actions is an important aspect of encouraging spatial awareness and physical development. Keeva Austin's ideas are best done in a large space. They can be used as a one-off session or planned over a number of weeks to ensure progression

The language of **movement**

Children need to know where they are in space and how they relate to objects and people around or near them. This involves the understanding of direction (up/down, over/under, to the right/to the left, forwards/backwards) and position (inside/outside, on/in, under/over, top/bottom, high/low). Actually doing an action linked to a word will help develop a clear understanding of the word and give them the ability to comprehend the dimensions of space and the relationship of their own bodies to space.

Children love the security of repetition and knowing what comes next and when given the opportunity to practise, repeat, copy and explore what their bodies can do their self-confidence increases and their movements become more controlled and co-ordinated. Start each movement session, then, with a familiar routine. Sit in a circle and play a copying game, encouraging the children to watch and imitate small movements, for example, clapping rhymes, head nodding, foot tapping, fingers clicking, or shrugging shoulders. Give older or more able children the chance to take the lead and see if they can also describe the movements they are making.

...Chug..chug..chug..chug!!

Follow this by asking the children to find a 'space' (young children may need help with this). Encourage the language of instruction and introduce action songs, for example, 'Simon says.' When they are ready, make the instructions more difficult and add position as well – 'Simon says touch your left ear'. Other songs to try are 'The hokey, cokey', 'The grand old Duke of York' and 'Here we go round the mulberry bush'.

With children who are finding these activities easy, introduce some of these ideas:

Watch and copy

Children love showing others what they can do. Sit in a circle and ask 'What can you do with your bodies?' Give each child in turn the opportunity to answer – the remaining group can watch and copy. Encourage them to describe the action or movement. At the end of the session, try to group the actions according to the language used – position, descriptive, controlled.

Fast and slow

Encourage the children to use the whole space provided. First let them move in any way they wish but then introduce start and stop sequences, encouraging them to use space effectively. When the children are ready, introduce different speeds, moving very slowly, slowly, quickly, very quickly. Children enjoy this activity but it may take several sessions of discussing the language of speed and refining it before they are able to do it! Older or more able children can begin to

follow more complex instructions involving speed and direction – stop, turn right, move forwards and then reverse. All these descriptive words will need to be introduced slowly to ensure children understand their meaning and can follow your instructions.

Directions and positions

With the children create a road layout (similar to an obstacle course) using small and large equipment. Such an activity will develop directional language, for example, moving round in a circle, rotating and moving between obstacles. If more than one child is using the layout, introduce positional language - 'Who is behind you?', 'Who is opposite you?' This demands good control and use of space.

Discuss different types of transport. Include tractors, bulldozers or a steamroller. Sit in a circle and encourage each child to think of a vehicle. Once it has been named ask them to describe how it moves in terms of speed and motion. (Is the vehicle fast or slow? Does it chug, trundle along or fly? Does it move jerkily or smoothly?) In pairs, ask them to produce a series of movements to show how their chosen vehicle moves. Encourage movements that show the strength and control of the vehicle.

Alternatively, ask the children to think of an animal and explore the way in which it moves.

Keeva Austin

Down's syndrome is a condition we have all heard of and perhaps think we know something about. Sarah Rutter explains the facts and makes the point that we should not make generalisations about people with Down's syndrome but look at each person as an individual

Including the child with Down's syndrome

The human body is made up of cells. Each cell is like a tiny factory, which makes the materials needed for growth and maintenance of the body. Contained within each cell is a set of 46 chromosomes (23 pairs), half of which come from the person's mother and half from the father. The chromosomes carry the genes that are inherited from a person's parents.

What is Down's syndrome?

Down's syndrome is a condition that occurs at or around the time a baby is conceived. Most people with Down's syndrome have an extra copy of chromosome 21 in every cell, making 47 in all. It is not yet known what causes this to happen. However, it is something that occurs in all races and all social classes. It is known that the chance of having a baby with Down's syndrome is higher in older mothers, although, because more babies overall are born to mothers in the 25- to 30-year-old age group, the majority of babies with Down's syndrome are born to 25- to 30-year-old women. We do know that, in the vast majority of cases, Down's syndrome is not passed down from generation to generation.

The presence of the extra chromosome has the effect of disrupting the growth and development of the baby. Quite how much effect the extra chromosome has varies from person to person, although all people who have Down's syndrome have a certain degree of learning disability.

People with Down's syndrome are as different from each other as any other unrelated members of the population. Like the rest of us, they get all their genes from their parents, so they look and act much more like members of their family than someone else with Down's syndrome. Their abilities and skills, strengths and weaknesses are just as variable as they are amongst the rest of us.

It is important not to make generalisations about people with Down's syndrome, but to look at each person as an individual.

How common is Down's syndrome?

In every 1,000 live births, one baby will be born with Down's syndrome. That is about 600 babies every year in the UK.

Diagnosis

In most cases, it becomes clear quite soon after birth that the baby has Down's syndrome. Doctors and midwives are usually alerted by certain signs that are more common among babies with Down's syndrome than among other babies. For example, if doctors detect a heart disorder it may alert them to the possibility of Down's syndrome because about 40 per cent of babies with Down's syndrome also have a heart problem. Diagnosis can be confirmed by a blood test to analyse the chromosomes.

It is important to stress that it is not possible to tell how disabled a child will be at this early stage. The number of physical characteristics of Down's syndrome a child has bears no relation to his or her degree of developmental delay.

Developmental delay

For a variety of reasons, such as poor health and/or hospitalisation at an early age, some young children with Down's syndrome will be more delayed than others. By the time children reach three or four, it may be apparent that they are not as advanced as their ordinary peers. Nowadays, most young children with Down's syndrome will have benefited from an early intervention programme (sometimes known as Portage) designed to help them gain the skills that other children learn naturally. Such programmes can be encouraging to parents who feel they can be actively involved in promoting their child's development. An early intervention worker will help parents to teach their child by breaking down tasks into small manageable steps. In some areas of the country, Portage is available from the age of six months; in others it starts later.

Speech and language delay

Speech and language difficulties are common in young children with Down's syndrome. Most children will be under the care of a speech and language therapist who will give parents and carers (including early years workers) guidelines on how to encourage the speech and language development of the child according to an individual programme.

'Most parents of a child with Down's syndrome will have become experts on their child's condition and needs. They need to feel that their views and knowledge are being respected and taken into account. Communication is the key to successful inclusion and many potential problems can be avoided by both parties keeping the other informed.'

Special Needs

Common health problems

Children's development can be delayed because of health problems that are more common in Down's syndrome.

Hearing

Many children with Down's syndrome have hearing problems caused by a condition called glue ear, which can be a consequence of repeated upper respiratory infections such as colds, or infected or enlarged adenoids. The fluid in the ear becomes thick like jelly and cannot drain away and hearing is affected. This can happen in all children but it is more frequent in children with Down's syndrome. Glue ear can cause deafness, infection, pain, delayed speech development, and temporary behaviour problems. Glue ear can be successfully treated, but early years workers need to be aware that the effects of hearing impairment can be reduced by a few simple steps outlined below:

- Always give the child plenty of time to respond to anything you have said - they will get frustrated if you start saying something new before they have had time to respond to the first thing you said. (This applies to most children with Down's syndrome whether or not they have any degree of hearing loss.)

- Try to face the child when speaking to them.

- Don't shout but speak clearly.

- If the child does not understand, don't just repeat what has been said but try to rephrase it.

- Make sure the child is paying attention before you start speaking.

- Give the child lots of visual clues - signs and gestures - to help them understand what you are saying.

- Keep your hands and any visual aids away from your mouth.

- Don't use exaggerated lip movements.

Vision problems

Some young children with Down's syndrome need glasses to correct their vision and, just as with other children who wear glasses, you may need to make sure that the child does wear them when necessary.

Where to go for help

Your local education authority's Special Education Department should be able to provide advice and support to staff who are involved in including a child with Down's syndrome in a pre-school setting.

The Down's Syndrome Association has an information service and also a number of advisers it can call on for specific information about such things as speech therapy, medical and behaviour problems. Lists of the DSA's leaflets and recommended reading are available to anyone who sends in a stamped addressed envelope to:

The Down's Syndrome Association,
155 Mitcham Road,
Tooting, London SW17 9PG.
Telephone: 0208 682 4001.

E-mail:
info@downs-syndrome.org.uk

Website address:
http://www.downs-syndrome.org.uk

Lack of muscle tone

Many babies with Down's syndrome have poor muscle tone and tend to be 'floppy'. In most cases, this improves as the child grows. However, it can contribute to delay in learning how to run, skip, throw and catch (gross motor skills) and affect the development of skills such as writing (fine motor development). Most children will master these skills eventually, but may take longer than their peers to do so. Many young children with Down's syndrome will have regular physiotherapy sessions either at home or at a child development centre. These sessions are designed to give parents exercises to do with their children to help them achieve particular skills.

Monitoring development

The developmental progress of children with Down's syndrome will usually be monitored by staff at the local child development centre. In the early years, parents are often offered extra support by a specialist health visitor or a social worker who is able to keep them informed of facilities for children with special needs in the area.

How to cope with questions about difference

Pre-school children in general tend to accept differences in colour, behaviour and so on much more readily than older children might. Most of the time, if children in a group ask questions about a child being different, it will be enough to point out that we are all different - 'You have blonde hair but Jessica has black hair'. The Down's Syndrome Association (see box) has a list of recommended reading books for children which deal with issues of difference.

Relationships with parents/carers

Most parents of a child with Down's syndrome will have become experts on their child's condition and needs. They need to feel that their views and knowledge are being respected and taken into account. Communication is the key to successful inclusion and many potential problems can be avoided by both parties keeping the other informed. It may be helpful to remember that a child with Down's syndrome is a child first and foremost and that his or her condition is secondary.

Sarah Rutter, The Down's Syndrome Association.

Dyspraxia or developmental coordination disorder (DCD)

Until ten to fifteen years ago the term dyspraxia, meaning a deficit in movement planning, hadn't been heard of in the UK. Children with motor coordination difficulties would probably have just been thought of as clumsy.

Dyspraxia - also known as developmental coordination disorder or DCD - is about ten years behind in terms of its acknowledgement and research in comparison to dyslexia. It is part of a spectrum of specific learning difficulties along with AD/HD (attention deficit/ hyperactivity disorder), Asperger's syndrome and dyslexia. It affects between four and six per cent of the population and about three times as many boys as girls.

What causes DCD?

There has been little research completed looking at the causes of developmental coordination disorder. There are both environmental and genetic factors at play. This means that often someone else in the family may have had dyslexia or other learning difficulties but when they were growing up they may not have been recognised.

Is the incidence of DCD on the increase?

More children are now being identified as having dyspraxia and this may be due to an increase in the condition because of different parenting styles today.

'More children are now being identified as having dyspraxia and this may be due to an increase in the condition because of different parenting styles today.'

How have parenting styles changed?

The 'Back to sleep' campaign now encourages parents to place babies on their back for the majority of the time. In the past, they would have put babies to sleep in prams or cots during the day and placed them prone as well as on their backs.

Nowadays, most babies are usually either in a car seat, which is carried in and out from the car, and placed on the floor, or in a pushchair. In both cases the child is supine (on the back) rather than in a prone (on the front) position. Children are not placed on a baby mat on the floor as often as they used to for fear of it being dirty. The use of playpens has also been limited as they are now seen as trapping the baby, rather than allowing them to explore their environment safely.

For most babies, these changes won't have a long-term affect. However, for the low-toned, floppy child, the opportunity to gain greater head and shoulder control and hip stability is essential for future development. The floppy baby is also likely to cry when placed prone,

as he is not able to lift his head for any length of time. This, combined with changes in parenting styles, may be the reason why there is a growing incidence of non-crawlers as well as more cases of DCD being identified.

The prone position is important as it allows the child to strengthen the neck muscles, do push-ups (ready for crawling) and learn to reach for toys (helping hand-eye coordination and bilateral integration).

The child with DCD may also walk later and for this reason may be put in a baby walker. Yet the child with DCD often has poor hip stability and the modern baby walker tends to make them sit down rather than use it as a support. He then moves around not just in a forward direction but also sideways like a crab! The older style walker with bricks in it made the child stand up to hold on to the bar in a good walking style.

Children with DCD also often have sequencing and rhythm problems that affect them in games and with activities like writing and mathematics. Early games played at

home such as singing nursery rhymes, catching and throwing balls are less common as children turn to television and video for entertainment, even at a young age.

Fewer children are eating together with families at mealtimes and this means that they are not getting the chance to practise key skills such as using cutlery (helps bilateral integration skills - a pre-cursor for writing) and sitting at the table and taking turns (helping, listening and social skills).

Children's diets have also changed. Today we eat more processed foods and less fish regularly. There is growing evidence that fatty acid supplements such as cod liver oil or Eye-Q (available over the counter at chemists) are especially helpful because it is thought that some children with dyspraxia have problems metabolising certain fatty acids needed for brain and eye activity.

How would you recognise a child that may have dyspraxia?

- Late motor milestones - this means that the child may have been later sitting, crawling, walking or talking. Some children may not have crawled at all.
- Balance problems – the child may be unreasonably afraid or conversely unaware of danger in precarious situations. Climbing on a climbing frame or along a wall or walking downstairs may make the child very nervous. The child may also be unstable if not sat properly in a chair with their feet on the floor.
- Poor bilateral integration – the child may find it difficult to coordinate both sides of the body. This may make using a knife and fork or handwriting harder to do.
- He may seem to run in a rather ungainly manner, may need to use his

arms to help balance, and find that stopping is quite hard to do. Catching and throwing a ball may be harder to do as well as being able to stand on one leg, skip or jump.
- Younger children often find a bicycle is harder to pedal.

Fine motor skills

- Immature grasp and poor dexterity – There may be difficulty holding and manipulating small objects, for example doing up buttons, holding and using a pencil, using scissors and playing with jigsaws.
- Poorly established dominance – the child may not seem to be clearly right- or left-handed. He may use whichever hand is nearer to reach.
- The child may have poor pencil control, and find drawing and colouring in harder to do than his peers.

Learning difficulties

The child with DCD may experience difficulties with:
- Letter and shape recognition
- Writing - their writing may vary in size and quality from the top of the page to the bottom. The letters may go above and below lines on the page. (Even at the age of seven or eight the child may still have writing that looks more like a four- or five-year-old's.)
- Counting and recognising numbers

Language and communication

- The child may have been slower to acquire clear speech and may still have poor speech which may be less distinct when the child is tired.
- The child may not join in with other children, playing alongside rather than interacting with them.

- He may appear at times not to be listening.

Behaviour and emotion

- Distractible- the child may appear to be distractible but this may be because of his inability to balance on a chair or filter out unwanted sounds, movement or a visually busy environment.
- Frustration – this usually presents for the younger child with behaviour which is better in school than at home. The child may have tantrums even as he gets older, especially at home.

So what can be done?

If you suspect that a child may have dyspraxia, early recognition and prevention is better than intervention. Therapy will help some children if their symptoms are more severe but plenty of play experiences to build up muscle control are important. Some schools even provide programmes to promote motor development. For the younger child, the best advice is to encourage big play, such as setting up obstacle courses, playing on the floor and swimming. Give them a big paintbrush and a bucket of water and let them 'paint' the walls or fence outside.

Make sure the child has their basic building block skills in place before moving onto more complicated work. The child with DCD often seems younger and just needs a bit of extra time to learn new skills.

They should see their GP or health visitor who could refer them on to a children's centre for a full assessment.

For parents, one of the most important things is to be kept informed of what help and support their child is receiving in your setting and who they should liaise with (SENCO or class teacher) and where they can get further advice through the education authority and local support groups.

Dr Amanda Kirby, Medical Director, The Dyscovery Centre, Cardiff.

It's important for all children, whatever their age, to have quiet periods during the day. This may mean a sleep, especially for younger children, or it may just be a quiet time when children do quiet activities, or have a story

Providing opportunities for **rest and sleep**

When they are newly born, babies sleep for a large part of their day. As they grow, the need for sleep becomes less until, by about two and a half or three they don't need a sleep during the day. Of course, sleep patterns vary, and some children will sleep more than others. If you work in a nursery which takes children from a few months old until they go to school, you will probably already have noticed the difference in the amount of sleep they need, and the different routines to cater for this. It would be helpful for you to spend a little time in each of the rooms at sleep or rest time, and observe the different needs of the children in each age group. You will find that even children of the same age have different sleep patterns. Talk to the staff about the sleep and rest arrangements in each room.

In the baby room, the younger babies will follow their own individual sleep and feed pattern. By about six months, they will begin to get into the routine of breakfast, dinner and tea as they start being weaned, but this will still need to be varied if a baby is asleep. For instance, the normal dinnertime in one nursery is 11.45 in the morning, but by 11 o'clock Alfie is very tired and obviously needs a sleep. He sleeps until 1 o'clock, and has his dinner when he wakes up.

It's important to ask parents about the children's sleep patterns when they start at nursery, especially with very young children, so that you can keep as far as possible to the same routine. Another important thing to consult parents about is where their child sleeps and how they go to sleep. They may sleep in a cot or

a pram, a pushchair, or a rocker. They may go off to sleep on their own, or need patting or stroking, or be rocked to sleep, or use a comfort object such as a soft toy or blanket. It's important that you follow the same routine at the nursery. This will help the children to feel more secure in their new surroundings.

Up to about two, children will normally have two sleeps in the day, but by about two, they will usually only need one sleep in the afternoon. As they get older, some will continue to need a sleep while others only need a quiet time to rest. The usual routine in a nursery is to have a sleep or rest time straight after dinner for children up to about two and a half. Ideally, sleeping children should be in a separate room so that they are not disturbed, but this is not always possible, so it's important to provide quiet activities for the children who are awake. They need to rest at some time during the day, because it's a long day for many of them. Activities such as books, jigsaws, playdough and other quiet table-top activities are ideal. It's good for the

adults to sit quietly with the children, rather than rushing around getting jobs done, to create a restful atmosphere in the room. There are other times of the day, too, when children have quiet times, such as snack time, story and singing time.

Parents may ask you not to put their child down to sleep at all, because they have difficulty in getting them to sleep at night. This can be stressful for parents, so you need to respect their wishes. However, if you find that the child really needs a sleep, you will need to discuss this with the parents, so that you can come to a satisfactory agreement. One way you can help to ensure that children are ready to sleep at night is to give them the opportunity for plenty of exercise, activity and fresh air. It's also important to establish a relaxed, calm atmosphere and routine for sleep or rest, whether it's in the nursery during the day, or a bedtime routine at night. At home, it may be by having a quiet playtime after supper, followed by a warm bath and a story, so that the child gets into a good bedtime routine.

Sleep routines vary a great deal from family to family, both within the same culture and between different cultural groups. Some families have strict bedtimes, others keep their children up until they go to bed. Where parents are working, they may want to keep their children up a bit later, so that they can spend some time with them. You need to respect different parents' preferences, and agree a sleep or rest plan which fits in with both the child's and the parents' needs. This will ensure a healthy, happy child and contented parents.

Mary Townsend

Chapter 3

Unit C4: Support children's social and emotional development

About this unit

Unit C4 is a really important unit in your NVQ because it's about helping children to feel happy, confident and secure, which is the key to children's well-being, learning and development. You can have a wonderful building with all the best equipment, but if children are not happy and secure they will not learn and develop normally.

Think about how you felt when you first started working in your setting. If the other staff were welcoming and helpful, you would have soon become happy and confident in your work, but if they were unfriendly and unhelpful, you would still be feeling very insecure. Remember this when you're welcoming the children and caring for them during the day. You and the other adults in your setting are taking the place of the child's parents while the children are in your care, and so you're a very important part of the children's lives.

note:

It's better to leave this unit until later in the training, and to complete it over a period, so that your assessor can see how well you help support children's social and emotional development in different situations. She will cross reference some of the evidence from other observations

Read through the elements and think about whether you're ready to do this unit yet. You do need to have done some training for the unit, to make sure that you have a good understanding of the important issues. You may like to leave the unit till later, after you have done Units C8 and C9.

Links with other units

You will be providing some of the evidence for this unit while you're doing the activities for Units C8 and C9. For instance, when you're playing games and organising activities you're encouraging the children to relate to each other and to take turns (C4.2), to make choices and to do things for themselves (C4.3), encouraging positive behaviour and dealing with unwanted behaviour (C4.5).

There are also links with P1, Relate to parents, because of

course, the better your relationship with the parents, the more secure the child will feel. Don't forget to keep a record of anything you can cross reference on your cross referencing sheet for this unit. Your assessor will be able to help you with this if you're not sure what to do.

Values

Have a look at the values section in C4 in your candidate handbook. As you might expect, the **welfare of the child** is important in every element. You also need to be aware of **keeping children safe** and **working in partnership with parents and families** in every element.

The best way to help a child to feel secure is to work closely with their parents, so that the way you care for the child is as near as possible to the way she is cared for at home. Parents need to feel confident that their children are receiving the best possible care, so you need to keep them well informed.

You also need to think about children's **learning and development** throughout the elements. Children will not learn and develop normally unless they are happy and secure.

As in all units, you need to be a **reflective practitioner**. You will be well aware by now how important it is for you to think about how what you do affects the children you work with.

In Element 3, for **equality of opportunity** you need to think about how you make sure that what you expect of children is appropriate for their stage of development and that you're not making assumptions based on stereotypes. For instance, do you expect girls to do more for themselves than boys? Do you expect children of different ethnic groups to be more or less independent? Do you have high enough expectations of children with disabilities?

In Element 2 on relating to others, you need to think about **anti-discrimination** and **celebrating diversity**. How do you help children to learn about and respect children and adults of all backgrounds and cultures and relate positively to them?

You need to be aware of **confidentiality** and **working with other professionals** in Elements 4 and 5. For instance, if you are worried about children's ability to express their feelings or about persistent problem behaviour, you should only discuss this with the relevant staff, and not with anyone who doesn't need to know. As an assistant, your role is limited, and you need to know when to pass on responsibility to a more senior member of staff.

Getting started

In this unit you are aiming to show how you can help children to:

◆ adjust to new settings

◆ relate to others

◆ develop self-reliance and self-esteem

◆ recognise and deal with their feelings

◆ develop positive aspects of their behaviour

Read through the elements and use your personal skills review to help you decide which you feel most confident about and which you need more practice or training in. You should have done some training before starting this unit. If you haven't, check with your assessor when it will be available. There are some useful articles later in the chapter and suggestions for further reading. You also need to understand your setting's policies on settling in and behaviour management. Ask for copies and discuss them with your supervisor.

> You need to time Element 1 carefully, because this is about helping children to adjust to new settings. If you're in a school you need to time this for the beginning of the year. In a nursery, timing is not so difficult, because children tend to start all through the year.

Plan with your assessor how you will provide the evidence for the unit. She may gather evidence over a period of time, rather than through particular activities. Don't forget to cross reference evidence from other units. Ask your assessor to help with this if you need to. We will suggest activities or routines for each element, but you may have done them already as part of the activities you have carried out for C8 and C9. Use your assessment plan to record how you will gather the evidence.

Element C4.1 Help children to adjust to new settings

Key issues

When a child starts going into a care setting it may be the first time she has left her parents, so it's a difficult time for both parents and children, and you need to be sensitive to this. The way you welcome children and parents will have a big effect on their happiness and confidence in the setting. As an assistant, you will not be responsible for the setting's policy, but make sure you know what it is, and do your part to put it into practice.

The parents and child will visit the setting before the child is left for the first time. The manager will gather the necessary information from parents at this meeting (you will cover this in P1, Relate to parents). Records will be kept confidential but your manager will tell you anything you need to know in order to care for the child - for example, they may have a medical condition or allergy.

In a school, the first meeting will usually be a formal open day, with all parents and children attending together. This may happen in a nursery school or playgroup, too, where children tend to start at the beginning of a school year. These settings may also carry out home visits, so that the children see the staff in the security of their own home. Staff may take an activity pack for the children as well as information for the parents. Often, parents are encouraged to stay with the children for a while at least for the first few days, and to make the child's stay short at first. Some schools only take children for half a day in the first few weeks.

In some settings it's difficult to have the ideal settling-in arrangements because parents have to work, but it's important to settle the child in as gradually as possible. This is especially true of children between the age of eight months, who are beginning to be wary of strangers, and two and a half, when they are beginning to want to be with other children. They are too young to explain that mummy and daddy will be back, so they can get distressed. Of course, children's ability to cope with separation will vary a lot, whatever their age, because all children are different.

On the first visit, encourage the parents to stay as long as possible with their child, and encourage them to visit at least once more before they leave the child. The first time the child is left should be short, gradually building up to a full day. Never let a parent sneak out without saying goodbye. It often happens, but it's the worst thing they can do. The parent should say where they are going and when they will be back. The child might be upset when the parent says goodbye but at least they won't feel abandoned. Always let the child have something from home to hold, to give them comfort if they need it.

Encourage the child to do an activity with you to take her mind off feeling insecure. Be friendly and reassuring. You need to build up a relationship in which the child feels she can trust you. Some settings have key workers with responsibility for a small group of children. Ideally, there should be two, so that if one is away or off duty, the other is there to comfort the child if necessary. Show the child around the setting, and make sure that she knows where the toilet is. It's important that children have a place of their own - their coat peg, and a drawer to put personal things in. It's good to involve the other children in helping a new child to settle in. Tell them before the new child arrives, and suggest ways they might make the child feel welcome.

Children whose first language is not English may find it particularly difficult to settle in if they do not understand the language. In this case, your body language, gestures, smiles and hugs will be helpful. Again, something from home for them to hold is really important. Your setting should also have displays and activities which reflect the cultural backgrounds of the children if they are from minority ethnic groups. Some settings are fortunate to have a member of staff who can speak different languages. If not, your manager could ask a member of the family if they can come in for part of the day until the child is settled.

The **knowledge evidence** statements for this element are 2, 5, 17 and 22. You will need to show that you understand:

◆ how individual children's needs might vary in terms of social and emotional development, change and separation (also C4.4)

◆ how you can make children feel welcome

◆ why you need flexible settling-in strategies

◆ the importance of preparing adults and children in the setting for new children.

Your training sessions will help you to develop a good understanding of these issues. Your evidence for the element will give you some of the evidence you need. Your assessor may give you assignments or questions to fill any gaps.

> **Don't forget** to check with your manager what training is available through the local EYDCP.

Which type of evidence?
Ideally, your assessor should **observe** all but one of the PCs and one aspect of each range section, but it's sometimes

difficult to arrange a visit at the right time. If your assessor works in your setting it's easier, but most assessors only visit the setting when they're carrying out observations.

If your assessor is not available when a new child is starting, keep a **diary** of how you helped the child over the first few days, and ask your supervisor to write a **witness testimony** to say you handled the situation competently. Your assessor will want to ask you **questions** about settling-in arrangements. If you have a written **settling-in policy** include it in your evidence, with a brief note to say how you used it, or discuss it with your assessor.

Element C4.2 Help children to relate to others

Key issues
Children who have come to a care setting for the first time may only have had a close relationship with their own parents and family, so they may need help to learn how to relate to other children and adults. They need to see good role models around them. It's important for children to see the adults in the setting being caring and co-operative. If the staff are calm, friendly and caring, the children are more likely to be the same. If adults are always shouting at the children and each other, the children probably will, too. Watch the staff in your setting, and think about your own practice. Which category do you fall into? Or is it somewhere in between the two? You are probably not in a position to tell other staff what to do, but

you can ensure that you are always calm and caring yourself. You need to treat the children and other adults with respect if you want to be treated with the same respect.

There are ways of doing things that encourage children to be co-operative, like taking turns to give out the drinks and snacks and helping each other to tidy up. Particular activities and group games like 'Farmer's in his den', parachute games (you don't need a parachute - a big piece of stretchy cloth bought cheap from a market stall will do), and activities where children work in pairs, like a computer game, are good for encouraging co-operation.. You need to remember, though, that very young children - up till at least two years old - are not yet ready to share and take turns, so don't expect them to.

Don't be too quick to jump in if children are having a small disagreement - they may solve it themselves. If you do need to step in, get them to reach a solution that's acceptable to both. Perhaps two children want to ride the same bike. Help them to decide who has it first, and for how long, and an alternative for the one who has to wait, and make sure that it happens. Children are good at seeing when something is fair or unfair.

It's important that children learn to relate to adults as well. In a nursery or other group setting, they will naturally get used to relating to several adults, through circle times, stories, singing and other group activities. They may get to know parents, too, if your setting invites parents in to help. It's good for them to see other people in and outside of the setting. Professionals such as child psychologists or health visitors may come in to see children. You can invite people in to talk to the children, like the local police officer, or visit local places of interest like the fire station, or a place of worship. Of course, you will need to ask your supervisor if you want to arrange anything like this. These things are probably part of your setting's curriculum plan. Try to be at team meetings where these things are likely to be discussed.

Children are quick to pick up attitudes, so you need to make sure that you show a positive attitude to children and adults from all backgrounds. Look around your setting and see if it displays positive images of a variety of ethnic groups, people with a disability in an active role, girls and boys in non-traditional roles; look at the displays, the toys and equipment, and notices. If you hear children making negative, abusive or discriminatory remarks to another child, you must challenge it. Children learn these attitudes from adults, so don't blame the child. Discuss it with the child in terms of how hurtful it is to someone and how they would feel if someone was that unkind to them. Comfort the child who was the subject of the attack. Report it to your supervisor, who may feel she needs to discuss it with the parents.

The knowledge evidence statements for this element are 1, 6, 12, 19, 23, 24. You need to show that you understand:

- children's social and emotional development and how it's linked to other areas of development (also C4.4, C4.5)

- the effects of discriminatory and anti-social behaviour on children, how to challenge the behaviour and console the abused child (also C4.3)

- how to provide activities and strategies, materials and equipment which help children to relate to each other, respect different cultures, backgrounds, genders and special needs

> Discriminatory behaviour is treating one person or group of people less fairly than other people or groups.

You may have already covered the first knowledge statement in your child development assignment. Try to cover as much as you can in your evidence for the element. You should by now have attended a training session for this unit.

Which type of evidence?
Check with your assessor whether you have already provided evidence for this element through other activities, and **cross reference** if you can. If not, your assessor will need to **observe** you working with the children for four of the seven PCs and one aspect of each range category, so set up an activity which encourages them to relate to each other and co-operate. Write an **activity plan** if you need to. Write a **diary** or **reflective account** of times when you have helped children to work co-operatively; think about routines you have organised during the day, or an occasion when you had to intervene in a conflict.

> **Remember!**
> If you already have evidence for this unit, don't do extra unnecessary work. Check with your assessor.

Element C4.3 Help children to develop self-reliance and self-esteem

Key issues
This element is about two things - self-reliance - doing things for yourself and having choices - and self-esteem - feeling good about yourself. You need to give children the chance to be self-reliant, to choose and make decisions for themselves. Children need to become independent as they grow older, so you need to start by giving them little opportunities early on. If a baby shows signs of wanting to hold the spoon when you're feeding her, give her another spoon to hold. As soon as you think she is able, let her start feeding herself.

Give children little jobs to do as soon as they're able to walk. A toddler loves to copy mummy or daddy dusting or sweeping. As children grow, give them more responsibility. Let them dress themselves, as far as they can, and allow extra time for them to do it. Allow plenty of time for tidying up, so that children can do it with help from you without it being a rushed, stressful time.

Give children praise and encouragement for trying. Do help them where they need it, but don't undermine their confidence by doing so. For instance, you could say something like 'You've done really well with … but would you like a bit of help with … because it's really difficult? Perhaps we can manage it together'.

Look at how your setting plans activities. Do you let children choose activities or do you set them out? Do they have a choice of drink or snack? Can they choose when to have their snack? What other choices are they given? Sometimes, children are allowed to make their own rules within the setting. This is a really good way of getting them to accept responsibility for their own actions. You may not be responsible for making these decisions, but you can give children choice in small ways. At story time let the children choose the story or songs sometimes. Try to bring some choice into the activities you are supervising - even if it's only what colour paper to paint their picture on, or a choice of collage materials to make a picture. Ask the children their opinion about simple things and listen to what they are saying. Role play is a good opportunity for children to make choices and decisions.

Some children find it more difficult to be self-reliant and to choose. In some families and cultures children are not expected to be self-reliant. Parents may have done everything for the child. Sometimes it's necessary for the nursery manager to discuss this with parents, because of course when children go to school they need to be independent and take responsibility for looking after their personal needs, such as dressing and going to the toilet.

Self-esteem is feeling good about yourself. Children need to feel valued and respected if they are to feel good about themselves. When children are self-reliant and independent, it gives them a lot more confidence and self-esteem. Think about how you feel if you know you can do something well, or that you have been given a choice about something. You feel pretty good. But they also need to feel that their efforts are valued, and that they are valued for themselves. If you know you've done a good job, or you've made a special effort to look great, and no-one acknowledges it, how does that make you feel? Remember to give children praise where it's due. Remember that what's easy for one child may be really difficult for another, so it's important that you recognise the effort a child has put into a piece of work.

In extreme cases where children have very low self-esteem there may be a serious underlying issue such as abuse. If this is suspected, the senior staff will need to take further action.

The knowledge evidence statements for this element are 7, 12, 13, 21, 25, 26 and 27. You need to show that you understand:

◆ how self-reliance and self-esteem develop and how they are helped by the development of communication skills

◆ how to listen and encourage interaction between children, and between adults and children

◆ how to encourage negotiation with children

◆ how to provide activities, strategies, materials and equipment to develop self-reliance and self-esteem, and respect for individuals, taking account of different cultural backgrounds, genders and special needs

◆ why this is important

◆ different cultural expectations about independence

◆ when to praise children, and why it is important

Try to cover as much as you can in your evidence for the element. Your assessor may give you an assignment or oral questions to fill any gaps.

Which type of evidence?
Your assessor may be able to **cross reference** some evidence from other units. If not, she will need to **observe** four of the nine PCs and one aspect of each range category. Some of these need to be done in the context of the normal routine, although you could **plan an activity** such as art, to show how you give children a choice of materials, and at the end of the session get them to join in with tidying. Keep a **diary** of the times you have helped children to do things for themselves, or given children choices.

Element C4.4 Help children to recognise and deal with their feelings

Key issues
Young children experience a whole range of feelings, just as adults do, but they are not able to express them in the same way, because of their limited ability to communicate. A baby will cry when she is hungry, or when she wants some attention, and smile when she is comfortable or being talked to. As she begins to move around, she may scream in

frustration if you take away from her something unsafe to play with. A toddler is full of curiosity, has no concept of waiting or sharing, and has no sense of danger. She is not yet able to talk well enough to make adults understand what she wants. No wonder she has temper tantrums! By the time a child is three, she should normally be better able to communicate, but will still sometimes have difficulty in expressing her feelings. You need to develop strategies for helping children to think about their feelings and how to express them in appropriate ways.

The important thing is always to stay calm yourself when a child has a temper tantrum. Children can be quite frightened by their own outbursts, and you need to reassure them. If you start shouting it will make things worse. If you need to, remove them from a situation where they might hurt themselves or other children, and stay with them until they calm down. Then discuss gently what the problem was. It may simply be frustration at not being able to do something they wanted to do.

With a child who is usually happy and even-tempered, there could be another reason why she is behaving in this way - perhaps something has happened at home, such as a new baby or family break-up. You need to report any incidents to your supervisor, who may talk to the parents if she feels there is a problem. Watch for children who are withdrawn, and don't express their feelings at all. There could be a serious problem here such as child abuse, which must be dealt with.

> **Remember** how crucial it is to maintain confidentiality. Never reveal anything about a child or their family to anyone except your supervisor or other staff who need to know.

It's important to talk to children about their feelings once they're old enough to understand. You can do this through a story or a game. Puppets, dolls and role play are useful for getting children to act out feelings and situations which make them anxious and unhappy. If you use a story, perhaps about a child who was sad, talk about why he was sad, and what makes them feel sad. A game you can use is to make faces with different expressions, and ask the children to make the same expression. Use mirrors (unbreakable ones) to make it more fun. Talk about what makes them happy/angry/sad and so on. Talk about how they can deal with negative feelings by talking about them rather than lashing out at another child or adult.

If you know a child is feeling angry or anxious there are some activities which are beneficial. Clay or playdough is good for punching and pummelling if they want to let off steam. Water and sand are quite soothing. Role play enables children to act out anxieties.

Remember that this element is about positive feelings, too. It's

important that we don't lose that feeling of enthusiasm, joy and wonder about the good things in life. Point out to children the exciting and interesting things you experience - listening to a bird, seeing a beautiful flower, feeling the wind in your hair or the sand in your toes. Remember to look for the good things that children do and praise them, so that you make them feel good about themselves.

The **knowledge evidence** statements for this element are 4, 8, 9, 11, 15 and 16. You need to show that you understand:

◆ how to liaise with others in the team and outside professionals when there are concerns about a child, and the boundaries of confidentiality (also C4.5)

◆ the importance to social and emotional development of children being able to recognise and deal with their feelings

◆ how to recognise signs of distress

◆ how powerful children's feelings can be and their difficulty in controlling them

◆ strategies for encouraging children to express their feelings in appropriate words and actions

◆ why you need to remain calm

Your training sessions should give you the necessary knowledge and understanding. Cover as many points as you can in your evidence for the element. You can cover any gaps by writing a **reflective account** using examples from your own work practice where possible, or complete the assignment set by your assessor.

Which type of evidence?

Your assessor may be able to **cross reference** some of the evidence for this element. She needs to have observed four of the seven PCs and one aspect of each range section. She may want to **observe** you carrying out a practical activity such as using a story, a game, dolls or puppets, to talk about feelings with the children. She may ask you **questions** about why you do certain things. Ask your supervisor to write a **witness testimony** if she has seen you dealing effectively with a child having an emotional outburst. She could include this with one for Element 5, stating how you have dealt with unwanted behaviour.

Element C4.5 Assist children to develop positive aspects of their behaviour

Key issues

This element is about your overall approach to helping children develop positive behaviour. The other elements all contribute to this one. It's about making children's environment interesting and varied, so that children are always occupied and don't get bored; and about making sure that they know what the boundaries are and stick to them.

Your setting should have a policy for managing children's behaviour, which all the staff agree on and work within. Children need consistency. It's confusing and frustrating if one member of staff expects one thing and others expect something different. Make sure you know the policy in your setting, and discuss it with your supervisor. If you're not sure about how to handle a particular situation, or what the boundaries are, always check. Find out whether your setting has rules, and whether they have been agreed with the children. Rules should be positive, rather than negative. For example, instead of saying 'No hitting' say 'Always be kind to each other'.

Children are more likely to behave positively if they are kept occupied and interested, so have a range of activities for them to choose from, and make sure they're at the right level for them. Very young children can't concentrate for long, so they need frequent changes of activity. Once you see children getting restless, it's time to change the activity. If you are doing most of the activity and the children are just watching, the activity is at the wrong level.

If you're enthusiastic, the children will be, too. If you look bored and don't talk to them, they will quickly become bored, too. Give plenty of praise and encouragement. Remember, it's the effort that's important, not the finished product. Remember to praise them for being kind and helpful - this is much more effective than telling them off for when they are behaving badly. Try to think of something positive to tell the parents about their child when they come to collect them.

Never say things like 'You're a naughty girl, I don't like you when you do that'. Make it clear that it's the behaviour you don't like, not the child.

Tell children why their behaviour is good or bad. For instance, say 'That was helpful of you to tidy up the bricks' or 'It was unkind to snatch the doll from Isaac, he had it first'. If a child who is normally well behaved suddenly starts being difficult, it may be an incident that has upset her - for instance, a new baby, or the death of a grandparent. You need to inform your supervisor, who will follow it up with the parents. If a child is persistently showing negative behaviour, the staff need to agree a strategy for dealing with it. There may be serious reasons for the child's behaviour. The manager will need to discuss this with the parents, and it may be necessary to call in a child psychologist to assess the child.

It can be quite tricky dealing with difficult behaviour. Be calm and try to avoid a confrontation. For example, if a child refuses to tidy up an activity when you have asked, say something like, 'Let's do it together, and then you can tell your mummy how helpful you've been'. It's better to ignore the bad behaviour as far as possible and to praise the child when she is behaving well. Watch how other members of staff deal with difficult behaviour. You can learn a lot in this way. Try to get onto a behaviour management course. Your supervisor or nursery manager will be able to tell you what is available through your local EYDCP.

Never use physical punishment on a child.
Never shut a child alone in another room.

The knowledge evidence statements for this element are 10, 14, 18 and 20. You need to show that you understand:

◆ factors and circumstances which may cause children to display negative and difficult behaviour

◆ the importance of boundary setting and consistency

◆ techniques for managing behaviour

◆ the behaviour management policy of the setting

You should undertake some training for this element, because it's crucial that you learn how to manage children's behaviour effectively. Your other evidence will cover some of the knowledge, but if necessary write a **reflective account** or complete the assignment or questions your assessor has given you.

Which type of evidence?

Your assessor only has to **observe** two PCs for this element, because it's not always possible for her to see you dealing with unwanted behaviour. She won't have to do a specific observation for this element, because she will probably have picked up evidence when she has been observing other units. She may want to ask you **questions** to check your understanding. You need to keep a **diary** of times when you have dealt with unwanted behaviour. Ask your supervisor to write a **witness testimony** that you are able to deal with unwanted behaviour competently. She could include this with the one for Element 4.

You need to be absolutely clear about what your setting's policy is on settling in. Mary Townsend offers some advice on how to make it a positive experience for young children

Settling-in procedures

For young children starting in an early years setting, it may be the first time they have spent any length of time away from their parents. Children will come to the setting with very different experiences. Some may be used to seeing other children and adults because they are part of a close-knit family, and they have spent lots of time with grandparents, aunties and uncles and cousins. But this is often not the case nowadays, with families moving to different parts of the country for their work. They may have met other adults and children in a mother and toddler group, or they may have been at home without much contact with anyone outside the immediate family. Starting nursery may be quite a distressing time for some children, so it's important to try to make the transition as painless as possible.

It's important to consider the particular difficulties associated with the age at which the child starts to attend an early years setting. Young babies will generally settle without any difficulty as long as they are well cared for, and their routine is more or less the same as at home. They should as far as possible have a key worker who carries out most of their care.

From the age of about eight months, when babies begin to be wary of strangers, until about two and a half years, when children begin to enjoy being with other children and adults, is the most difficult time for a child to be separated from their parents, so it's crucial that extra care is taken to settle them in gradually. My most distressing memory during a visit to a nursery was a little girl of about 15 months old who was absolutely inconsolable. She had just started at the nursery, and had no understanding of what was happening to her. So how can this be avoided?

Full day care providers such as nurseries and childminders, who take children at any age,

need to emphasise to parents the need for a gradual introduction to the setting. Most do insist that parents at least have one pre-start visit with their child. Some pre-schools, nurseries and childminders have developed their own effective settling-in strategies to suit the circumstances of working parents. It's not always easy when parents are working, but with a little thought and care, you can usually arrange for the child and the parent to spend some time together in the setting before the child is left for long periods. Most parents are anxious about leaving their children and will be only too happy to make sure that they are happily settled.

Most local authority schools and nursery schools have a well planned settling-in procedure which may include some or all of the following:

■ A visit to the child's home to talk to the parents and to the child. Sometimes it will be the teacher and the nursery nurse who will visit so that while the teacher is talking to the parents and filling in any relevant forms, the nursery nurse will

bring an activity to do with the child. They may leave a pack for the parents and child to do together, to prepare them for starting in the setting. Some parents may find a home visit a bit threatening, so it's important to explain beforehand what the purpose is, and to respect their wish if they don't want a visit.

■ An initial meeting at the nursery or school to give parents information about the school's policies and aims, and to explain the curriculum. Often, the children will go into the classroom and do activities with the teachers and nursery nurses or classroom assistants while the parents have a meeting with the

headteacher, and fill in any relevant paperwork. The parents may then be encouraged to spend some time with their children in the classroom.

■ The parents may be invited to bring their child in for several short sessions, staying with the child the first time, then leaving the child for short periods, before attending for full sessions at the nursery or school.

■ On starting school or nursery, parents are encouraged to stay and play with the child until they are settled, then leave. Often, children only attend for half a day for the first few weeks. There may be a staggered intake, so that staff can give plenty of attention to each child.

Sharing information

It's important to gather as much information about the child from the parents as possible. Every setting must have records which include the child's dietary needs, medical background, relevant family details, contact addresses and telephone numbers and permission for emergency treatment. But there is other useful information which will help you to get to know the child better. Some settings have an 'All about me' book or something similar, which parents are asked to fill in about their children's development, and their likes and dislikes, fears and anxieties. Parents are their children's first carers and educators, they know their own child better than anyone, and you need to show them that you respect them as such. Too often, carers see themselves as the experts, and don't take enough account of what parents can tell them. You need to work in partnership with parents, so that you provide continuity of care and education for their children.

Many nurseries, especially those who care for babies and young children, have a diary in which both carers and parents write important events in the child's day - from how much feed they took, how many nappy changes and the amount of sleep they have had to milestones in the child's development and exciting activities the child has done. This is an important part of helping both children and parents feel secure and happy with the setting, and for ensuring continuity of care. Children need to see that their parents and their carers have a good relationship, too. It will make them feel more secure.

Most early years settings have a brochure which they give to parents. This will contain useful information about the nursery aims, policies and regulations, but they will often contain much more:

■ how they ensure children's health, safety and well-being at all times

■ how their equal opportunities policy is put into practice
■ an explanation of the Foundation Stage and what it means
■ detail about the educational value of activities, to show parents that children are not 'just playing'
■ how they will support children with additional needs
■ an explanation of how their behaviour policy works in practice
■ how they will ensure quality of care and education
■ how they value parental involvement, and suggestions about how parents can be involved

This may well be supported by parents' evenings and open days to give parents further insight into how they work.

Making new children and their parents feel welcome

This is the most important aspect of helping children to settle in. If they are greeted by a happy, smiling member of staff, who takes the trouble to know their names, and has time to listen to them and their parents, they are far more likely to settle in easily. You need to be aware of the particular difficulties and anxieties of children and parents from different cultural backgrounds, whose home language may not be English. The notices and displays in your setting should reflect the different cultural groups in our society, so that children and parents don't feel that the setting is completely alien to them. Many people from minority ethnic backgrounds have grown up in this country, and won't have difficulty with English, but you do need to check this beforehand, so that you can have an interpreter present if you need to. You may be able to get support from your local intercultural support service to work with a child who doesn't speak English.

If the new child has additional learning needs or a disability, the parent will be able to tell you what the child's particular needs are. Find out if the child is supported by a specialist agency, and make contact with them. You may be able to get additional support in the setting for children with additional needs.

Show the parents and child around the setting, pointing out their coat peg with their own name or picture on it, their drawer or other space for their own possessions, and the toilets. Point out and explain things that may be unfamiliar and worrying for the child. Talk about the routine of the day, bearing in mind the age of the child and how much they are able to cope with. Make sure there are lots of interesting activities which will encourage the child to join in, and encourage their parents to play with them for as long as possible. With older children, it's nice to get a confident child to go and talk to the new child, or explain to the group that Jacob may be feeling a bit nervous as he's only just started nursery, so could they be particularly kind to him today and invite him to join in their play. The parents will perhaps be able to tell you what approach the child is most comfortable with. Some children like just to watch for a while until they feel confident to join in, others will prefer to sit with an adult. Some like a cuddle, others hate being touched. Some children will join in with no difficulty. Children may like to keep a comfort object with them - something from home which makes them feel more secure.

When the parents are ready to leave, insist that they say goodbye to their child. Some parents think it's better to sneak out once their child is absorbed in an activity, but that is the worst thing they can do. There may be tears when they go, but at least their child won't feel as if they've been abandoned. They should tell the child what they are going to do, and when they will be back, using an event the child can relate to, such as 'after lunch'. Then the carer can remind the child what the parents said, to reassure him. Once the parents have gone, give the child as much attention as you think he needs, and make sure that you explain the routine as new things happen, such as snack time, outside play and so on. For some children, being separated from their parents is always going to cause them distress, but if you follow these guidelines, you will know that you have done everything you can to minimise their anxiety.

Mary Townsend

The way we are and the way we behave really matters. Children absorb the words, the values and the actions of adults with great ease. That means we must pay careful attention to the way in which we present ourselves to the children in our setting

Adults as effective role models

Children learn by watching. You only have to spend a short period of time in the company of young children before they are copying your actions, repeating your language and mimicking your gestures, sometimes with infuriating accuracy!

Children are keen observers of adults. They have eagle eyes and don't miss a trick, and as if that wasn't bad enough, they also have excellent listening skills! We may think we are being discreet, but they can overhear what we say with little difficulty, especially when we don't want them to. So where is all this leading?

What does this mean for us?

Once we have come to terms with being under the constant surveillance of the children with whom we work, we can begin to work out what that really means: young children model themselves on the adults with whom they spend their time. They learn to talk by listening to adults using language to communicate.

We shape their values and behaviour. Children's attitude to learning will reflect the attitudes of the adults in their lives. When we work with young children we cannot avoid having an impact on the way they see the world and make sense of it. We shoulder a heavy responsibility. The way we are and the way we behave really matters.

It is important to acknowledge that we have this responsibility and do our best to present ourselves as positive role models to the children we work and spend time with. Sometimes this is easier said than done. It

requires that we pay attention, not just to our own behaviour, but also to the behaviour of all the adults working within the setting. If what we do differs even slightly from what we say we can be sure they will catch us out! It is what we do that really matters, not what we say or what we think we do.

Examples from practice

■ Rosie is three years old and the daughter of professional parents. She spends much of her time in the company of articulate adults from whom she has absorbed a rich vocabulary. One day, when Rosie was washing the dishes, her grandfather questioned whether she had washed a particular plate properly. 'Why Grandad!', said Rosie, upon closer examination of the plate, 'I think you'll find it's adequate!'

■ John, who is four, was looking out of the nursery window.

Pointing at a car parked in the street he proudly announced, 'That's my Dad's car that is!'
'It's very nice', responded the practitioner.
'He nicked it last night', said John, with great pride.

■ Then there was Tony who attended a setting in an area where it was not unusual for males to become involved in household chores. When he played at washing dishes he was told by Sophie in no uncertain terms, 'You can't do that! The mummies have to do that - the daddies have to sit on the sofa and read the paper and watch the telly!' Already comfortably seated on the sofa was Jason, who was pretending to puff away on a cigarette.

'Oh!' said the practitioner with disapproval, 'You shouldn't be smoking. It's very bad for you.'

'Why not?' came the swift reply. 'You do! I can smell it on you.'

As we can see from these examples, children easily absorb the words, the values and the actions of adults. Consequently, if we are committed to being effective role models, we must pay careful attention to the way in which we present ourselves to the children in our setting. It is not enough to leave it to chance. We need to take positive action to ensure that what is being absorbed by the children is what we want them to absorb, and where the values of the setting conflict with the values of the home we must act with appropriate sensitivity. It is not for us to offer value judgements about the adults in children's lives or make

negative comments about what happens for them at home. Our role is to be clear about the values and beliefs of the setting and then ensure that our theory is matched by our practice.

What can you do?

Once we have become fully conscious of the way in which our own behaviour affects children we have to make sure that our influence is as positive as we can make it. It is not enough to leave such important work to chance.

If you work alone this is a relatively simple matter, but if you work as part of a team this process will need the whole team to come together. It is also worth considering inviting voluntary helpers to join you in drawing up what will effectively become a code of conduct for everyone associated with the work of the setting. For some settings assembling such a group of people together may not be easy, especially where there are extended day facilities and practitioners work shifts. Having said this, the ultimate advantages of such work outweigh logistical difficulties.

Once you have got people together you can begin to unpick the complex issues around adults as role models, and in so doing, you may find the following process helpful. Ask yourselves the following questions, and write the responses on a flipchart. Be as honest as you can and then measure 'what is' against what you would like things to be. This will enable you to define: the current situation, and any changes you may wish to make.

■ Do we model positive relationships for the children?

■ Are we courteous and respectful in our dealings with each other?

■ Are we able to disagree respectfully, and where there is disagreement, can we

compromise and arrive at a consensus with which everyone can work?

This is really important. It is not helpful for children to grow up thinking that all adults see things the same way. Neither is it useful for them to observe adults backbiting and bickering about each other. Children benefit most from spending time with adults who can help them begin to understand that community life is based on cooperation, compromise and consensus. Children need to spend time in the company of adults who can express their feelings appropriately - this will enable them to learn that it is OK to be angry, but not OK to express our anger in a way that abuses and hurts someone else!

We can improve their understanding in this area by asking ourselves:

■ How well do we listen to each other and how well do we listen to children? Children who are listened to are much more likely to listen to others than children who have not experienced being listened to.

We need to ask ourselves:

■ Are we effectively modelling positive attitudes to learning?

■ Do we talk to the children about our interests?

■ Do they see us writing and reading?

■ Do we show them the books we read and the various ways in which we use writing?

■ Are we helping them to understand that literacy and numeracy are life skills that help us to organise our lives and get things done?

■ How do we react when things go wrong for us?

■ Are we showing the children how important it is to have a positive attitude to mistakes and see them as an opportunity for learning?

■ How is our self-esteem? We all want children to develop into confident adults with good self-esteem, but we won't help them to do this if what they see is adults constantly putting themselves down. So next time your colleague tells you that she admires your outfit, don't say, 'Oh it's nothing much really, it's only from the market.' Hold your head high and say, 'Thank you for noticing!'

■ What sort of messages are we giving the children with regard to making health-promoting choices? As children observe us they unconsciously absorb massive messages. We are powerful in their eyes and the things they observe us doing become acceptable things to do. Irrespective of what we tell them, if they see us smoking or eating crisps and chocolate for lunch every day instead of making healthier choices they will make the assumption that those things are good things to do. Here again, polarisation is not helpful; what we need to model is balance. Children need to know that it is fine to eat crisps and chocolate some of the time, but that we also need to eat fruit and vegetables to stay healthy.

The imaginative play area provides excellent opportunities for modelling health promoting choices and many other positive attitudes to life and learning in general.

Giving out the right messages

Spending a little time addressing these questions may well give you a few surprises. How we perceive something to be is not necessarily the way it is in reality, but once we are conscious of this we are in a great position to do something about it. Children learn by watching, and as they watch us we give them massive messages. What we do is much more important than what we say, and by paying attention to these messages we can narrow the gap between perception and reality. In short, we can make sure that the messages the children are picking up are the ones that we want them to.

Ros Bayley

Children aren't born prejudiced. It is something they learn. Can you be confident that they are not learning from you?

Dealing with prejudice and discrimination: **the issues**

Do some young boys really believe that they are superior to girls? Can some young white children think that they are superior to black children? Are there some young children living in affluent parts of our towns who feel that they are superior to children living on a local authority housing estate? If young children believe they are superior to others on these grounds they are beginning the process of learning to be prejudiced - pre-judging, basing their attitudes on false or no information.

Learning prejudice

We would surely like to think that young children believe all other children to be as 'worthy' as themselves, deserving to be treated with equal value and respect. But although many children may voice these principled sentiments when asked, the reality is that further investigation often results in them saying things that do not support their initial reactions. Research and personal anecdotes also tell us that young children often do not say what they really think in front of potentially critical adults.

There has been far more research about children's racist attitudes than about their sexist attitudes or attitudes to social class. The early years are an intense period of learning and children learn their attitudes, including their attitudes to differences, at an early age. Evidence shows that children as young as three may express racially prejudiced attitudes and behaviour. It also shows that young white children are far more likely to be racially prejudiced than young black children. This is not surprising when we acknowledge the deeply embedded racism in our society, reinforcing racist attitudes and behaviour and perpetuating them from generation to generation. There is no reason why the equally deeply embedded practices and procedures, based

on sex/gender and social class, do not influence young children in the same way.

Children are not the innocents that we might wish them to be. They may be learning to be prejudiced under our very noses. They may be learning false notions of superiority based on prejudice.

Where does prejudice come from?

It is important to recognise and accept that prejudice and discrimination exist everywhere in our society. Wherever we live the principles of addressing prejudice and discrimination are the same, although the practices may differ. Because men and women and able-bodied and disabled people live in all parts of the country, most people accept that any negative attitudes based on sex/gender or ability/disability are not confined to particular areas. Yet we sometimes hear people say they do not have any problems with racism because there are no black people living there, that racism only exists in multiracial areas of Britain because that is where it is most commonly seen. The fact is that racism exists everywhere, including in rural and suburban areas. It is only when black people are seen and live in these areas that racist attitudes and behaviour surface. Research in rural areas has demonstrated the deep racial hostility felt by many people.

No baby is born prejudiced. Children learn all their attitudes from all that is around them - from their toys, books, the media, their friends, their family, their teachers and carers, what they see, what they hear and what they do. If they see women portrayed in the media and elsewhere as always in the kitchen and caring for children, then they learn that this is women's role in our society. If they hear racist comments about asylum

'If we do nothing to help children to learn that everyone has a right to be treated with equal respect then what goes on around them will be of great influence on them. And we may be shocked at what our children say if we have not talked to them about these things.'

seekers and 'Pakis' and no-one counters this, they learn that such people are not seen as valuable members of our society. If they never meet children who live in poverty they may learn that it is somehow the children's fault that they are poor. And all these things may be reinforced by what else they hear and see in their everyday lives.

Responses to prejudice

But they learn these things only if we allow this to happen. If we do nothing to help children to learn that everyone has a right to be treated with equal respect then what goes on around them will be of great influence on them. And we may be shocked at what our children say if we have not talked to them about these things.

If we believe - whether consciously or unconsciously - that men are more important than women, that black people are unwanted in our society and that people living in poverty have only themselves to blame for their situation then

Building a Portfolio Level 2 • • •   **Personal, Social and Emotional Development**

these very beliefs may influence our young children.

These attitudes may not yet be fully fledged prejudice in young children but they may be the beginnings. They may continue into their later lives and develop into putting prejudice into practice - discrimination, treating someone less fairly solely because of who they are - and, if unchecked, such attitudes may become part and parcel of institutional practices and procedures, the damaging and discriminatory effects of which most of us are unaware. It is vitally important that early years policy makers, trainers, administrators and practitioners recognise the powerful consequences of these institutional practices and procedures on the life chances of those affected.

If, on the other hand, we wish our children to learn positive values and attitudes to differences, we cannot leave this to chance. We must consider all the influences on our children and reflect on what they might be learning that reinforces any negative attitudes to differences. We need to plan and prepare for this in strategic ways.

Children learn other attitudes, too

There are other aspects of the lives of young children that we need to consider. We know that young children are likely to be curious about children with physical or learning disabilities. They may even be apprehensive about meeting a person who is disabled because of their lack of experience. They may not know how to behave or be friends with them. We need to guide and support children to value equally and respect them in positive ways.

Some children may believe that certain roles can only be portrayed by particular people because that is all they have ever seen. For example, they may only have seen women as nurses and so cannot comprehend that men can be nurses, too. This shows the importance of providing a variety of role models for children.

Institutional practices and procedures

Institutional practices and procedures (oppression) may discriminate against particular groups of people. Institutions include early years services and settings.

Being part of a discriminatory institution does not mean that you or I, as members of such an institution, are personally prejudiced or even collude with any discrimination. It just means that we are part of that institution whose practices and procedures have an unfair (disproportionate) effect on particular groups of people.

It is, consequently, those very practices and procedures that need to be scrutinised to identify any discriminatory impact.

There are some groups of people, including young children, who are often blamed for many of society's ills. For example, the children of Travellers/Gypsies, Muslims, refugees and asylum seekers may have experienced ostracism, overt hostility or forms of trauma that most people could never imagine or only ever see from a distance. Caring for each and every child with sensitivity and an awareness of their experiences is the responsibility of all practitioners.

We know that some children may repeat hurtful things that they have heard from others, perhaps with little idea of what they mean. For example, implying that another child's family lifestyle is unacceptable when they live with two 'mummies' or two 'daddies'. We need to be aware of these issues and make sure that the families of all children are equally valued and respected. No child should ever be made to feel guilty, not included or 'different' because of who they are or who their families are. Attitudes towards divorce and single-parent families have changed over recent decades so that children living in such families now are far less likely to be stigmatised than in the past. We can only hope that other negative attitudes towards families and children will change in the same way in the future.

Attitudes to religion

Whereas we can be confident in saying that prejudice against children based on ethnicity/'race', sex/gender, social class, family lifestyles, ability/disability is not acceptable, the issue of religion raises different and complex factors. While many religions accept the valid existence of other religions some do not. This is difficult because, in accepting differences equally as we do above, sometimes this is not possible with religion. We need to be sensitive and accepting and try to consider every situation according to the particular circumstances pertaining at the time. And, of course, taking account of those who practice no religion.

The damaging effects of prejudice and discrimination

Prejudice, discrimination and their institutional aspects are damaging to all children. Clearly, those experiencing them are likely to feel hurt, excluded, lack self-esteem, have their motivation and ability to learn diminished, and their confidence undermined. Such children need to learn that what has happened to them is not their fault or the result of anything that they have done.

'No child should ever be made to feel guilty, not included or 'different' because of who they are or who their families are.'

But prejudice, discrimination and their institutional aspects are also damaging to the children who practise or perpetuate them. They may lead them to believe that they are somehow superior and more 'human' than others. They may blunt their sensitivity to others and distort their perceptions of reality by failing to provide them with the full range of information on which they can make their own judgements. But fundamentally, they may prevent them from learning concepts of empathy to others, concepts that are basic to respecting and valuing each other.

Building a Portfolio Level 2 • • •

Early Years Equality (formerly the Early Years Trainers Anti Racist Network) has developed a Framework for Equality which offers a strategic approach - a way of everyone involved in the early years working together towards the same objective.

A Framework for Equality is in *Planning for Excellence: Implementing the DfEE Guidance Requirement for the Equal Opportunity Strategy in Early Years Development Plans* (EYTARN 1998).

In 1998 the D*f*EE sent a copy of this publication to every Early Years Development and Childcare Partnership.

What we need to do

So how do we make sure that all children in our care are given equality of access and opportunity to fulfil their dreams and their potential? To have their cultures, languages and faiths acknowledged? And to be free of discrimination?

We need to adopt an approach that not only promotes equality but also counters any negative attitudes and behaviour that children may have already learned. This is more than just being positive about everyone. It is about learning to unlearn any existing negative attitudes. This is often called an anti-discriminatory or anti-bias approach.

Some people argue that this is negative. It is negative only in the sense that it tries to remove something that is damaging. Anti-discrimination should be viewed in the same way. Its specific aspects, for example, anti-sexism, anti-racism and opposition to prejudice and discrimination based on social class are all parts of the whole approach to these.

The dual approach of promoting equality and countering negative attitudes and behaviour is important. For example, providing a range of resources reflecting our multicultural, multilingual, multifaith and multiracial society is really important. But alone it is not enough. This is because cultures, languages and faiths are, in our society, often ranked in a hierarchy where some are considered more important, more worthy than others. This ranking can be racist. So although, for example, Urdu may not be a language that everyone should learn in Britain, it should nevertheless be seen as an equally valid and valued language to English in all its aspects. All children need to know that all languages are equally important and can say what they wish to say even though some may play a greater role in particular societies. This demonstrates the difference between a multicultural approach and an anti-racist approach, both of which are critical in breaking down racism.

The crucial role of families

But, as practitioners, we cannot do all this alone. Children's primary carers and the people with the greatest influences on their lives are their families. What they say and do is of critical importance in their children's developing attitudes and behaviour. While they are not the only influences, they play a complementary role with practitioners in early years settings in their involvement with children. Consequently, to be effective in providing opportunities for young children to consider issues of equality, we all need to work together with family members towards this objective. This crucial role means involving families in all aspects of policy making, in thinking about why equality issues are important and in discussing the curriculum. Without the support of families, practitioners will only be able to deal with prejudice and discrimination in half-measures.

The way forward

If we are serious about helping our children not to be prejudiced and not to discriminate against others we need to take positive action. This means that we must move from *ad hoc* responses to a specific carefully thought-out strategy so that every aspect of our work is considered.

Jane Lane , Early Years Equality

'We need to adopt an approach that not only promotes equality but also counters any negative attitudes and behaviour that children may have already learned.'

The best way to deal with prejudice and discrimination is to have an equal opportunities policy. Jane Lane looks at what this should cover

Dealing with prejudice and discrimination **in practice**

It would be easy if dealing with prejudice and discrimination just required us to think about resources, the curriculum and the Early Learning Goals. But it involves more than this. Not only are there additional issues to do with who is employed and who has places in the setting, but there is the fundamental issue of the attitudes that we, as adults, bring to the setting. We need to consider these very carefully before there is any point in examining the details of the curriculum. We need to make sure that we understand what a setting that is positive about equality looks like in reality first.

Thinking before we act

Dealing with prejudice and discrimination is a process not a one-off activity. It is a way of thinking and behaving. Everything you do needs to be considered and evaluated to ensure that it deals with prejudice and discrimination in effective and practical ways. Eventually, it will become a way of working in the same way as working with sand and water play.

This means it is no use attempting to deal with prejudice and discrimination in an *ad hoc* way. Just looking at resources, while important, is not enough. Just celebrating festivals on one occasion but ignoring the people whose festivals they are for the rest of the year does little to remove prejudice. Learning about other people's cultures does not necessarily make you like them better - it just provides more information about them. Unless everything we do is identified in a comprehensive way to consider prejudice and discrimination our response is likely to be ineffective.

We can start by talking to each other about the issues. This is not always easy at first because most of us come from different backgrounds and perspectives and perhaps we are not used to discussing ideas together. But it is important to be able to talk to each other in general before we try to discuss issues that may be difficult, challenging or controversial.

We also need to try to talk together within a 'no-blame culture' where we accept each other's different viewpoints - recognising that we all come to the situation with differing backgrounds and experiences - and where we deal with the issues and do not criticise each other personally. This is the only way that we are likely to be able to get consensus. We need to agree on what we are trying to do, why we are trying to do it and that it is important to do it.

What we need to know

In order to understand and recognise the importance of dealing with prejudice and discrimination we need to know that the evidence shows that children begin to learn their attitudes at a very young age - at least by the age of three. Unless we ensure that they are given opportunities to learn positive attitudes and behaviour about differences between people they are likely to reflect the attitudes and values of the society around them. Our society has discriminatory attitudes embedded in it - so children are likely to learn to be prejudiced.

Although children may not talk about these attitudes in front of adults this does not mean that they are not learning to be prejudiced. We need, therefore, to take positive action with all young children to provide them with an environment where differences between people are valued. We also need to enable them to consider their existing attitudes, those that they have already learned, and to give them opportunities to 'unlearn' any that are based on prejudice.

Because children come to our settings nearly always as members of families, we need to involve and include family members in the work we do to deal with prejudice. They are crucial influences on their children, so we need to talk with them about the importance of equally valuing and respecting one another and how, together, we can make it come about in practice. Many may be supportive or never have thought seriously about the issues. Some may be reluctant to agree but they may be receptive if we approach them with care and sensitivity.

Sexism, racism and attitudes based on social class are deeply embedded everywhere in our society. So, wherever our settings are, the principles of the work we need to do with the children are the same, although the methods may be different. Even if there are no black children in our setting, the issue of helping white children to value black children and unlearn any negative attitudes are equally as important as in multiracial settings. Similarly, sexist attitudes and prejudiced attitudes about social class, ability/disability need to be dealt with in every setting.

But the key issue to remember is that, alone, it is insufficient to just help children to value each other by providing positive resources and practice. All children need to be given opportunities to consider, reflect and unlearn any negative attitudes that they may have already learned. This means putting a specific programme into place that is anti-sexist, anti-racist and counters negative attitudes and behaviour based on social class.

Planning a programme of initial action

So where do you start? There are lots of resources and reading materials that will help you to understand the issues better and it is useful to use these because you can take them home and digest them at your own pace.

We need to see ourselves working within a framework in which members of the Early Years Development and Childcare Partnership (EYDCP), those working in the early years service and ourselves, as practitioners, play equal parts. Our joint objective is to provide equality in employment and all services for children

and their families in order to remove prejudice and discrimination from their lives. This framework approach will be fundamental to the plan which the EYDCP has to prepare for the government.

Adopting a strategic approach may seem formal, but there are clearly structural aspects that need to be addressed in settings - for example, the law, record keeping and policy making, as well as the more specific details such as dealing with name-calling, selecting resources and language support. All form essential parts of the whole strategy.

Everything that is done in the setting needs to be identified, analysed and assessed with regard to its implications for removing prejudice and discrimination. Following this process you need to decide whether you need to take any action. If so, what action do you take, and how do you ensure that it works in practice? This is the only way that you can be sure that any prejudice and discrimination are removed - by looking at employment practices and what goes on with the children. For example:

■ In considering the words you use to describe people - are they appropriate, respectful and acceptable to the people concerned?

'We need to agree on what we are trying to do, why we are trying to do it and that it is important to do it.'

■ Do you need to talk with people about the words you use?

■ When thinking about skin colour differences in your setting or in the world outside, we know that some skin colours are often seen as more acceptable than others. What do you need to do to help children learn that all skin colours are equally beautiful? And how can you check that what you do helps this to happen?

Key issues for practitioners to address

A policy for equality

The most effective way to put the strategy into practice is to develop a policy covering employment, admissions and everything that goes on in the setting. (Early Years Equality publishes *A Policy for Excellence: Developing a Policy for Equality in Early Years Settings*) It should include a policy statement, an implementation programme and a monitoring and evaluation mechanism.

Such a policy should not be seen as a chore or a nuisance or even as raising issues that are too difficult. Some people feel that by developing a policy they will be raising a hornet's nest of trouble with which they will be unable to cope. By being clear about why a policy is necessary and how it is a help rather than a hindrance these barriers can be overcome. And, in any case, the Department for Education and Skills (DfES) requires the EYDCP to report on the progress made in ensuring that all settings have an equal opportunities policy.

It is particularly important to have a policy on all forms of harassment, name-calling and inappropriate comments - a policy that involves and includes all family members, decides what action to take on the various forms of harassment, name-calling and comments and checks whether any subsequent action taken was effective.

Family members should be equally involved in developing the whole policy - this is crucial as families need to understand and support the principle of why a policy is necessary. They, too, need to 'own' it, for their children's sakes and for the effectiveness of the policy overall.

Legislation

Everyone working in the setting should be familiar with the principles of what the laws say, but someone in authority needs to know them in detail. In particular, admission policies and employment procedures need

A policy for equality.

children to learn that every language can say what it wants to say and that all languages are equally valid - none is more worthy than another although some languages may be used more than others? For example, although Standard English is the main medium of communication it is an English dialect, just like other English dialects.

■ Home languages

Are children encouraged to speak their home languages in the setting? Do all practitioners know and understand that children learn English as an additional language better if their home languages are valued and encouraged to be spoken in the setting?

■ Differences

Are differences (for example, physical features, hair textures and styles, skin colours, abilities/disabilities, impairments) between people talked about openly and in positive ways? And are such discussions conducted according to the situations concerned, in sensitive ways and with thought given beforehand as to any potential consequences of the discussion? Are differences between boys and girls and between black and white children discussed? Are opportunities provided for drawing such differences using accurate colours of crayons, pens and paper? Are disabilities and impairment talked about positively, and not with pity, in sensitive caring ways?

■ Expectations/stereotypes

Are practitioners clear about the damaging consequences of having low expectations of children's abilities and of holding stereotyped attitudes and opinions about what they can and cannot do?

■ Childrearing practices

Have practitioners had the opportunity to think about the differing childrearing practices in our society? Have they considered that, with rare exceptions, all such practices are equally valid for those who practise them? And, perhaps, that we can learn something from each other. For example, bedtimes may vary in different communities and many people may take equal responsibility for bringing up a child.

to be examined to check that they do not discriminate. Records should be kept and analysed of who applies for and gets jobs and who applies to come to the setting and who is offered a place, by ethnicity, sex and disability.

Treating everyone with equal concern

■ Resources

Do children and their families see people like them reflected in the resources? Have all the jigsaws, books, toys and posters been examined to check they are balanced, accurate, have positive images of people and do not reinforce stereotypes? Do the dolls have a range of skin colours and are they accurate representations of people? Is there a check-list for selecting resources that identifies all the issues about equality? Do all practitioners understand that it is the way the resources are used that is important, not their mere presence?

■ Terminology

Have the words colleagues use to describe people been considered to ensure that they are not offensive and are appropriate?

■ Assumptions

Have practitioners had opportunities to think about any assumptions they make about children and their families - how they live, what they eat, what their faith is, what languages they speak? Are the assumptions correct?

■ Ethos

Does the setting make everyone feel welcome, valued and respected? Do the visual images reflect accurately the people who live in our society? Are the languages used by children and their families seen in writing in the setting?

■ Languages

Are all languages equally valued? How does the setting ensure that this is put into practice? Is there a programme for helping

■ Observations

Do practitioners have opportunities to observe what each child is doing and whether particular groups of children (for example, boys and girls and black and white children) are having equal access to all the available learning opportunities?

■ Incidents of name-calling/ harassment/inappropriate comments

Is there a specific policy for dealing with these? Does everyone understand that the first objective after such an incident is to comfort and support the child who has been hurt? And then support the child who has caused the incident and try to find out why it happened and what level of understanding there is. Incidents need to be followed up by recording them, deciding on appropriate action to be taken with all the children so it does not recur and monitoring the result. Details of what to do should be in the policy.

■ Employment

As well as keeping data on who is working in the setting, by sex/gender, ethnicity and disability, does the composition of the staff at all levels reflect that of the locality? If it does not, do you consider taking positive action to recruit appropriate staff under the legislation and do you examine your recruitment procedures? Groups of people who are under-represented deny children the positive role models they need. Does your setting make sure that it only appoints staff who are committed to deal with prejudice and discrimination and have the knowledge, understanding and skills to address them in practical ways?

Fundamentally, do you and your colleagues reflect on your practice regularly with a view to making sure prejudice and discrimination are addressed? Do you talk about issues together and practise what you might do in particular situations? Do you make sure that

the resources help children to reflect on their attitudes by providing a full range of positive images?

Strategies to support the learning of positive attitudes and behaviour to differences and the 'unlearning' of any negative attitudes and behaviour already learned

■ Working with families together

Do practitioners and family members have opportunities to discuss the policy for equality and the reasons for working together to learn positive attitudes to differences and unlearn negative ones?

■ Talk with children

Do practitioners provide opportunities to discuss issues of differences with children in sensitive and carefully thought-out ways? For example, in circle time.

For information about the 1976 Race Relations Act and ethnic monitoring see *From Cradle to School: a practical guide to racial equality in early childhood education and care* (Commission for Racial Equality 1996) and *Planning for Excellence* (EYTARN 1998).

■ A variety of viewpoints

Do practitioners provide opportunities for children to consider and discuss a variety of points of view so they can make up their own minds about what they think, based on evidence?

■ Persona dolls

Persona dolls tell a story about their feelings through an adult to develop empathy with children. Have practitioners considered using these to aid them in dealing with prejudice? (For further information on a publication and training, contact Persona Doll Training, 51 Granville Road, London N12 OJH. Telephone 0208 446 7056.)

Above all, do practitioners provide children with the skills to be 'critically aware' of the world around them, to empathise and reflect, so that they can make up their own minds about what is fair and just?

Jane Lane, Early Years Equality

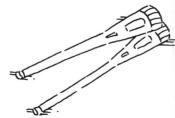

Useful addresses

Early Years Equality, PO Box 28, Wallasey CH45 9NP. Tel: 0151 639 1778. This is a national network of people working to encourage anti-racist practices and procedures in the education and care of young children. It campaigns for racial equality and justice, holds conferences, publishes relevant information and materials, offers advice and support, responds to proposed and existing legislation and publishes a newsletter.

Commission for Racial Equality (CRE), St Dunstan's House, 201-211 Borough High Street, London SE1 1GZ. Tel: 020 77939 0000. The Commission offers advice and information to individuals and groups.

Teaching young children to take turns is an important part of their personal, social and emotional development. However, it cannot be taught in isolation; it takes practice and some children will learn more quickly, whilst others will need sensitive adult support and encouragement

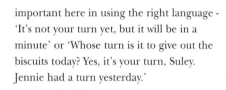

Learning to
take turns

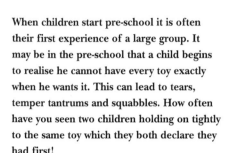

When children start pre-school it is often their first experience of a large group. It may be in the pre-school that a child begins to realise he cannot have every toy exactly when he wants it. This can lead to tears, temper tantrums and squabbles. How often have you seen two children holding on tightly to the same toy which they both declare they had first!

The role of the adult and the language they use is crucial. Fairness and consistency are paramount. There are many ways adults could respond to this scenario:

- The adult takes the toy away completely and says something like - 'Well, if you're going to argue about it, neither of you will have it'.
- The adult finds another similar toy and suggests that 'You have this one and let Jonathan have that'.
- The adult takes one of the children away from the situation and says 'Come and help me do this puzzle'.
- The children are left to sort it out for themselves.

Whilst all these responses may be appropriate at certain times with certain children, and may even stop the fight and the tears, they do not necessarily help the children understand the idea of turn taking or incorporate the language of 'turns'. Instead, the adult could spend a few minutes with the children and make the most of the opportunity. If it were a toy car, for example, the adult could say:
'You both like the car do you? It's a lovely car.' *(Acknowledges the children's feelings and gains attention)*

'Let's all have a turn with it. First it's my turn, then David's and then Sophie's. Well done!' *(Allows the children to know they will*

actually get to play with the car and introduces the idea of 'turns'.)

'Yes, you're taking turns now, well done!' *(Gives positive reinforcement when the turn taking takes place, rather than negative for squabbling.)*

Many activities lend themselves naturally to encouraging turn taking. Begin with only two children taking turns, for example, pushing a car to each other, then build up to a small group situation and finally to the wider context of a large group.

Activities include:

- table games such as picture matching, lotto, Kim's game, games involving dice
- baking - each child takes a turn to stir the cake mixture or add ingredients
- feely bags or smelly jars - passing it around, taking turns to have a 'feel'
- taking a turn to give out the cups and biscuits
- taking turns to help feed the fish, water the plants, get the bikes out of the shed, hold the book or turn the pages in story time
- taking turns to pick his or her name card from a table and hang it on the name board
- taking turns to be the leader of the line

At the painting easel or sand and water tray, children need to learn that numbers are restricted perhaps to two, three or four at a time. Adults need to explain this and make sure children understand that if it's not their turn, they will eventually have a turn. Sometimes you can put out less resources than the number in the group, deliberately creating a situation where the children have to take turns, for example, three rolling pins between four at the dough table. The adult role would then be one of observing and intervening when necessary. Adults are so

important here in using the right language - 'It's not your turn yet, but it will be in a minute' or 'Whose turn is it to give out the biscuits today? Yes, it's your turn, Suley. Jennie had a turn yesterday.'

Singing time
Many popular nursery songs and rhymes lend themselves to taking turns. For example, number rhymes where children can take turns to be the five little speckled frogs. In circle games children take it in turns to choose each other. Games based on pass the parcel or hide the teddy also encourage turn taking.

Outdoor play
With the ride-on toys you could set up a system for turn-taking - there might be a station or bus stop and children could be allowed to ride up and down to and from certain points, then get out for the next child to have a turn. They soon learn to accept the rules and routine. It is important to observe the quieter children and make sure they have a turn on the popular toys, too. Again adult intervention and language will reinforce the message - 'One at a time'; 'Take it in turns, Katie first, then William, then Arminder'; 'Don't worry, you'll all have a turn!'

When the children are playing independently and you hear them saying to each other 'No, it's his turn now' then you know you've achieved your aim. However, remember, even teenagers will argue about whose turn it is to sit in the front of the car!

Caroline Jones

Cooperative games can make a real difference to the way in which children behave towards each other. But you need to give some thought to why and how the games are played for effective learning to take place

Organising cooperative games

Tolerance, empathy, confidence and communication can all be fostered through games that emphasise cooperation rather than competition. As they play, children will develop thinking skills, listening, attention and concentration skills at the same time as enhancing their self-esteem, but if this is to happen effectively, you need to give some thought to the following questions.

What do we mean by a cooperative game?

It is interesting to share your thoughts about this with other members of your team, as there is sometimes confusion about what a cooperative game really is. For a game to be genuinely cooperative no one is the loser and no one should be left out. Unless every child makes a contribution and works as part of the group, the group cannot achieve its aim or reach its goal. When the task is accomplished and the goal is achieved, everyone celebrates together and the sense of achievement is reward enough!

How should we plan for cooperative games?

Consistency is important. It is far better to play some games every week for shorter periods of time than to have a longer session every few weeks or just when it seems to be a good idea. By working this way, children will have the opportunity to revisit games, refine their skill and build on their learning. Little by little their understanding of cooperation and all it involves will grow, and the planning of such games, with all their benefits, will become an integral part of the work of your setting.

Think about where in the daily routine you will play the games, and this may be different for different games. A game requiring a high degree of concentration and cooperation is probably best played before the children are too tired, whereas

a game that can be played more easily and is more relaxing can be introduced towards the end of sessions. Whatever the time of day, when several games are played, the following pattern works well: start with a relatively easy introductory game, play the more exuberant ones in the middle of the session and finish with a quieter, calmer game.

You will also find that as the children become more familiar with the games, they will want to play their particular favourites.

Is there progression in cooperative games?

Quite simply, yes! Some games are much more difficult than others, and as the children gain mastery over the skills of cooperation they will become increasingly able to play more complex games. As you plan your programme and decide which games to play when, consider the skills involved and the degree of challenge offered to ensure that they are developmentally appropriate for your children. Just like linguistic or mathematical skills, a programme for cooperative games should be stepped and progressive.

How long should a session last?

The appropriate length of time will be entirely dependent on the skills and involvement of the children. The most important measure of success in cooperative play is that everyone is having fun. If the children are enjoying themselves and

want more, play on. If they become restless and cease to be engaged, then stop. By tuning in to the children you will know how long to make the session last.

How many children can I work with at a time?

Again, this will depend on the children and on the particular game you wish to play. The key question to ask is, 'How many children can I be effective with?' Some games can be played in a group of 30, others may need a group of six or ten.

What should we do before we start?

Before starting a session it is important to be clear with the children about what is expected of them. Set some ground rules and make them as simple as possible. For example:
- Try hard to be a good listener
- Stick with the group until the task is complete
- Call everyone by their names
- Help each other

Building a Portfolio Level 2 • • •

Personal, Social and Emotional Development

Throughout the proceedings you need to clarify the group process with the children, as this will enable them to build on their understanding of what is involved in a group working well together. Encourage them to evaluate how well the game went and discuss ways in which it might be improved.

You might ask the children:
- What did you like about the game?
- Was there anything you didn't like?
- Do you think there are ways in which we could make it more fun/play it better?

With children with communication difficulties you can use pictures to represent how they might feel about the game, for example happy, sad and 'in between' faces. Children can point to, stand by or make a mark by the picture that best matches the way they feel about the games.

Some games to try

Cooperative games have been played by children through the centuries, and we have a rich heritage of activities that have been handed down from generation to generation. For the most part, it is impossible to say where the game began or who first thought of it. Some of the games listed below may be old favourites and well known to some of you. For others, many of the games may be new, but hopefully, even for those of you who already play cooperative games on a regular basis, there will be some fresh ideas and some new challenges.

To help practitioners that are new to cooperative games, the games are listed according to their degree of difficulty and challenge, beginning with the most simple. Effort has also been made to avoid the most common games, for example 'The farmer's in his/her den,' and 'There was a princess long ago'.

■ **Pass the mask**
For this game the children sit in a circle and the person who begins the game makes a funny face – the next child makes the same face and then passes it onto the next child until the 'mask' has gone all around the circle.

To make this game more complex:
The first child makes a funny face – the second child copies it and then makes one of his/her own to pass on to the next child. In this version everyone has to imitate and invent a funny face.

■ **Electric squeeze**
The children stand or sit in a circle holding hands. One child gently squeezes the hand on their left (or right) and the next child then squeezes the hand on their left until the squeeze has been passed right around the circle. You can also pass a hug, a smile, an action or a rhythm.

■ **Pass the teddy**
For this game you need a triangle, tambourine or drum, or you can play some music. The teddy is passed around the circle, but on a given signal or when the music stops, the children stop. On the next signal, or when the music starts again, they pass the teddy in the opposite direction.

■ **Change seats**
Place enough chairs for each child in a circle. When everyone is sitting down the leader says:

Everyone who has a cat…change seats.

Everyone who has a dog…change seats.

Everyone who has black shoes… change seats.

Everyone who likes chocolate… change seats.

At first the children all want to change seats all of the time, but if you play this game enough they soon get the hang of it.

■ **Circle dancing**
Make a circle and devise a series of movements that can be linked together to form a circle dance. Demonstrate some of the ways in which the circle can move and invite the children to add their suggestions. If they have trouble keeping

together give them a length of rope, elastic or material to hold on to. Once you have devised your dance, do it for its own sake or perform it to a friendly, appreciative audience.

■ **Dragon dancing**
Use a cardboard box to make a dragon's head and attach a length of material to the box. Cut zigzags in the edges of the material and decorate it with ribbons and streamers. It may take a bit of practice, but with everyone underneath the material, the dragon should eventually weave its way along. Find a suitable piece of music or let the children use percussion instruments to make their own accompaniment. If you have a video camera, record the dragon dance so that the children underneath can fully appreciate the effect!

■ **Don't make a sound**
Place a bunch of keys, tambourine or other jangly object on top of a large piece of cardboard. The children all hold the sides of the cardboard and try to move it from one point to another without it making any noise. If it makes a noise the group return to the starting point again.

■ **The mystery object (circle game)**
Place a small object in an envelope or box so that the children cannot see it. The leader whispers the name of the object in the ear of the child next to her. They in turn whisper to the next child until the whisper has gone all the way round the circle. When everyone has had a go, take out the object and see if they have named it correctly!

■ **Pass the balloon (circle game)**
The object of this game is to pass the balloon right round the circle with nobody throwing it into the air. Play some quiet music. If anyone throws the balloon the pass must begin again. To make it even more difficult carry out the pass in silence! You may need to practice this one quite a few times until the children achieve it, but it is a great exercise for self-control!

Islands

Place several hoops, mats or sheets of paper on the ground. The children 'swim' around the room until a given signal when everyone must stand on an island. The game continues with an island removed each time. The object of the game is to ensure that no one is left outside when the time for standing on an island comes. It can be done if everyone helps.

Go for a blindfold walk

For this game the children work in pairs. Before playing the game it is important to be sure that:

a. Children are happy to wear a blindfold. (Some may be scared.)

b. Children have been taught properly how to lead another child who is blindfolded. (A good way to do this is to carry out a demonstration.)

The children then take turns to lead each other around. To make the game more challenging introduce some obstacles.

Bubble sculptures

For this game you will need some washing-up liquid, water, drinking straws, suitable containers and a few drops of glycerine to strengthen the bubbles. Prepare the bubble liquid and pour into small containers. Allow the children time to use their straws to explore what will happen when they blow into the container. At first, let them make their own bubbles and then get them to join the bubbles together to make one big bubble sculpture.

Across the river

For this game you will need either a length of material or some mats to represent the river, and an inflatable beach ball. The children stand in the 'river' close together with their

hands behind their backs. The object of the game is to pass the ball from one side of the river to the other without using their hands and without it falling into the river. If the ball does fall, the pass begins again!

The train

The children stand in a line with their hands on the shoulders of the person in front of them. The leader has a tambourine or drum and while she plays it the train moves around the room. As soon as she stops the train must stop. As soon as she starts, the train begins to move again, the object of the game being that of getting everyone to stop and start together without breaking the train.

Fire, fire!

This game is exciting but can only be played if your setting has an upstairs. You will need a large sheet and a collection of soft toys. The object of the exercise is to rescue the toys from the fire. The children hold onto the sheet as someone hurls the toys from an upstairs window, when hopefully, they will be caught in the sheet!

Useful resources

Let's Play Together Mildred Masheder (Greenprint 1989).
Cooperative Games, Activities for a Peaceful World (Peace Pledge Union, 41b Brecknock Road, London N7 0BT).
Winners All, Cooperative Games for all Ages (Pax Christi, 9 Henry Road, London N4 2LH).
Playing Around Susan Rowe and Susan Humphries (Forbes Publications 1994).

Using parachutes

Working with parachutes is a great way of getting children to work together. Parachutes are a marvellous resource that can be used both indoors and outside and if you can't afford one, don't despair. If you buy some cheap nylon sheets and stitch them into panels you can make a good substitute. The overall shape of the parachute doesn't matter. It can be square or rectangular as well as circular!

Powerful vehicle for learning

Cooperative games will have most benefit when played on a regular basis. The more children take part in them, the greater the learning will be, but it will not always be easy. As children play these games, they are often called upon to work with children they might normally avoid, but this in itself is valuable learning as it reflects what is asked of us in the real world. When we help children to deal with this level of discomfort, we help them to begin to understand some of the complexities of human relationships and equip them with important life skills. But for the most part, these games are tremendous fun, at the same time as being a powerful vehicle for learning across a wide range of contexts. So much so, that it's got to be worth making them a regular feature of the work of your setting.

Ros Bayley

Being able to dress yourself is an important part of personal and social development and leads to a greater sense of independence. But it also requires considerable physical skill, so you need to build opportunities for this into your planning for physical development as well

Developing dressing skills

It was only last year when I broke my arm that I realised just how much is involved in putting on and taking off clothes! It made me more aware of the abilities of children within my setting. I thought that most of them could put on their own coats at home time but I noticed that the younger children often asked an adult or a friend for help. Getting dressed requires lots of practise and you need to plan for this, providing children with meaningful opportunities to explore different clothes.

What fastenings can you do?

Do you know how well your children can dress themselves? Observe them to find out. Talk to them in small groups about what fastenings they can manage. You could make a big chart featuring children's names and drawings of different fastenings to record their achievements. Encourage the children to fill in the chart with you so that they can see how they are progressing. You might want to award stars or certificates after each successful fastening.

At this stage, you also need to assess children's understanding of the words used to describe different types of clothing and fastenings. Do they know the difference between a skirt and a dress, shorts and trousers, a buckle and a toggle? What about the names for parts of garments - a hood, cuffs, pockets, waistband, and so on?

Basic skills

A table set out with a variety of fastening objects is an easy way to help the younger children develop their fine manipulative skills. Simply provide a tray with various lengths of zips and Velcro just for them to play with and explore. Then introduce large buttons sewn onto fabric with another piece of fabric with a hole in it so they can practise doing and undoing buttons.

Once the children have developed the basic skills and gained confidence, make some self-help cards. Self-help dolls are effective but they can be expensive. I always put a few out when we talk about 'Ourselves'. Some of the fastenings can be tricky because of the smaller scale - and don't let children worry about learning to tie shoe laces.

Contexts for clothes: role play

Provide a variety of dressing-up clothes, old and new. Try to build up a collection of coats and jackets with different fastenings and in different textures from plastic to fake fur. Don't worry if they're too big - the children are going to be putting them on top of their own clothes. Anyway, wearing 'real' adults' clothes is part of the fun and fascination.

Each day introduce a few new challenging items of clothing, for example one day put out an outfit with Velcro fastenings, then put out a waistcoat with large buttons. Belts are good for buckles. This gives the children a choice of what to wear and also presents all children with different challenges depending on their abilities.

■ Jumble sale

Sometimes you find that the same children always dress up in the same clothes or the children lose interest in the dressing-up area. Fire their imaginations by creating new scenarios and situations - such as a jumble sale.

Pile all the clothes on a table - you'll find that this alone sparks off great conversations with the children. You can then decide together whether you want to sort them into different categories - men's, women's and children's garments, for example, or put all the coats together, all the trousers, all the shoes. You could make price tags, then sort and label the different items - all the coats £1, all the trousers 50p. Or you could group garments according to their fastenings - coats with buttons, toggles and zips, shoes with Velcro or buckles.

■ Fashion show

If you have any extrovert children who enjoy an audience, a fashion show gives them the chance to take centre stage. With the children's help, write down some short descriptions of various garments or outfits - mention the colour, type of fastenings and occasion when it would be suitable to wear. Let children take it in turns to put on the clothes and walk slowly up and down - all the better if you can mark out a catwalk with a strip of carpet. Children who don't want to take part can help the models dress and undress.

■ Clothes for all weathers

Put out a box of clothes for a range of weather. Encourage children to talk about when they might wear different outfits. Play games whereby you call out the weather and they have to find and put on the right clothes.

Leanne Davies

Children are usually happy to express their likes and dislikes. They are not always aware that other people's likes may not be the same as theirs. Brussels sprouts don't taste nice and ice cream is yummy. For young children, these things are facts not opinions!

Expressing **opinions**

Helping children to begin to see that, even within a broad consensus, people will hold different opinions gives them a good foundation for building empathy, tolerance and understanding. It also helps them develop a sense of self. As they reflect on how their likes differ from others they can begin to see what kind of individuals they are. My five-year-old daughter recently invited a friend to tea and asked me to find out 'what kind of girl' she was, by which she meant what kind of toys she liked playing with.

The Personal, Social and Emotional Development guidelines call for children to:
- Have a developing awareness of their own needs, views and feelings and be sensitive to the needs, views and feelings of others and to
- Understand that people have different needs, views, cultures and beliefs, that need to be treated with respect.

Encouraging children to talk about their opinions and feelings is a useful beginning to this process. It is important, however, to prompt them to think about how they have come to have these preferences, what these choices say about them as individuals and as members of wider groups such as family or community and to realise that other children have acquired their preferences in the same way.

What's my favourite?

A good place to start is with children's favourite toys. Ask children to bring their favourite toy with them to nursery. Give each child a label on a string to write their name on and attach to their toy. This will be useful in the guessing activity but is also a practical way to make sure toys don't get muddled and children upset. It's also a chance to encourage children to write their own names.

As a group, take it in turns to look at a toy and see if children can guess whose favourite toy it is. Look on the label to see if the guess was right. Challenge children to say what made them think this would be a certain person's favourite. Once all the toys have been looked at, talk about any surprises. Are other children's likes easy to predict or can we find out new things about our friends when we listen to their ideas?

You can extend this activity to enable children to see that some of our preferences stem from our culture. Ask each child to bring in packaging from their favourite food (or a picture). As before, ask them to attach a label with their name to the packet or tin. Can children guess which favourite food belongs to which child? Why not look at how many children like the same food. Choose four or five of the favourite foods and ask children to put their hands up for each kind of food they

like. Encourage them to think carefully before they answer and not just put their hands up every time. Older children may be able to work in a smaller group and talk about what it is they like or dislike about certain foods. This would help them to see that even when people appear to like the same thing, they may do so for different reasons.

Talking books

If children have enjoyed finding out more about their friends, why not make a big talking book on 'Things we like and don't like'. Rather than have a page per child, try making a page per item so that children can see a range of opinions on each page. Ask for children's drawings and write their comments, perhaps using the computer. To each page, glue an envelope big enough to hold a cassette tape. Record children's opinions on each object, creature or event onto separate cassettes, label the tapes and put them into the relevant envelopes. Store the book near a cassette player so that children can listen to their own views or those of their friends whenever they want to.

Asking children to bring their own things into nursery is important as it:
- makes connections with the rest of children's lives
- gives them real reasons to share and to talk and listen
- enables children to develop a sense of self within the nursery community

If you do this, however, it is important to establish rules about what things are suitable to bring, where things are kept, how the nursery knows what belongs to whom, who can use the things in nursery and whose ultimate responsibility the safekeeping of the objects is.

Jo Graham

Children like to explore new ways to play and learn and puppets are a remarkable tool which can encourage them to experience all areas of learning, especially personal and social development

Puppets and emotional development

Puppets are fun and easy to make. Once you have given your puppet a definite look, character and most importantly a name, they come to life. They are a great aid when telling stories and make good visual props. A child is captivated when puppets are performing and can be encouraged to communicate with the puppet and even instruct it what to do. Their imagination will be stimulated and you will be encouraging their language development.

Storytellers

In the past, puppets were used to retell stories about everyday events that happened around the country. Travellers would earn their keep by relating what was happening in neighbouring towns and villages. Not only was this a good way of hearing the news but it was entertaining and was a means of escaping into the wonderful world of imagination.

Puppets come in all shapes and sizes and in various forms - finger, hand, glove, string, shadow and rod. Most can be made out of junk materials - card, fabric, socks, gloves, tubes, tissue, pipe cleaners and plastic containers and boxes, the list is endless. It is a good idea to start a bitbox for small items

The value of puppets

Children will work independently to make a puppet, choosing the materials, solving any problems that arise and asking for help when they need it. They will also develop their concentration skills

When performing with a puppet children work as part of a group, taking turns and sharing. They gain in confidence and are able to express their feelings by using the puppets. A shy or sensitive child can be comforted by an adult manipulating a friendly puppet. Puppets can be used to encourage a withdrawn child to communicate. Role play with puppets can highlight ways to behave, how to use good manners and children will experience joy and achievement when given the opportunity to use their creation.

such as buttons, eyes, ribbons, lace, wool, felt bits, and so on, and a scrapbox for larger pieces of card, boxes, tubes and fabric. Here are some simple ideas.

Finger puppets

Hand/finger puppets were the most popular form of puppetry in this country. The simplest of finger puppets is Thumbelina, made by placing a small oblong of material over

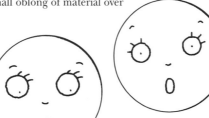

the thumb, fastening it with an elastic band or piece of ribbon/thread and then drawing a face onto the fabric. You can retell the Hans Christian Andersen story and create some more visual aids.

Faces are not difficult to draw, the simpler the better. (Some basic looks are given here.) Children can express their emotions by using puppets with different features. They can use skills of communication, planning, memory recall, language and concentration when they create their own puppet and stories.

Another form of finger puppet is a walking one, where your finger becomes the legs or nose of the puppet. These can be made out of card or

felt and can be a great aid when singing nursery rhymes. Make a spider to use for 'Incy Wincy' or 'Little Miss Muffet'.

Pinocchio

Use your finger to make a nose grow or make up a story about a bad mannered person whose nose grew when he got angry!

Hand puppets

Hand puppets can be made as simple or as elaborate as you want. The two main methods are sewing or gluing, the latter is easier for small children. When making a hand puppet template do make sure that your hand fits it!

Children can be encouraged to sew using plastic bodkins and brightly coloured wool. They will be using skills of planning, cutting, threading, joining, manipulation, design, handling tools and various materials.

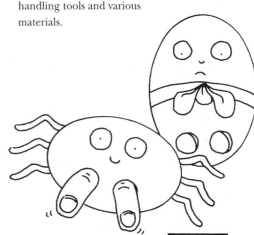

Socks can be turned into wonderful puppets. Create a mole by using a dark or grey sock, add buttons for eyes and nose, some pink felt pieces shaped like feet and a pink tongue.

Take a shoe box and make a hole in one corner big enough for your hand and arm and then paint the box an earthy colour. Place some small twigs, leaves, acorns and stones in and push your mole puppet through the big hole. Cut some smaller holes for your fingers and use them as worms.

For a more realistic mole, use black fur or velvet, make into a tube and then attach decorations.

An 'emotional' puppet can be used to encourage a child to talk about why they think the puppet is sad (please don't forget to give your puppet a name). What would they do to make him/her happy again?

The puppet can be made from felt or fabric. This is best done in small groups of three to four children. Adults may need to cut the material out first.

What you will need:
Two pieces of fabric or felt - size will depend on child or adult's hand.
Oddments of wool for hair
Small pieces of felt for hands
Wiggly eyes (optional)
Glue
Felt-tip pens
Oddments of sequins, lace, fabric to decorate

What to do:
Make a template, place it on the material and cut out two pieces.
Cut strands of wool to length of hair required.
With wrong sides together place wool along head between the two pieces of fabric and glue down.
Continue to glue the wrong sides together. Do not glue bottom or end of arms.
Cut out two felt hands and glue into place.
Draw happy face on one side of head and sad face on the other side with felt-tip pens or use eyes or buttons.
Decorate body with oddments of fabric or sequins or draw with felt-tip pens.

Elizabeth Coller

Felt hands cut 2.

Template.

Not full size – enlarge on a photocopier.

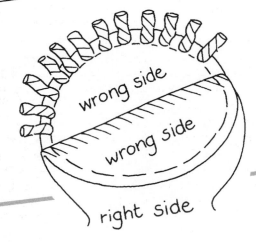

wrong side

wrong side

right side

Emotions affect all of us in each part of our lives, whether we're at work or play. Children deserve to be given the opportunity to discuss their emotions and time to reflect on appropriate ways of expressing their feelings

Expressing **feelings** and **emotions**

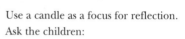

Young children experience a wide range of emotions and they need to learn to express them appropriately. Many children will learn this almost instinctively, but others will need reassurance and encouragement to express themselves appropriately or they may simply explode with joy, sorrow or anger in a confusing or disturbing manner.

One of the most effective ways of doing this is by introducing a topic such as 'Happy and sad' which gives children the opportunity to talk about their own feelings and gives staff an insight. We may be able to discover what makes children happy or sad and why.

Wonder

As adults we rarely use the word 'wonder' and sometimes forget that first thrill of a new experience because we are seeing with eyes that have seen before and are rationalising with experienced or understanding minds. The sense of exhilaration and wonder that children feel needs to be fostered and valued so that their experiences become meaningful. We must ensure that we give proper attention to times of wonder and reflection.

Sorrow

Children's sorrow often arises from situations that they cannot understand and may find confusing. Young children don't have an understanding of the life-cycle and are quite likely to show sorrow when flowers that have grown from seeds die when the season ends. Perhaps one of the things that saddens children most is experiencing relationships that they find confusing such as bullying, the new baby who now has all the attention, the death of a pet or the distress of a close adult. Children need an opportunity to discuss these feelings in a safe and secure environment with adults whom they trust.

Joy

This is another word that adults do not use often. Joy is a deeper emotion than happiness. It implies a singing from the soul. For young children we hope that joy is an emotion they experience often:

- the joy of realisation, when they understand something for the first time
- the joy of independence, perhaps when riding a two-wheeler bike for the first time without stabilisers
- the joy of close relationships
- the joy of bathing a baby brother or sister and seeing them smile 'just at me!'

Children need to have these feelings of joy valued and confirmed or they learn not to share or even not to value them.

Suggested activities

Play a variety of taped music. Ask:

- How does it make them feel?
- Why? (talk about fast/slow, instrumental/vocal)
- Extend into appropriate gestures, movements or dance to express the feelings evoked by the music

Look at different paintings, drawings or other expressive artefacts.

- How does it make them feel?
- Does it make their friends feel the same way?
- Why? (talk about colours, subject matter and so on.)
- Can they paint their own picture to evoke the same feelings?

Grow plants from seed.

- Give opportunities for the expression of wonder as the first shoots appear, joy when they flower and sorrow when they die.

Use a candle as a focus for reflection. Ask the children:

- To think about what makes them happy.
- What could they do to make someone else happy?

Discuss happy times such as different cultural and religious celebrations - birthdays, weddings, births, Easter, Eid.

- Plan your own celebration, think of a reason to celebrate.
- Organise invitation cards, fancy hats or costumes, food, candles, music, and so on.

Use music as a focus for reflection. Ask the children:

- To think about what makes them sad.
- What makes other people sad?
- What makes them feel better?

Visit places in the community:

- Places of worship
- Homes for senior citizens
- Baby clinics

Talk about welcoming and rejecting people.

- Discuss feelings caused by having a new baby in the family. How can we help to welcome the baby? (set up a baby clinic or bath a doll with care.)
- Discuss the feelings of new children joining the group. How can we welcome them and show them the activities we enjoy and ask them if they would like to join in?

Naomi Compton

You should always acknowledge children's fears as they experience them, but you can also develop their understanding of this painful emotion through a range of planned activities

Exploring emotions: feeling afraid

Fear is a natural part of life, and something that young children experience in varying degrees. Our role lies in enabling them to understand that everyone is afraid sometimes and that being afraid is all part of being human. If we fail to do this, children's feelings of fear may be compounded by shame or guilt.

It is also important that we help children to see that fear can be a personal thing; that although some things may be frightening for everyone, different things frighten different people. Whilst one person may be fascinated by spiders, another may be terrified of finding one in the bath!

Activities that support children in understanding some of these complex issues can be beneficial and rewarding, but it is important to exercise great sensitivity. When asking children to think about and talk about fear you may be focusing on things that cause them pain and discomfort, so it is really important to establish a climate of trust within which everyone can feel safe, and confident that they will not be laughed at.

The most important starting point is acknowledging children's fears as they experience them. If you can do this they will get the message that there is no shame in feeling afraid, understand that the feeling is something that happens to all of us and feel confident that they can look to you for help and support.

You can then develop their understanding of this sometimes difficult emotion through a

range of planned activities. You might like to try out some of the following ideas.

Puppets, toys and dolls

Find a soft toy or teddy bear that looks appealing and will engage the children's emotions. Place your toy in a special box or basket and hide it under a towel or blanket. Explain to the children that there is someone who would really like to meet them but that he is too frightened to come out of the box. Ask them for their ideas about why he may be frightened and encourage them to suggest ways in which they could help him.

Once they have done this, let them try their ideas out. They usually have no difficulty coming up with ideas but if they do, support them by asking questions like: 'Do you think it would help if we all stayed very quiet and passed him round so that everyone could say hello and make friends with him?'

If you have any large puppets, create a

scenario where one character frightens another. Children are always fascinated by props, so if you can bring credibility to your story by using some plastic snakes, spiders or stick insects, for example, so much the better.

Explain to the children that one character has been invited to stay at the other's house and that both of them are very excited about it. Build the story by talking about what they packed to take with them, the games they played and what they had for tea. (The children can help you build the story.) Then tell the children about how, when one character was cleaning their teeth in the bathroom, the other hid some toy spiders in the bed, and go on to explain that when they got into bed and saw the spiders they were so frightened they cried and cried to be taken home.

Encourage the children to talk about and name the feelings that were experienced by everyone concerned and consider how the story might have ended and how the parents might have felt.

This scenario works with most children in the Foundation Stage and, by the end of Reception, children are usually able to discuss the issues with considerable complexity, and can even use the scenario as a basis for their writing.

Use the story as a springboard for discussing the children's feelings. Talk about the things that frighten you, and let the children add their own fears to the list. If appropriate, make a chart of all the different things that everyone is afraid of.

Stories and scenarios

Create further scenarios with your doll or puppet characters, for example the day one of them got lost in the supermarket or got locked in the toilet.

Tune into the children's fears and, over time, explore them through simple story scenarios. Many children, for example, have experienced tremendous fear when they have become lost in a big store or on a beach. Have this happen to one of your characters and encourage the children to generate strategies for helping. Encourage them to focus on what they would say to the character and the things they would suggest they do.

A visit to the dentist can be frightening for some children. Again, explore these feelings through your character and let the children make suggestions for how this situation can be handled.

Circle games

Play circle games that help children explore ideas about being afraid. You could collect pictures or make a list of some of the things that frighten the children, such as being in the dark, riding on a fast ride at the fair, being lost, climbing to the top of the slide, dogs, snakes or going to the dentist or doctors. Then play 'Change seats'.

Make a circle of chairs then go through your list and say, 'If you're frightened of spiders, change seats!' This is a concrete and practical way of helping young children to understand that people are all frightened by different things. With younger children, you can simply use your collection of pictures as a basis for conversations about feeling afraid. With older children, go round the circle with a tag line: 'I feel frightened when ....'

Fairy tales

Tell fairy tales which feature characters that are afraid, for example 'Little Red Riding Hood', 'Goldilocks', 'The Three Little Pigs', and talk about the feelings of the main characters, identifying the points in the stories when they were frightened. With older children, read some of the more scary stories like 'Hansel and Gretel' and 'Jack and the Beanstalk'.

Story books

Use storybooks like *The Park in the Dark* by Martin Waddell, *A Dark, Dark Tale* by Ruth Brown, *The Bear Under the Stairs* by Helen Cooper and *Can't You Sleep Little Bear?* by Martin Waddell as a basis for discussion. For older children, the *Helping Hands* series published by Evans Brothers has some excellent titles that deal with fear. *Could You Leave the Light On?* is all about a little girl who is afraid of the dark and *Mummy, Mummy, Where Are You?* deals with all the feelings associated with being lost.

Adult visitors

Invite adults into your setting to share their stories about when they have been frightened and talk with the children about how they overcame their fears. This really helps children to understand that everyone feels frightened some of the time and enables them to see that fear is something that can be dealt with and worked through. It can also help them to begin to understand that fear has a positive side; that it can both help to keep us safe and help us to grow as human beings. Taking your driving test or parachuting from an aeroplane can be frightening but we can be extremely proud once we have done it successfully !

Props and role play

Create prop boxes and role-play situations that enable children to explore scary situations, for example a jungle expedition. Provide backpacks, binoculars, torches, sleeping bags, cameras, clothes to dress up in and pop-up tents. Make a place for the children to play in by draping blankets over a climbing frame, clothes' horse or table. Use a torch or battery-powered lantern and hold story-telling sessions in the dark, dark place. For a really scary experience, add cobwebs and bats and hang things from the roof to give the feel of a 'ghost train.'

Read and dramatise *We're Going on a Bear Hunt* by Michael Rosen and Helen Oxenbury. Explore the family's feelings at each stage of the story, allowing the children to sense the change in atmosphere when they discover the bear!

Play a game where everyone hides under the covers on a given signal. (The children can choose the things that they are going to be scared of!)

The beauty of all these activities is that they allow children to explore their fears in a safe context, to develop empathy for others who are afraid and begin to develop strategies for helping and supporting them. Carried out with thought and sensitivity, this work can really help young children to accept fear as something that is not only a natural part of life but something through which they can grow and develop as people.

Ros Bayley

Most young children co-operate because they want to please you. Developing this further, so that the child realises that his or her own actions or intentions affect others, is quite complex and needs our help.

Teaching **right** from **wrong**

Children come to your setting from different cultures, traditions and religions and bring with them differing moral values. What is right for one may be wrong for another and it is important that we recognise this when developing moral codes.

The children will already have learned a great deal at home, particularly about role expectations, so it is important to recognise this and provide opportunities for these values to be explored. It may be acceptable at home for the first child not to share their toys or to eat lunch with their fingers, but in a group situation like pre-school, these actions will have an impact on the group.

We have developed a set of moral codes linked specifically to conduct and attitudes within the nursery. Parents smile when they first hear their children say 'We don't do it that way, we do it this way in nursery', but this way we tackle difficulties such as sharing and good manners without undermining the values present at home.

Role play

Role play can be a great way to explore the impact of our own actions. You might like to try playing a board game using two adult helpers as actors. One adult can be domineering, not allowing the other to take his or her turn, challenging where the counters are placed, telling the other what number they have thrown, moving their pieces for them, and so on, and eventually pushing the board away.

- Use your helpers as actors, set the scene and ask them to act it out.
- Ask the children to watch and think about what is happening.
- Don't make the scene too long or complicated.
- Discuss the outcome. *Was that the way to behave?* (Wait for a response.) *No? Why not? What did they do wrong?* (Again, wait for responses.) *What would you do?* Encourage the children to give you explanations.

- Replay the scene with the children.
- Make it fun. Even though these issues are serious, for children to learn and take on board the messages, they must enjoy what they are doing.

You can continue this throughout the session when situations arise. Rather than telling the children off or just saying 'well done', try asking them to think and talk about what was good or bad and why.

The theory

Morality is what you perceive as being right or wrong within your own environment, an agreement of a group of people as to the acceptability of a type of behaviour. Many theorists see morality as a set of developmental stages, which need to be learned. One such theorist is Lawrence Kohlberg. His theory is based on the idea that the stages build on each other in order of importance and significance to the person. He also found that 'moral growth' begins early on in children and that by the time they begin pre-school education, most of them will have reached the stage of wanting to co-operate as it reaps a reward which they find pleasurable. Developing this further for the child to realise that his or her own actions or intentions affect others is quite complex and needs our help.

Story time

During story time introduce books such as *Look What I've Got* by Anthony Browne. (Jeremy has difficulty sharing and shows off about all the new things he has. Each time he loses the chance to have a friend to play with by being self-centred and rude.)

Aesop's Fables, published by Ladybird Books, has tales told in simple language with an outcome to discuss at the end. These can be used to illustrate everyday occurrences that the children will understand. I am asked daily to tell the tale of 'The dog and his reflection' which highlights the effects of greed.

These activities enable the children to feel what it is like to be someone else, to explore emotions and to understand rules and fairness. By making children aware of their actions, we can build on those experiences and encourage development to the next stage of understanding, awareness and empathy for others.

Vicky Hislop

Building a Portfolio Level 2 • • •   **Personal, Social and Emotional Development**

Young children often find it difficult to say sorry and understand that their actions can affect others in a negative way. Judith Harries explains how you can help children to forgive and forget

Saying **sorry**

Young children should not be expected to say sorry spontaneously until they can understand what it means, and this requires an empathy which is only just beginning to emerge in the pre-school years. However, we should all be encouraging the development of this quality in the children in our care. The Early Learning Goals highlight the importance of setting a good example. If practitioners show awareness of the needs of others and consider the effect of their actions and words, children are also likely to develop such skills and attitudes.

Why is it important to say sorry?

When our actions or words have hurt someone else, even if the hurt was accidental or at best unintentional, as adults we usually manage to say sorry. Hopefully we can see that by apologising we can help to improve a situation and make others (and ourselves) feel better. Children need to be taught this.

Many pre-school children are just beginning to realise that their actions have consequences for themselves and for others. When Tom rides his bike into Liam and makes him cry, has he consciously thought 'I am going to hurt Liam', or is he experimenting with how fast he can ride and seeing what happens if he doesn't stop? The practitioner needs to help Tom realise that whatever his intentions, his actions have hurt another child and that saying sorry will help Liam to feel better.

Just saying sorry is not enough

A child may find it easy enough to say the word sorry, and then go on to repeat whatever caused the original hurt.

Encourage children to say exactly what they are sorry about, for instance 'Amy, I am sorry I knocked down your tower'. You can suggest to a child that they could also do something to make amends - 'Shall we help Amy rebuild the tower?' Some children need help to see that saying sorry should also signal a change in behaviour. You can also talk about forgiveness and encourage children not only to say sorry but to forgive each other. Intervene calmly in times of conflict between children and gather information about what has happened and how the children are feeling. Ask the children for their ideas and solutions and offer them the vocabulary with which to articulate their feelings.

Why do some children find it harder than others?

Some children find it especially difficult to say sorry to other children or adults. They may become withdrawn or distressed when asked to say sorry and this needs careful handling. Do they really know why we are asking them to say this magic word? Try to help them imagine how the other child is feeling as a result of their actions. The key is to help them see situations from another's point of view.

The feelings bag

Role play gives children the opportunity to make sense of their world. This role-play activity is designed to help children talk about their feelings and recognise when and how saying sorry can help make a difference. It works best with a small group of six to eight children but can also be helpful in a one-to-one situation with a child who has challenging behaviour.

You will need:

Two hand puppets; a soft draw-string bag; eight to ten plastic or cardboard discs showing different facial expressions, for example happy, sad, angry, scared, hurt, and so on (see diagrams).

Sit in a circle with the children and introduce them to the two hand puppets. Ask the children to give them names and help them to feel at ease.

Invite two of the children to pull out discs from the bag. Talk with the children about what feeling is shown on each of the faces. Can they make their own faces look sad or angry?

Ask them why they might be feeling angry. Using suggestions from the children wherever possible, make the puppets re-enact situations where they feel sad or angry. Can the children think of how to help the puppets feel better? Would it help if one or both of the puppets said sorry? You obviously need to guide the children so that the message you are trying to share comes across clearly! You can extend this activity to allow the children to act out the different situations within the security of a circle game.

Here are some simple situations for you to try resolving:

- One child pinches or slaps another child without reason.
- One child accidentally knocks another over.
- One child snatches a toy from another.
- A group of children won't let another child join in a game.

Judith Harries

As adults we appreciate the differences between right and wrong, but how does our understanding develop? Keeva Austin suggests some general ways in which to support children's understanding

Establishing **codes** of **behaviour**

Children reach conclusions about right and wrong not so much from what staff say, but from the examples they set and the atmosphere within the setting or school. Codes of behaviour and positive attitudes should be implicit in the learning environment. For example, the choice of books, toys and equipment should show the children that it is right for all people to be equally valued and respected.

Your attitude to sharing and turn-taking should be obvious in the way you choose children to help you with daily tasks, for example, giving out drinks, taking the register. Do you have a rota so each child gets a turn or is it pot luck? You also need to be explicit in explaining your values. Racist or sexist remarks or bad behaviour should be challenged immediately by giving the child an explanation as to why they are wrong. Good behaviour should be reinforced through praise.

Use spontaneous interactions as a means of reinforcing right and wrong. For example, a small group of children are playing in the water tray. One child says, 'Don't keep dropping that big bucket in the water, I'm getting splashed and my dress is all wet'. Take this opportunity to discuss with the children why the child is dropping the bucket into the water. Why is it wrong to splash another child? When and where would it be acceptable? Why doesn't the child want a wet dress?

Drawing up rules

Consider any rules you may have. Rules help children with the concept of right/wrong but must be based on good reasons. Children need to discuss these reasons so that they come to understand the principle upon which these decisions have been made. Encourage the children to draw up the rules for themselves. For example, decisions on sand tray rules may depend on the answers to the following questions:

- How many children should be at the sand tray at any one time and why?
- How can the sand tray equipment be shared fairly?
- Should we throw sand? Why not?
- What do we do about spilt sand?
- How should we respect the creations others make?

Once you and the children have reached some conclusions, clearly label the rules near to the sand tray. Do this for each activity area within your setting.

Using stories

Understanding right and wrong will also help the children be sensitive to the needs, views and feelings of themselves and others. They learn that it is right to form good relationships, take turns and understand the need for agreed values and codes of behaviour. In addition they are encouraged to consider the consequences of their words and actions.

Alongside these general points you need to plan activities specifically to promote an understanding of right and wrong. Take the story of *Bad Mood Bear.* *

The story is about Bear. Bear can't sleep. The next day he is very tired and in a bad mood. He throws his porridge on the floor, screams and pokes his tongue out at his mum, is rude

Other stories which could be used in a similar way:

A Duck so Small by A H Benjamin (Magi Publications). Duck is teased and made fun of because of his size. This book gives adults the opportunity to discuss the importance of treating everyone with respect and understanding.
Peaches and Plum in Trouble by Caroline Repucick (Paragon Book Service). Peaches and Plum play a trick, which results in someone else taking the blame. This book encourages children to consider the consequences of their words and actions on others.

to his friends and kicks his grandad, causing him to fall over. His dad sends him to his room where he screams but eventually falls asleep. When he wakes up he thinks about all the wrong things he's done and goes downstairs to apologise.

Young children often find it hard to look at themselves critically. Stories help them to discuss issues in a non-threatening way. Use this story initially for discussion:

- Why was Bear in a bad mood?
- What did he do wrong?
- How would his friends and parents have felt about his behaviour?
- Is it right to use a bad mood as an excuse to do wrong?

Once they are able to recognise Bear's wrongdoing encourage them to think about themselves. When have they ever done wrong at pre-school? Do they know why? What did the adult do? Extend the discussion and explore feelings and emotions. How do we feel if we have done wrong? Do we feel better if we are doing right? Perhaps make happy/sad bear faces to express their feelings. Encourage the children to draw things that are wrong, then ask them to draw the right things they should have done instead.

* *Bad Mood Bear* by John Richardson (Random Century 1991).

Keeva Austin

Building a Portfolio Level 2 • • •   **Personal, Social and Emotional Development**

Chapter 4

Unit C8: Implement planned activities for sensory and intellectual development

This chapter is all about the activities you carry out with the children every day, such as playing games, cooking, painting and other art work. These activities help them to develop their senses of sight, hearing, touch, taste and smell, and their intellectual development - that is, their ability to learn and understand.

Play is absolutely central to children's learning and development, and to their overall well-being. You must give them as much opportunity as possible for free play, because it's through exploring their environment that young children learn best. You need to learn when it is appropriate to let children play alone and when it is beneficial to join in. The best way to do this is to observe the children. Watch a group, for instance, playing in the sand. If they're using their imagination to create hills and roads, and they're using lots of language, leave them to carry on playing, because they're gaining a lot from it. But if you see a child struggling to make sandcastles with dry sand, that's a good time to intervene and suggest that they try wet sand. You will be developing their learning.

Remember!
Play is absolutely central to children's learning and development, and to their overall well-being.

This may be a good unit for you to start with, because these activities are things you do every day with the children. It will be useful for you to work with different age groups, so that you get a feel for which activities are best for each age group. It's important that you stimulate children right from birth. Babies will respond to your voice and touch. They will enjoy watching mobiles placed near them, or toys which you hold and shake, and listening to music and singing. By four months old they will begin to reach for objects and will enjoy exploring them with their mouth, so it's vital that toys are clean and safe, with no small or sharp pieces which could choke or injure them. Between six and nine months, babies will begin to be more mobile, so you will have to watch everything they do, and make sure their environment is completely safe.

From the time children are able to grasp, sit up and move around, they will need a great variety of activities and experiences. Try to spend some time with each age group and write down all the activities they do during a week. Make a list of which activities are suitable for each age, and which children can enjoy at every age. Think about which of the senses each activity is helping to develop. It may be more than one. For instance, cookery can develop every sense.

Children play in different ways at different stages of development, and you need to be aware of this so that you can plan appropriate activities:

◆ **Solitary play** - children play alone up to about two years old, although they will take an interest in other babies; they are unable to understand sharing.

◆ **Parallel play** - from about two to three years old, children play alongside each other, with some interaction, but little cooperation.

◆ **Cooperative play** - from about three years old, children play together and are beginning to cooperate and cope with sharing and taking turns, although there will still be disagreements.

Of course, older children will still sometimes play alone or alongside others. It depends on the individual child, the activity and how the child is feeling. Some children are more solitary than others.

Early years settings which receive nursery grant funding and schools with nursery and Reception aged children will be working towards the Foundation Stage curriculum and the Early Learning Goals. They will use the *Curriculum Guidance for the Foundation Stage* to plan the curriculum - that is, all the activities and experiences you provide for the children which help them to learn. This includes free play as well as planned activities. The guidelines are based on six areas of learning:

◆ Personal, Social and Emotional Development

◆ Communication, Language and Literacy

◆ Mathematical Development

- ◆ Knowledge and Understanding of the World

- ◆ Physical Development

- ◆ Creative Development

It would be helpful to think about these when you plan your activities. Ask your supervisor if you can see a copy of the guidelines. Your centre will probably explain them more fully during your training.

Links with other units

This unit is closely linked with C9 which is all about helping children to develop their language and communication skills. Whenever you are with the children it's vital that you talk and listen to them about what you and they are doing, and encourage them to talk. There may also be opportunities to provide evidence for C4, to show how you support children's emotional and social development. For instance, you will probably be encouraging children to share and take turns, letting them choose and try things out for themselves, and helping them to gain confidence. There will certainly be links with E1 about keeping children safe. Some of the games you play may have links with C1.3, which is about encouraging children's physical skills.

Values

Find the values page for C8 and look through it carefully. Throughout the unit, as in all the units and everything you do when working as a carer and educator of young children, you will need to be aware of the first two values - **the welfare of the children** and **keeping children safe**. For every activity you plan, you must think about these key issues. As this unit is all about **children's learning and development**, that will be important to consider in every element. You also need to develop your skills as a **reflective practitioner** - thinking about why you do things the way you do, what the children will gain from them, and whether you could do it better.

Working with parents is important in Element 3 - Assist children with cooking activities - because you will need to check with parents whether their child has an allergy, or is not allowed certain foods. Choose a recipe that is suitable for all of the children if you can, so that no-one feels left out.

You need to think about **equality of opportunity** and **anti-discrimination** in Element 2 - Playing games with children - by making sure that all children have an opportunity to choose and that all children are treated fairly. In Element 3, Cooking with children, you need to make sure that through the recipes you choose and the explanations you give, you enable all children to participate, and avoid any stereotyping such as expecting the girls to wash up.

Celebrating diversity is important in Elements 1, 3 and 5.

When providing paint and other drawing materials, make sure you provide paper, paints and crayons which reflect the skin colours of all the children. Through cooking, you can help children to learn more about food from their own and other cultures. For instance, if you're making bread, you can also make, say, chapattis, or show the children a range of bread from a variety of cultures. Many kinds of bread are available from supermarkets. When you choose interesting objects to show to children, include things from various cultures - your local intercultural support service or parents may be able to help you with this. There is a useful article later in the chapter which helps you to think about how well the toys and equipment in your setting help children to develop positive attitudes to diversity.

You need to be aware of **working with other professionals** in Element 1, insofar as you need to report any faulty equipment to the appropriate people in your setting, and in Element 5, where you need to have agreed with the appropriate staff that the objects or displays you are using fit in with the curriculum plan.

Getting started

In this unit you are aiming to show how you can:

- ◆ provide activities, equipment and materials for creative play

- ◆ play games with children

- ◆ assist children with cookery activities

- ◆ provide opportunities and equipment for manipulative play

- ◆ examine objects of interest with children.

Read through the elements, and the knowledge statements, and make sure you understand them. If there is anything you don't understand, discuss it with your assessor. She will be able to tell you what training sessions are available for this unit. Then use the personal skills profile to identify which areas you feel most confident about and which you need some more experience in, or where you need to gain more knowledge and understanding. Ask your supervisor if you can get some practice in doing activities you don't feel confident about. Plan with your assessor which activities you will start with. She may need to observe you several times for this unit because there is a lot to cover. Your assessor will fill in an assessment plan with you, so that you are clear about what you need to do.

note

You have access to a range of courses run by the Early Years Development and Childcare Partnership. Your setting should receive details of these. Check with your supervisor.

Element C8.1 Provide activities, equipment and materials for creative play

Key issues

Free play is really important to give children the opportunity to be creative. If you restrict children's choice too much, you will limit their creativity. Let them experiment and try things out. Avoid getting children to colour in outline pictures or fill in templates with bits of material or paper. This stifles their creativity.

> ### Remember!
> It's the doing that's important, not the end product.

There are many different activities you can provide for creative play. Look at the range, and the notes for the element, for ideas. Ideally, they should all be available so that children can choose what they want to do, but if you don't have space for them all to be out at the same time, try to make sure that children have regular opportunities to use them. Use the outside space as well as indoors. Sand and water are great favourites with children, and they learn a lot from them. Watch children playing and make a list of why sand and water are good for their development, and what they learn from it.

Here are a few ideas. Add some more of your own:

◆ science -why dry sand pours and wet sand doesn't

◆ maths language - full, half full, empty

◆ imagination - being at the seaside, or in a boat, or making a car track

◆ they enjoy it!

Children also love malleable materials - things they can squeeze, shape, knead and pummel - such as playdough, clay and Plasticine. Plasticine can be difficult for small children. You need to keep it in a warm place, to keep it soft. Clay is messy, but well worth the effort. Playdough is easy for children to use, because it's soft. You can also colour and scent it, to make it more interesting. You can buy it, but it's much cheaper to make. There are various recipes for playdough but here is one you may like to try:

> 4 cups plain flour
> 2 cups salt
> 3 teaspoons cream of tartar
> 2 tablespoons oil
> food colouring
> 2-3 cups water

Mix dry ingredients, add oil, water, colouring. Cook over a low heat stirring with a wooden spoon until dough thickens and begins to form a lump. Allow to cool slightly and knead. Store in an airtight container. Lasts for up to two weeks.

You can use a cold mix and let the children make it. Use the same ingredients but leave out the cream of tartar. Try different sorts of flour for different textures.

Cornflour and water makes a wonderful tactile (touch) experience for the children. Just mix a little water with the cornflour, and try it out yourself before giving it to the children. You can colour it with food colouring if you wish.

Let children start using creative materials as soon as possible. Once babies can sit up and hold things, they will enjoy the experience. Of course, you will need to be watchful, to prevent them putting things in their mouth. You will need to do these activities one to one with a baby. Whatever the age of the child, you need to provide protective covering for floors and tables, unless you have a wet area with washable tables and floor, and protective clothing for the children. It's useful to provide hats for sand play, especially for children with tight curly hair or plaits, because sand is difficult to remove.

The **knowledge evidence** statements for this element are 1, 3, 7, 8, 19, 20, 21 and 24. You need to show that you understand:

◆ sensory and intellectual development (also C8.2, C8.4)

◆ how different types of play help children's learning and development (also C8.2, C8.3)

◆ why a curriculum plan is important when choosing activities (all elements)

◆ what activities and materials to provide for creative play

◆ what are the hazards of playing with natural materials, and what safety measures to take

◆ different ways to set out materials attractively (also C8.4, C8.5)

◆ health and safety requirements of the setting

◆ how to select or adapt equipment for children with additional needs

You will normally need to go on training to make sure that you have the knowledge necessary for the unit, unless you feel you already have the understanding through previous experience or training. You may have already been asked to write an assignment on child development, which will show your knowledge of all aspects of child development for each unit. You will be able to show some of the knowledge and understanding through your assessor's observation and the other evidence we have suggested below. If there are any gaps in your knowledge evidence, your assessor may ask you questions, or she may want you to provide written answers to questions.

Which type of evidence?

Your assessor will need to **observe** all but three PCs and one aspect in each section of the range, but she may be able to observe more than that. She will probably ask you **questions** about the activities she has observed, to check your understanding.

You should complete an **activity plan** to show your assessor that you have prepared everything properly. When you have completed the activity make a comment on how it went, and whether you would change it next time to make it better. You will find the activity plan form on pages 28-29 in the introduction.

If you have carried out other activities as part of your normal work, write a **reflective account** or a **diary account** to cover the range. Your supervisor could also write a **witness testimony** to say you have carried out these activities competently.

You must make sure that you have covered all of the range and the PCs, either through your assessor's questions or your own written accounts. For instance, one section of the range asks you to show how you would provide equipment to enable children with additional needs to participate in activities. If you don't have any children with additional needs in your setting you will have to show a good understanding of the issues through your other evidence. Your assessor will help you with this.

> ### Remember!
> If you find writing difficult, ask your assessor if she can ask you more questions, or record your reflective account onto a tape.

Element C8.2 Play games with children

Key issues

Children love to play games almost from the time they are born. One of the first games a mother plays with her baby is 'peek-a-boo'. By the age of about one year, babies find it a great game to throw the toys out of their pram over and over again for someone to pick up. As children grow older, their games become more complex, so that by about seven years old, children can play team games and cope with rules -

although they may still break them!

Playing games introduces children to their own culture - many playground games are rooted in history, and almost all cultures have passed on games from one generation to the next. Some of the common ones you may remember are 'Ring-a-ring-o' roses', 'Oranges and lemons', 'The farmer's in his den', 'Simon says', 'What's the time Mister Wolf?' It's important to keep these games alive, but you need to be aware that they often stereotype, so you need to counteract this. For instance, instead of Simon, use Sara or Sanjeet, and sometimes choose a girl to be the farmer, or have Mrs Wolf. Find out about games from other cultures by asking parents or your local intercultural support service.

> **Stereotyping** means labelling an individual or group with a particular characteristic, often negative.

Many games, such as board games like snakes and ladders, and races during sports and physical education, are competitive and some early years workers would argue that they have no place in an early years setting because they cause children to be winners or losers. Others would say that life is competitive, and children have to learn to cope with that. It would be useful to discuss this with your colleagues and see how they feel. It's important that you don't put too much emphasis on winning or losing, and emphasise that it's the fun of playing that's important. You also need to balance competitive games with non-competitive ones, like parachute games and games which give every child a turn. There is a helpful article on co-operative games in Chapter 3 (pages 74-76).

The younger the child, the smaller the group needs to be for playing games, so that every child is actively involved. Young children up till about two to two and a half years of age are not capable of sharing and taking turns, and are unable to concentrate for long. Games need to be appropriate for the children's stage of development and level of understanding. If children are sitting doing nothing for long, the game is not appropriate. If you start a game, and it's not working, or the children are getting bored, change to another activity.

The **knowledge evidence** statements for this element are 2, 3, 4, 18, 22, 23 and 26. You need to show that you understand:

◆ the sequence of development of children's play

◆ the effects of competitive games and losing on children's self-esteem and behaviour

◆ how to handle children who are disruptive or don't want to join in

◆ how to devise and improvise your own games

◆ why you choose particular games and activities

◆ the effect of stereotyping in traditional games and how to counteract it

There are some quite difficult topics here which your training sessions will help you with. Your assessor may have some written questions for you, to make sure you understand. You can cover some of them in your evidence for the element.

Which type of evidence?

Your assessor will need to **observe** all of the PCs and one aspect in each section of the range for this element. She may also ask you some **questions** about what you have done and how it has helped the children's development. Read through the requirements for the element to make sure you cover everything you need to. It would be helpful to prepare an **activity plan** to make sure you are well prepared for the activity. You will see that there is quite a wide range you have to cover, so your assessor will probably want to watch you playing more than one game. For instance, you could play a game like colour matching or 'Kim's game' with a small group of children, then take all the children outside for some singing games. You will need to arrange this with your supervisor to make sure it's convenient, because you will need a qualified member of staff with you outside. Check how much of the range this would cover - nearly all of it! If you have played some games with the children before, you could write about these as a **diary** or reflective account, or describe them to your assessor.

> **Remember!**
> If your assessor has observed you and asked questions, or if you have written evidence for the elements, you will have covered some of the knowledge evidence already.

Element C8.3 Assist children with cooking activities

Key issues

Most children really enjoy cooking, especially if they can eat what they have made! Before you decide what to make, you need to check with your supervisor whether any of the children have allergies or additional dietary needs. You will also need to check what cooking facilities there are. If you don't have a cooker, you will have to make sandwiches, fruit salad or ice biscuits. There are some other ideas in the notes on this element in your candidate handbook. You need to be particularly careful with hygiene. If you have done a basic food

hygiene course for C1 that will be useful in this element. Check whether you have any other evidence from C1 which would be appropriate.

> **Remember** to use your cross referencing sheets to record any evidence which might be useful for other units.

If you're using a cooker, you need to be careful that children are well away from it but able to see what you're doing. Don't choose a recipe that's all done on the cooker - that would be unsuitable because the children couldn't join in, and they need to be involved as much as possible. Keep the group small and let the children do the measuring, pouring and mixing. Several small bowls rather than one big one is better so that everyone has a turn without having to wait too long. Think about the age of the children - the younger the children, the simpler the activity needs to be. Choose a healthy recipe if possible, and think of ways to widen children's experience of other cultures. There are some articles later in the chapter which will help you with this.

The **knowledge evidence** statements for this element are 5, 9, 10, 16 and 17. You need to show that you understand:

◆ which cooking processes are appropriate for children at different ages and levels of development

◆ the general principles of healthy eating

◆ a variety of recipes, including recipes from different cultures, to use with children

◆ how to adapt cooking activities so that children with additional needs can take part

◆ hygiene and health and safety

Try to cover as much as possible in the evidence below. For instance, in your activity plan, you could say how you would change the activity if you were working with older or younger children, or children with an additional need.

Which type of evidence?

Your assessor will need to **observe** all but three of the PCs in this element and one aspect of each section of the range. She will also ask you **questions** to check your understanding - for example, she may ask you how you have ensured that the ingredients were stored safely, and if you have checked whether any children have additional dietary needs. You will certainly need an **activity plan** for this element, because you need to plan carefully, so that you are sure you have all the necessary ingredients and utensils before you start. If you have any evidence from C1, don't forget to **cross reference** it. If you need help with this, ask your assessor. It would be useful to collect a **book of recipes** suitable for making with children of different ages, including healthy eating and recipes from a variety of cultures. If you haven't covered all of the range, you can ask your supervisor to write a **witness testimony** describing other cooking you have done.

> **Remember!**
> You may not need all these types of evidence. If you have covered everything, don't give yourself extra work. But do try to cover the knowledge evidence in your observation, oral or written evidence.

Element C8.4 Provide opportunities and equipment for manipulative play

Key issues

This element looks at gross motor skills and fine manipulative skills. Gross motor skills show children's ability to use their arms and legs, and control their body, so that they can run, climb, throw, catch and move large objects. Fine manipulative skills show children's ability to use their hands and fingers for small construction, jigsaws, using pencils, paint brushes and other tools. They learn to do these things naturally if you give them the right equipment, materials and activities. If you can, watch different age groups and see how the children's skills develop as they grow. Young babies are not able to control their limbs or their hands and fingers. By four or five months they are beginning to grasp things. By about six months they can sit up, and by eight or nine months they will crawl. By around a year old they will walk. But it will take several years for them to fully develop their gross and fine motor skills.

Make a list of all the equipment you use in your setting to develop gross motor skills and another for fine motor skills. Watch how the children use them. Here are some ideas, but you will be able to add more:

Gross motor	Fine manipulative
Large construction toys	Small construction toys
Bat and ball	Playdough
Music and movement	Cutting and sticking
Climbing frame	Jigsaws
Tricycles and other wheeled toys	Drawing and painting

Other fun ways of developing children's manipulative skills are finger rhymes like 'Tommy Thumb', 'Five fat peas' and 'Incy Wincy Spider'. Join in with singing sessions in your setting and learn some of the finger rhymes the other staff use. It's useful to write them down in a book, to refer to if you forget them. There are some good song books available such as *This Little*

Puffin by Elizabeth Matterson (Puffin) and for some, audiotapes are available too.

Playdough and clay are good for strengthening children's hand and finger muscles. Threading beads and lacing cards, jigsaws and small construction toys all help children to gain good finger control. A writing corner, or pencils and paper in play areas such as the shop, encourage children to 'play' write. But avoid giving pre-school children worksheets. The other activities we have described are a more appropriate way of giving them the skills they need.

> **note**
> It is not appropriate to push children into formal writing too young. Instead, give them lots of opportunity for 'play' writing and other manipulative activities.

The **knowledge evidence** statements for this element are 11, 12 and 25. You need to show that you understand:

◆ how to support and encourage children in activities but still allow them to control the activity and develop self-reliance.

◆ the differences between fine and gross motor play

◆ games and equipment to help children with additional needs to take part

Try to cover as much of the knowledge evidence as you can in the evidence below.

Which type of evidence?

Your assessor will need to **observe** you for all but one of the PCs and one aspect of each section of the range. If you plan carefully, you could cover most of the evidence through observation. Plan two sessions together - perhaps a session where you supervise the children choosing a variety of activities, where they have large and small equipment out, getting them to clear away and followed up by singing some finger rhymes. Of course, you would need to have other staff helping to supervise, but you could ask your supervisor if you could choose the activities and set them out. Your assessor will probably ask you **questions** about why you have set out certain activities, and what the children gained from them. If there are other activities you have carried out in the past write about them in a **diary** or **reflective account**.

Element C8.5 Examine objects of interest with children

Key issues

In this element you will be looking at how you can use interesting objects with children. Children are naturally curious and will enjoy looking at, touching, smelling, feeling and listening to all sorts of objects. It's a good idea to start collecting things you think may be suitable and keeping them, so that you can use them again and again in different ways. The toy box can produce some interesting discussion - about different textures, hard and soft, big and small, and endless other possibilities. Second-hand shops and jumble sales are a good source. Also, lots of things around the house, like saucepan lids, wooden spoons and other things you can make sounds with are useful. Ask parents to bring in articles for a topic you may be doing. Try to include articles which reflect the different cultures of the world in every display. You do need to take extra care with these things, though, because they're not intended as children's play objects. Make sure that they're safe to handle, especially if you are using them with very young children. Check with your supervisor if you're not sure. As a general rule, children should be allowed to handle all of the objects on a display table, as long as they are taught to treat them with care and respect. You may need to make an exception if an object is precious or fragile, or dangerous to handle, but you really think the children will benefit from seeing it.

You also need to be aware of any child who may have a sensory impairment. For instance, for a child with impaired vision, you would need to think about how to provide objects which would stimulate their other senses, like things to smell, feel and listen to.

As you can see from the range for this element, objects have been divided into five categories. Here are a few examples of each. See if you can add some more:

Natural: growing plants, stones, pieces of wood, fruit and vegetables, nuts and berries (be especially careful with these)

Manufactured: clocks, kitchen utensils, objects made of wood, metal, plastic, jewellery

Thematic (that is, to go with a particular theme or topic): objects of a particular colour or shape, to do with the senses, food, clothes, a religious festival

Written: a beautiful book or poster displaying ornate letters, books in different languages, Braille

Pictorial: beautiful art work by famous artists

Of course, you can also go out to look at objects of interest. For instance, your setting might arrange a trip to a park or garden, a place of worship, the shops, a farm or a museum. Or you could simply take a walk around your outside area looking for minibeasts, stones, leaves and so on. Look out for unexpected things, like roadworks, a snowstorm, the refuse lorry, or a fire engine. One of the parents who collects particular things as a hobby might come in and show them to the children.

The important thing is that you let the children handle things and discuss them, answer their questions and extend their knowledge by explaining and describing things carefully.

The **knowledge evidence** statements for this element are 6, 13, 14, 15, 20, 27 and 28. You need to show that you understand:

◆ why and how exploring interesting objects helps children's development

◆ how to build on children's natural curiosity and not stifle it

◆ the range of themes, objects and materials which reflect the cultural background of the children and how to use them to extend their understanding of other cultures

◆ how to encourage children to treat cultural objects with respect

◆ how to enable children with a sensory impairment to examine objects effectively

Try to cover as much of this as you can in the evidence below. Your assessor may set you questions to fill any gaps in your evidence.

Which type of evidence?

Your assessor will need to **observe** all but one of the PCs and one aspect of each section of the range. She will probably ask **questions** to check your understanding. You could write a **list** of the interesting objects you have collected, and what you could use them for. For example, things to sort in different ways, like a particular colour or shape, wooden or metal things, soft or hard things, things which roll and so on. If you have set up a display, take a **photograph** for your portfolio. Write a **reflective account** on how you used it, if your assessor didn't observe it.

How does play in educational settings differ from play in other contexts? The Oxfordshire Early Years Team looks at the critical role of adults in establishing and sustaining high quality learning through play

Supporting children's play

Most early childhood educators would agree that play should have a central role in the early years curriculum. But increasingly, many feel that play is being squeezed out of children's experiences and that it is harder than ever to justify play as a significant part of the educational day.

What does high quality play look like?

Play is one of the most crucial ways in which young children come to make sense of the world around them. Through play, children acquire understandings, skills and strategies that will be the underpinning of all their future educational and life experiences. Play provides children with their first experiences of the astonishing range of their body's capabilities. It develops imagination, curiosity, ways of communicating and social competence . . . and all in contexts which children find absorbing and fun!

High quality play challenges children. It excites and stimulates them. It has purpose and relevance to what they want to know and what they want to achieve. It is an active process that demands the involvement of their body and their mind in a search for answers to the endless questions they pose for themselves. High quality play enables children to progress through exploration and investigation to mastery and control of resources, the environment and their experiences. It is the process of play that matters more than the end product. What children try out, do, refine and adapt in the process of play offers learning opportunities unparalleled in more adult directed learning.

Giving status to play

The problem with a great deal of play in educational settings is that it is reduced to the 'second division' of classroom activity. It is an activity that is done once the 'work' is

finished, it is under-resourced and is not assessed as rigorously as more adult directed learning. When play is reduced to this status in a setting then the quality of play suffers. If play is a key process of learning then it must be at the heart of children's educational experiences. It should form an integral part of the process of teaching and learning and be treated with the respect it deserves.

It is the adults in the setting who determine the status of play within that setting and their belief and enthusiasm which will raise

'There is a fine line between intervening and interfering. When adults interfere with play they can take it over, dominating both the process and the outcomes.'

the profile of play amongst fellow practitioners, parents and children. When adults understand the powerful nature of play then the learning environments they create and the experiences they plan all harness this most natural and effective process of learning.

Preparing an appropriate environment

An appropriate environment for play is one that attracts children to a range of play opportunities. It needs to be inviting, stimulating and cause children to ask such questions as 'What is this?' 'What does it do?' and 'What can I make it do?' The environment should reflect the breadth and balance of the early years curriculum, providing opportunities for personal, social and emotional development; interaction and

communication in a variety of situations; mathematical and scientific understanding; creative, imaginative and physical challenge. All of these experiences should be planned to take place both indoors and outdoors so that play can be extended and enhanced as children move from one environment to the other. An appropriate environment for play should include a rich variety of good quality resources.

It is important to remember that resources need to be selected with an awareness of the equality of access and opportunity which they provide for children. They should be appropriate for both boys and girls, for example providing dressing-up clothes that encourage boys into the role play area. They should reflect a wide range of cultures that have been introduced to children in meaningful ways, for example Chinese cooking utensils as part of Chinese New Year celebrations. They should also be appropriate for a range of special needs, interests and circumstances. No child should feel excluded from an activity or experience because the resources available reflect a cultural, gender, social or ability bias.

Planning for learning

Although children learn spontaneously through play it is the role of the adult to ensure that in an educational setting play is planned for in a rigorous and systematic way. This does not mean that children do what adults tell them in play situations but rather that adults select equipment and resources and give children experiences that enable them to play in purposeful and meaningful ways.

In their long- and medium-term planning, adults identify what it is that they want children to learn. These stages ensure that children receive their curriculum entitlement and that their learning

In a nursery school the adults had identified that the older boys needed more experience of role play, to improve their relationships with other children. A visit to the fishmongers in the local market sparked imaginative play of the highest quality as children, dressed in boaters and aprons, wrote a chalkboard of daily specials and weighed and costed lobsters, crabs, eels and whelks. The boys, stimulated by the male role models in the fishmongers, took an active part in the recreation of the market stall. The adults had given the children a purposeful stimulus, the appropriate resources, good role models and the time and space to interpret their experiences in meaningful ways.

progresses. It is at the short-term stage of planning that the detail of the activities and experiences are identified in order to ensure that the needs of individual and groups of children are being met. Well-planned play experiences cut across artificial subject boundaries and empower children to use and apply a whole range of skills, strategies, knowledge and understanding in contexts that are relevant, challenging and absorbing.

Observing and assessing play

If play is to have status in a setting then adults must observe and assess what children are learning in ways that are as rigorous and systematic as they are for any other activity. There are things that adults learn about children when they are playing that they will not learn from observing more adult directed activities. Very often adults need to stand back and watch and wait in order to see the rich variety of understandings and skills which children at play reveal. As adults watch children at play important questions will arise, such as, 'Are the children involved and absorbed?' 'What are they doing?' 'What are they learning?' 'Do I need to intervene at this moment?' 'Do I need to plan for something more challenging in the future?' Having made such observations it is important to record those which give evidence of significant development in order to show progress in learning. Then, adults are in a position to make use of their observations and records in deciding what play opportunities need to be provided in the future.

Interacting and intervening in play

There are times when children need the time and space to play uninterrupted. The role of the adult here is to have provided resources, experiences and stimuli so that as children play independently, everything possible has been thought about and planned for to ensure the experience will be of good quality. Even when children play independently they should not be abandoned! Adults may be involved with other children but still keep an eye on what is happening in the home area or the sand play and, perhaps, make sure that those children playing uninterrupted have the opportunity to talk about their independent experiences later in the day.

But there are times when the quality of play will be increased through adult intervention and interaction. The skill of the adult is in judging when this is appropriate. There is a fine line between intervening and interfering. When adults interfere with play they can take it over, dominating both the process and the outcomes. This mistake is usually made when adults have not observed for long enough before intervening. It can be all too easy to misinterpret the play that is taking place and to make assumptions about

what it is that children are doing and why. Adults need to recognise that even if they have provided resources for a purpose, for example climbing apparatus to develop children's physical co-ordination, that children might just turn this apparatus into a den because at that moment it meets their needs and interests to do so! This does not make the play worthless but rather shows the creative and fertile imaginations of children. The appropriate response to this scenario is to observe and record what children are doing and learning in their play and, in the light of what is seen, to readjust the short-term plans.

The role of the adult in supporting children's play is demanding and challenging. It requires great sensitivity and great skill. It rests on a deep knowledge of how children learn and an appreciation of what they are learning in situations which are usually far more complex than they may appear. If play is of high quality then it takes sustained observation and skilled interpretation before all its many layers are revealed. Those who undervalue the place of play are frequently not sufficiently knowledgeable to appreciate how remarkable play is as a vehicle for learning. All of us in early childhood education must do what we can to understand and promote the power of play.

Julie Fisher and the Oxfordshire Early Years Team

Play is the primary way in which children learn about themselves and about the world around them. Toys and games can be regarded as the building blocks of awareness of the rich diversity that surrounds children. Can you be sure that your resources reflect that diversity?

Evaluating your resources in an anti-racist framework

Children from a very young age pick up messages from everything and everybody around them - the language they hear, the toys they play with, the images they see in books, in window shops, on TV. The impressions that children form of each other and the assumptions that are made about each other are influenced by the nature of these messages - whether positive or negative.

The English language plays a part in this. Notions of good and bad are often associated with colour - the word black has connotations of evil or wickedness in many dictionary entries, whilst white is often associated with goodness or truth. It is obvious that assumptions should not be made about somebody's personality, potential or lifestyle on the basis of physical features such as hair texture or skin colour, yet we rarely stop to analyse the messages we are bombarded with every day.

Very early in life children are aware of their own and other people's skin colour. By the age of three many children are beginning to learn that white skin is viewed by some people as superior and black skin as inferior. As a result black children can experience rejection and abuse. White children can become insensitive by harbouring these false feelings of superiority and are then unable to value the accomplishments, activities and languages of people who are not white. This can damage the emotional and intellectual development of all children and lead to the reinforcement of racism in society.

Racist stereotyping denies children opportunities to develop in the early years. One example of this is the view often held that black boys are noisy and over active and should be encouraged to concentrate on energetic outside play. Labelling children in

this way denies them access to a full range of activities in their early years.

Few young black children can articulate how racism affects them. It can often be seen in changing behaviour patterns or a reluctance to acknowledge their own skin colour, particularly in largely white play settings - the black child in class painting herself white is an indication that the child has accepted the stereotype that white is the preferable colour to be. In many early years settings, particularly in largely white areas, there is still un under-emphasis on the importance of resources which reflect all communities positively.

Criteria for evaluation

Children need toys and books that reflect the overall diversity of the society in which they live. This is particularly true for children who live in predominantly white areas. In the absence of a positive reflection of diversity, white European culture will continue to be regarded as the norm and other cultural/linguistic groups will be marginalised to the detriment of all children's understanding of diversity.

All children need to see themselves reflected positively in the world around them. They should see people like themselves on television, on the fronts of magazines, in adverts, in books, toys and games. This tells them that they matter and are an integral part of society. However, this is not the normal daily experience of black children in Britain today. All the more reason that a positive stand is taken against racism to ensure that all human beings and cultures are equally valued in the resources used with young children.

However, it is not enough to ensure that toys and books reflect black people and

---

Points to consider:

- Do your resources reinforce the self-esteem and identity of all children? For example, do illustrations in books, posters and jigsaw puzzles feature black people in active and effective roles. Instead of using magazines aimed at the white majority, introduce those produced by African Caribbean and Asian press.
- Do your resources include items which extend the children's understanding and awareness of languages and cultures, food and celebrations - without making them exotic or strange?
- Do your resources extend the children's confidence and growth by challenging stereotypes and assumptions related to race, gender and disability ?
- Are the representations of people in dolls, models, puppets and miniature figures accurate and realistic so that children can experience and explore differences in a positive way? Rag-dolls should not have the exaggerated negative features of the golliwog.

---

communities. A lot of what passes for 'multicultural' could actually be reinforcing stereotypes. For example, a black doll with European features gives a clear message that European features are preferable. You should aim to provide resources with an emphasis on those which feature black characters in leading roles as well as a good variety of black dolls, not just one or two.

Resources for children cannot be positive unless they are also safe, durable, fun and inviting. While easy cleaning and value for money may also be considerations, it is important to note that many excellent resources are produced by small companies and may appear expensive by comparison - but these resources are usually not available anywhere else. It is important not to make price the main consideration.

Building a Portfolio Level 2 • • •

Check-list for evaluating and selecting picture books:

Date of publication

This is an important indicator of how issues are likely to be treated in the text. Books which were published some time ago may present situations and express attitudes and ideas that are no longer acceptable.

Author and illustrator

What is their connection with the subject of the book? What qualifies them to write or illustrate it? Where both are familiar with their subject, the result is much more appealing. Do the text and illustrations consciously or unconsciously present only a white Eurocentric perspective? This is still possible where both author and illustrator are non-European.

Publisher

Most good titles are produced by a very few small independent publishers such as Tamarind, Mantra and Magi. Some large publishing houses restrict themselves to publishing a single 'multicultural' title or a small sub-list. Few publishers have an overall anti-racist policy operating across the range of titles they produce. This results in inconsistency, where the same publisher can be recommended for an excellent book and simultaneously criticised for offensive titles which appear in the same catalogue, so make sure that you examine books individually.

Language and style

The way language is used is very important. When evaluating a book, check if 'black' is used only as a derogatory descriptive term associated with unpleasant, bad or frightening things. Are terms such as 'red skins', 'red Indians' and 'Bushmen' still used? Are words with insulting overtones, for example - 'savage', 'tribal', 'primitive', 'inscrutable' used primarily to describe black people? Do words like 'only' and 'proper' in the text convey value judgement? For example, 'He didn't have a refrigerator or an oven, or even a proper sink' (from the book *Nanda in India*). By whose values was the sink 'not proper'?

How are languages other than English referred to? Are speakers of other languages or those using English as a second language made to do so in non-standard English? Are they laughed at or ridiculed in the text? When referring to people speaking in their own language, is it referred to as 'mumbo jumbo' or 'chattering' instead of 'talking'? Where words are used which reinforce prejudice and inequalities, is this done in a way that makes it clear these are unacceptable terms? The demand for dual-language text remains high. But where a second language is used in addition to English - are they given equal status? Often English appears first on the page in a larger bold typeface. Often there is no indication where a language is to be read from right to left.

Illustrations

Children look to the pictures in a book to tell the story, even when someone is reading the text to them. In the context of current children's publishing in Britain, where black people are rarely represented, every picture carries far more meaning for both black and white children.

Stereotypes: Make sure that the illustrations are not stereotypes or caricatures making over-simplified generalisations of a particular community. For example, are Chinese people shown with hats and pigtails?

Faces: Too many illustrators appear to use a shorthand line to suggest particular facial features, for example, diagonal lines for Chinese people's eyes, or big circles for African and African Caribbean eyes and overly thick lips on African and Caribbean people. This not only makes everyone look the same, it is also inaccurate and offensive to the community it attempts to portray.

Tokenism: Is the solitary black character the only indication of a multicultural perspective? Are faces of all characters shown having exactly the same features, where some are simply coloured in different shades to indicate other cultures? Is there a

picture of a black child on the cover and no representation of black people in the book?

Comparison: When showing or describing lifestyles, what is left out is as important as what is included. Particularly where the story makes a comparison, is like being compared with like? What messages are conveyed to children being presented with pictures of poor rural children from one culture alongside middle-class affluent urban dwellers in another, for example 'A is for Africa'.

Overall content

Where is the black character in the text? At the periphery looking in, or at the centre? Many titles claim to be multicultural because they are traditional tales from African, South Asian, Chinese and other communities. These often distort perceptions of children who find it difficult to differentiate between fantasy and reality. Small children may conclude that Chinese emperors still rule over Chinese people who look and dress alike. Large mainstream publishers appear to be wary of using black characters in any children's books other than folk tales, photographic concept books and titles written or illustrated by established talent such as James Berry or Caroline Binch.

Accuracy

Far too often authors place a story in a particular country or even a continent without giving an accurate picture of the local scene thus over generalising the story and misleading children into thinking that Africa is a place rather than a huge continent with numerous countries and several hundred languages.

Nandini Mane, Working Group Against Racism in Children's Resources.

> The Working Group against Racism in Children's Resources (WGARCR) runs courses and offers advice. You can contact them at: 460 Wandsworth Road, London SW8 3LX. Tel: 0207 501 9992.

Early art and craft activities create the ideal time for talk and action to complement each other. By exploring ways of working with paint you are encouraging discussion between adults and children in a secure setting

Experiments with paint

Simple experiments with different techniques give children the opportunity to have control over the work they are doing and the confidence to talk naturally about work in progress. All these ideas need to be introduced through a structured session – children need to know the rules and boundaries of working in a different way. Some of them may be old favourites but sometimes we forget how the simplest ideas can give children pleasure and a sense of achievement.

Printing patterns

You can print with anything - natural or made - and make the most wonderful patterns or abstract pictures. There is no right or wrong way, whatever the children produce is individual and created by them alone. Make up the paint to a creamy consistency in a shallow dish. Dip the shape into the paint and print onto the paper. Use hands, dib and dab with fingers – children love getting messy for a purpose! To introduce a mathematical dimension, make up pictures of all circles, squares and so on or repeat colours. Talk about where they might have seen patterns used in this way – what about wallpaper or wrapping paper? Bring some examples in for them to look at. How could their patterns be used? Get them to comment on each other's work. Who'd like a jumper with Tara's pattern on it? Which ones do they like best and why? Do they have a favourite colour?

Bubble painting

Add washing-up liquid to a thinnish powder paint in different size containers. Get the children to blow through straws into the paint until the bubbles froth over the top of the container. Place the paper on top of the bubbles and gently press down. Fill the whole of the paper in this way and then cut around the shapes of the bubbles to create lovely bubble creatures. The children can add eyes and a mouth with felt pen.

Note: It's a good idea for the children to practise blowing through a straw before using the paint. Ask them to blow a ping-pong ball across the surface of a table - that way they learn the purpose of blowing and enjoy the fun of making the ball roll without touching it. You can then take this a step further.

Blow a picture!

Put a small spoonful of mixed paint onto the paper. Get the children to blow gently across the paper to produce lovely spidery effects. What happens if they blow gently? What if they blow hard?

Flick and splatter

Children love the freedom of being able to flick paint onto paper without worrying about the consequences! Flick it or dribble it onto one side of paper and then fold it in half to give you a butterfly painting.

Feathers for brushes

Use different size feathers to dip into paint and move across paper to make interesting patterns.

Using string

Use lengths of thick wool or string and dip into medium mixed powder paint. The children can wriggle the string around on the paper to create a pattern or place the string flat on the paper into a shape then carefully lift it off to see what they have created.

Painting with marbles!

Use black sugar paper and bright fluorescent paint for a dramatic effect. Place the black paper into a shallow tray and drop a paint covered marble into it. Get the children to tilt and rock the tray in different ways to send the marble around the paper leaving behind a trail.

Display

It's a good idea to have several of these activities set out on tables in one session or choose one a day over a period of a week. That way the children can get a real feel for the huge variety of effects they can achieve with the same basic materials - it just takes a bit of imagination. As their confidence grows you'll find them coming up with their own suggestions for techniques to try!

When you've finished, make a big display to show all the different effects and talk about which you like the best. Perhaps parents could join in and try to guess what their children used to make the pictures.

Pam Taylor

Creative Development

Art doesn't have to be limited to paint and easels. Develop children's artistic talents on the huge canvas which the outdoor environment provides

Ideas for outdoor art

Children's creativity and imagination thrives outdoors. Just being outside makes you feel different - there are different sights, sounds and smells as sources of inspiration, not to mention resources. The outdoor environment also offers opportunities for working creatively on a large scale - on huge sheets of paper or even walls and paved areas.

Painting with water

Give your children some large buckets of water and some clean painting tools such as rollers, large paintbrushes, sprays and squeezy bottles. Encourage the children to create a world of watery images on your concrete or paved play area. They will delight in the experience of using the tools and the water to create contrasting effects. Make long solid lines by painting with a roller or wide paintbrush, create spirals by twirling with a squeezy bottle, make a mist of spray or a splatter of droplets with the spray gun.

Natural materials

If you have a large outside area provide the children with an assortment of natural materials to encourage their creativity in two and three dimensions. Try:

- lengths of stick of varying size and thickness
- slices of log
- bags of acorns
- leaves
- wood shavings
- small pebbles and shells

Show the children how to use the materials to create a large outdoor collage of a face, a house, a flower (this works best on a large grassed surface). Encourage the children to create patterns and pictures of their own.

Exploring textures

If your outdoor area is more concrete jungle than enchanting woodland, make the most of your surroundings by exploring different textures. Give children some strong paper and thick wax crayons and encourage them to create different rubbings from the textured surfaces around them. Show them how to work in pairs so that one person holds the sheet of paper firmly over an interesting surface while their partner firmly rubs a thick wax crayon lengthways over the paper to create an impression.

Make a display of the different patterns created or play a detective game by laminating the textures and then using the laminated patterns as clues. Hunt around the outdoor environment trying to match the textures to the surface from which they were originally rubbed.

Try to find some photographs of the work of Andy Goldsworthy, the British environmental artist who works in the open air using natural materials, such as sand, stone, twigs, leaves and even ice and snow, often on a huge scale. He has published several books - try your local library or the internet for examples.

Wheeled toys

Place a very large piece of paper on the ground and make puddles of paint on it. Encourage children to ride their bicycles, scooters and wheeled toys through the paint to create a modern art masterpiece of colour and lines. (To avoid paint-splattered clothes, provide children with wellington boots to wear while riding through the paint.) You can achieve a similar effect by riding through puddles of water on a dry playground.

Coloured chalk

Brighten up your play area with some colourful chalk drawings. Chalk is a wonderful medium to explore and it has the benefits of being semi-permanent. Children will love to colour and make patterns. Try experimenting with crumbling powdery chalk to discover the effects you can create. Consider what happens if you work on a wet surface or add water to the chalk.

If you are worried about the overall effect this work may have on your outdoor area then tape up a small area and restrict children's work to this particular space.

Fence weaving

Another way to get creative with the fixtures around you is to incorporate them into the artwork. If you have a fence surrounding or segregating your outdoor area into sections put it to use as a medium for weaving. Designate an area of fence (chain link fences work especially well) and help and encourage children to weave and wrap strips of fabric, crepe paper, rope, ribbon, lace and wool into the fence.

Dianne Irving

Puppets are a great way to stimulate a child's imagination and creativity.
Elizabeth Coller outlines some ideas

Making shadow puppets

There are various types of puppets - string or marionettes, glove, finger, hand, rod and shadow. All of these can be made out of anything, from scrap materials, paper, card, socks, gloves, tubes, lolly sticks to yoghurt pots. New materials and resources are easily obtainable from most craft shops. Puppet making is an inexpensive appealing activity which is only restricted by the size of your imagination. An inanimate object can be transformed into a puppet by a few props and a voice.

Many skills and concepts are used in creating a puppet. Children use skills of planning, design, cutting, joining, handling tools and various materials, listening, working together, memory recall, concentration and manipulation. They learn concepts of size, shape (two- and three-dimensional), movement, time, light and dark, sounds, textures and emotions. By providing an assortment of materials we aim to enable children to express their own individual creative ideas.

By encouraging the children to use puppets we are promoting the need to use their imagination without fear of ridicule, develop social interaction, problem-solving, improvisation, use of language, communication, stories and thinking for themselves.

Many of the Early Learning Goals are incorporated into the creating and operating of a puppet - social interaction, vocabulary, role play of stories, shape, size, events and feelings, technology and design, textures, fine and gross manipulation, music, space, and most importantly, imagination.

Exploring emotions

Playing with puppets is therapeutic. It allows children to explore emotions in a safe situation, it releases tensions and anxieties about moving house, a new baby or going to hospital. A child can re-live an experience (good or bad) and give way to a fantasy.

A friendly puppet can comfort a shy or sensitive child or calm a tearful one. A withdrawn child will usually communicate to a hand puppet - they find that they can talk to them easily and share secrets with them. The puppet comes alive and becomes a small person to the child.

Achievements

Creating a puppet is as exciting as using it. Children delight in their achievements when the item they have made comes to life with a voice and some movement. Add a background and the imagination runs wild. Turn a simple nursery rhyme into a story by encouraging the children to add their own ideas about what comes next.

Shadow puppets

Shadow puppets are one of the simplest and oldest forms of puppetry. They were used in Asia more than 2,000 years ago to pass on or illustrate traditional stories and legends of gods, demons and heroes. The art of Wayang Purwa (wayang means shadow, purwa means ancient) is still performed in Indonesia today.

Stories and festivals

This form of puppetry is an ideal way of telling stories from other countries and religious festivals, the stories of Fox, Alligator and Rabbit from Jamaica; *Good Morning* from Bangladesh; *The Greedy Father* from Zimbabwe; Dog, Cat and Monkey, from Indonesia. All these come alive and have more meaning when retold by the shadows of the characters.

You don't need to be experienced in drawing or design to create shadow puppets. You can photocopy and cut out shapes, people, animals and objects from magazines or books as long as the outline is clear. Draw around stencils or use the stencils by attaching sticky-backed Velcro to the back of them and also onto a stick. All you need is a

Creative Development

sheet of tracing paper attached to a cardboard frame and a light source (torch or table lamp) and you have the start of a shadow production.

As a child, I remember making shadow shapes on the wall which is the most simplest way of shadow theatre. This is very limited, but add a few props and a story can be told. Take some black card and cut out a crocodile's head (two pieces). Cut out an eye and nostril, attach a loop of elastic or card with glue to the two parts and place your two fingers of one hand through the loops. Take it to a light source and you have a sad crocodile who has a toothache (your arm becomes the creature's body). Now add another animal silhouette, a mouse maybe, and start to tell a story.

Loops for fingers.

Angle the light so that it is higher or lower than the puppeteers so that the performer's shadow is not seen. Experiment by moving the puppet toward the light source to make the shadow bigger.

Music

If the children are unwilling to use their voice, add music to your performance. Make some shadow sea creatures, play the *Little Mermaid* song and create a screen with seaweed in the foreground. Add light and watch the children use their puppets to entertain.

The most important thing to remember is to have fun making and performing with puppets. Bear in mind that it is the puppet that is performing and all eyes are on it not you.

Don't be reluctant to have a go! It is surprising how many barriers come down when the stories and the character of the puppet comes to life. Don't forget to give your puppets names - these also add life.

Put lots of enthusiasm into your creations and lots of enjoyment will follow for you and your audience.

Elizabeth Coller

Screens

A screen can be made very simply by cutting out a frame from a cardboard box and gluing white tracing, tissue or greaseproof paper to it. You can also use stretched thin calico, linen or cotton sheeting. This is more suited for regular use and mounted onto a wooden frame. You can achieve good results from two chairs with a white sheet tied between them - shine a light on it and you can make a large screen. Screens don't have to be square - draw an oval or circle out of black card and paint an appropriate scene onto the translucent paper.

Lighting

Lighting could come from a torch, which children can use easily. Place some coloured cellophane paper over the light and create different lighting moods. An Anglepoise lamp or projector light is better as the light is much more intense and superior shadow effects are created.

Warning: these lamps get hot and adult supervision is advisable at all times when in use. Never place coloured cellophane too close to a hot bulb as it will burn, use cinemoid, a non-inflammable colour filler used for theatre lights, or use coloured bulbs.

It can be difficult continually planning experiences for children that are fresh and imaginative when you have the same, old familiar equipment out every day. Take a close look at your messy play area and ask yourself whether it needs a lift

Rethink, revitalise or rebuild
your messy play area

Start by reminding yourself what exactly you are hoping to achieve through messy play. It may influence the value you place on the messy play area and how much time and effort you devote to enhancing it.

In terms of the Early Learning Goals you are giving children opportunities to practise and improve the quality of their tactile skills, allowing them to handle appropriate tools, objects, construction and malleable materials safely and with increased control. But activities have many other benefits including social, intellectual, communication and emotional.

Never underestimate the power of play and the vast opportunities it offers for children to learn – watching, imitating and practising new-found skills and discoveries – either of their own making or with the benefit of that well-placed piece of equipment or well-chosen word.

Basic equipment

If you have limited funds and space, don't be put off – I remember starting out with donated baby baths and washing-up bowls. Small bowls are ideal for an individual child or a child with special needs who has limited physical movements. Improvise with equipment if you need to - empty tubs, old spoons, forks and pans are ideal – and savings made on these might pay for the sand or compost!

Water: Provide a water tray which has more than one depth to allow shallow and deep-water play. A clear tray allows children to see what is going on under the water. Always have a tray with a drainage facility.

Sand: The sand tray should be larger than

the water tray and where possible be wide and shallow (making it easier to move). Position it where children will not be continually walking through to cut down on mess. Sieve the sand regularly and change it often. Ideally you need three trays - one each for dry, wet and saturated sand.

Craft area (including dough and clay): Provide children with a flat, covered surface to work from. You may want to cover the floor as well. Make sure there is easy access to glue, scissors and paper when necessary. Ask parents to contribute collage bits and items suitable for junk modelling. If space allows, store the larger items in a dustbin accessible to the children. Large junk modelling may be best done on a covered floor.

Painting: The painting area should be close to a sink to make the mixing of paints easier. Provide easels or tabletops and a ready supply of paper. Have a selection of paintbrushes, rollers and sponges for the children to use.

The type and variety of resources you have in the messy area will depend on finances. What is important is to store the equipment so it's easily accessible for you and the children. Label it into sets – 'pouring and filling', 'floating and sinking,' for example. Keep the equipment near the activity base, in other words the water play items near the water tray. A vegetable rack or plastic laundry baskets are useful for sand/water items. Plastic buckets, especially with lids, are good for storage, and can be stacked, labelled and carried easily.

Buy sand/water trays with lids so they can be covered when not in use and also show

clearly to the children that the activity is not available.

Before you buy any large items, consider your storage facilities and remember to check the width of the doorway – will your equipment fit through it?

Introducing variety

■ **Salt:** Pours, takes the shape of the container temporarily, flows, sieves, feels gritty, rough, takes colour. Be aware of children with eczema. Could it be snow? Add plastic vehicles, animals, miniature people, bricks, scoops, containers.

■ **Compost:** Damp this down as it can be dusty for children with asthma. Feels soft, has a smell, can keep a shape. Add small plant pots, seeds, scoops, rakes, dinosaurs, any creatures.

■ **Pasta:** Makes a lovely sound, particularly with metal containers, such as old saucepans. Comes in different shapes, colours and sizes. Add tipper trucks, diggers, empty cartons, tubs. It's also wonderful for gluing/collage, but you'll need to use card for the base.

■ **Rice:** Flows, pours, takes colour, but needs to be dried overnight. Give children a tub with a lid, add rice and food colouring and shake – magic!

■ **Pan scrubbers:** Different textures, colours, shapes, sizes. Add

Good buy
Ever thought of buying a Tuffspot? It's a sturdy plastic rubber octagonal base - a bit like big dustbin lid - that builders use mixing cement on. It sits on the floor table top and is invaluable for all of activities, not least messy play costs around £10/15 from a builders' merchant.

washing-up liquid, a little water and scrub on a smooth surface to create suds that children can write and draw in. Add colour or glitter.

■ **Shredded paper:** Can be dusty but it rustles beautifully. Hide creatures or vehicles or any small toys, like a lucky dip!

■ **Shells:** Different shapes, colours, sizes, names. Add water and see the colours change. Match the shapes, count them, add sand, boats, people to make the seaside. Listen to the sounds, talk about memories, experiences.

■ **Stones and pebbles:** Similar to shells but different textures and weights. Add vehicles, tools for moving about.

■ **Sand play:** Alternate between wet and dry sand – it behaves quite differently. Dry sand flows, pours, sieves, and wet will keep a shape, take impressions, stay where you put it. Look at hand prints, footprints, different patterns on shoe soles. Use tubs, scoops, old jigsaw pieces (the ones with little knobs) to make impressions, wide toothed combs or make your own out of card.

Use different types of sand – play sand, builders' sand or silver sand.

Make paper cones. Can the children vary the amount of sand being poured through by altering the size of the hole in the cone?

Using chopsticks or lolly sticks, encourage children to create early writing patterns, horizontal and vertical lines and circles, drawing a man or crosses.

An easy way of revitalising your sand area is by organising resources well. Separate the equipment and label it clearly then allow free play. At other times limit the choice to avoid the sand tray becoming overcrowded and focus on one skill.

Starting from scratch

☐ Where will you site it? Think how far you need to carry equipment. Do you need to be near the water?

☐ How many children can safely and comfortably use the equipment? Will it be in the way? Is there enough space around each activity?

☐ Dry sand, wet sand and water behave in different ways and, if space allows, there should be provision for all three.

☐ Position water away from the dry sand - children can't resist mixing the two!

☐ Where possible locate the messy area on an uncarpeted, non-slip floor, separated from other activities.

☐ Locate the area near to your water supply and/or sink and if possible near the bathroom so children can easily wash their hands after an activity.

☐ Have clearly labelled aprons, positioned so children can help themselves.

☐ Try and have a member of staff designated to the area each session.

☐ Provide equipment at the correct height. (Trays and tables at waist height are best).

■ **Water play:** Despite its familiarity, water is a rich resource which children enjoy exploring.

Coloured water: create different effects – use crepe paper, which loses its colour when placed in water, or food colouring.

Bubbly or scented water: try using bubble bath, washing-up liquid, bath balls, peppermint or almond essence. (Check that no child is allergic to these products.)

Add cooked spaghetti – it feels wonderful!

Cut out coloured cellophane fish shapes and use tubs or hands to catch.

Add glitter, sequins, swirl and watch.

Turn the messy area into a launderette - provide washing powder boxes, washing, airers and pegs. Other ideas include a hairdressers or a doll-washing session.

During warmer weather use paddling pools for water activities and give the children large containers such as buckets and saucepans rather than the smaller ones used inside.

Try really messy activities outside such as cornflour slime. Provide the children with some cornflour and slowly add water, encouraging the children to mix it with their hands. This is a perfect medium for early writing skills.

Mix and match equipment, and remember, not all children like to get their hands wet or messy, but if they see adults and other children having fun they might just risk it!

Ideas supplied by Sue Riley and Keeva Austin

Building a Portfolio Level 2 • • •

Water play is a routine activity and can be overlooked - just putting out a water tray and waiting for it all to happen won't work! Vicky Hislop explains how to make your water corner provide really positive learning experiences for your group

Organising **water play**

Just putting out a water tray and waiting for it all to happen without you will not work! You must have a plan for the activity and be prepared to make the most of the questions you will be asked as you would with many table-top activities. Plan ahead and decide what skills or information you are aiming to share with the children at each session and aim to deliver it. Linking in with previous discussions or ongoing themes makes sense.

How you talk to the children during any activity is crucial. Use new words, test understanding of new words and repeat them several times. Don't be afraid to try quite difficult concepts such as 'waterproof' or 'saturated' - the exposure to new vocabulary is always positive. Be prepared to 'go with the flow' (no pun intended!) when playing in water; you can come back to your plans if needs be. You have the advantage that water is not a new concept to any child. They will all have something to say about bath-time and washing seems to hold great fascination for young children. The washing machine may well be out of bounds but is nonetheless of great interest!

Introduce variety

Start by looking at the equipment you use. Children enjoy the jugs and colanders but there is more to be had from the activity by offering more varied equipment. Don't be tempted to overcrowd the tray, though; too much equipment can ruin a good idea - keep it simple.

- Colour the water with food colouring.
- Scent the water with essential oil of lemon, lavender or peppermint.
- Add bubbles, colour the bubbles.
- Use toys - dolls, doll's clothes, play people, cars, construction kits, marble run games, and so on.

- Add natural objects - cones, stones, wood, sand, pebbles.
- Experiment with junk - yoghurt pots, cardboard tubes (for a short time!)
- Change the temperature - add ice cubes, freeze whole trays of water then pour on warm water.
- Use sponge rollers and paint the outside walls.
- Thicken with cornflour - a thick mix is a fascinating play medium. You don't need to heat it up, just mix it in. Experiment with consistency. Pour the mixed cornflour and water into a shallow tray and let it run through your fingers and hands. A packet of cornflour, some water and a tea tray are all that is required.

When you have your new idea plan the group size carefully - most water trays do not work well for more than two or three children. With this small number you can be really involved, leading discussions and pointing out new ideas and interesting happenings. Note changes to the items you have added, suggest different ways of experimenting, link one discovery with another when appropriate and encourage the children to express their thoughts and findings as they explore. Troubled children often find the therapeutic effect of warm water, absorbing toys and close adult attention a good time to chat - be sensitive to this and make the most of the opportunity.

When you are planning your water play remember to check which children have skin problems. Scented or coloured

water would play havoc with eczema sufferers. Rubber gloves are an option but finding ones small enough is a challenge. Mildly sensitive skin might survive a short session if smeared with Vaseline first - always check with the parents beforehand.

To make general sessions easier to manage you could collect equipment together and group it into subject trays for easy access. Having trays labelled would remind you what the objective of each session was.

- A 'floating' tray might contain: plastic tubs, boats, fish made from wood or

Cross-curricular

plastic, corks, empty film cases, bottle tops, sticks and straws.

- A pouring tray could have: jugs, cans, tubing, plastic bottles (Body Shop empties are great), funnels and tea sets.

- A wash day/washing-up tray would need: towels, flannels, soap, pegs, line, sponges, plastic dishes, tea set, plastic cutlery and drainer.

Water in the natural environment

Don't forget natural water when you are thinking about the children's learning. Who didn't enjoy jumping in puddles? Rain, condensation, taps, drips, drains, pipes, puddles, streams, rivers, sea, lakes,

Water stories

Mr Archimedes' Bath by Pamela Allen (Picture Puffin)

The Turtle and the Island: a Folk Tale from Papua New Guinea by Barbara Ker Wilson (Frances Lincoln)

The Owl and The Pussy Cat by Edward Lear (Walker Books)

Harry by the Sea by Gene Zion (Red Fox Books)

Alfie's Feet by Shirley Hughes (Picture Puffin)

An Evening at Alfie's by Shirley Hughes (Red Fox Books)

Bumpa Rumpus and the Rainy Day by Joanne Reay, Adriano Gon (Picture Mammoth Books)

Action songs and rhymes

Get in the Bath - Play along songs (Faber music)

Water in Bottles - This Little Puffin (Puffin Books). (This reinforces the message that water always takes the shape of what it is in.) *This Little Puffin* also has many rhymes about the sea and water. A good resource.

Drips and drops - experimenting with water and paint

Using eye droppers (available cheaply from chemists) drop drips of marbling paint on to the surface of water in a shallow tray. Stir the water a little, very carefully and slowly, then briefly lay a piece of paper on top of the water. The pattern you made with the marbling paint will have transferred on to the paper.

This activity helps you to explore patterns and change, sound, colours, form and space. You can begin to look at two- and three-dimensional concepts and you can concentrate on the slow and careful movements required!

hose and sprinkler - they all represent natural water and offer a wealth of activity ideas. For example:

- Find a puddle, draw around it in chalk and come back later to it to see if it is bigger or smaller.
- An outdoor game of musical puddles is great fun.
- Puddle jumping (in wellies of course) is a joy on its own.
- Measure the rain in a rain measure and discuss where rain comes from.
- Make an aquarium - plastic or wooden fish work just as well as real ones, require less food and offer more play opportunities!
- Umbrellas lead you on to discussing waterproof, shelter, shapes, weather.
- Pond dipping for those with access to such a resource is a lovely way to spend time - scooping out insects such as water boatmen (remember to put them back), looking at weeds.
- Salt and fresh water is interesting to compare - salt water will make children instantly sick, never allow them to swallow it.
- Snow and ice are a perennially interesting topic - frozen water is as interesting as liquid.
- Floods and droughts are good topics to tackle in the water tray and work well as part of a larger nursery theme.

Outdoor play

Outdoor equipment to play in water with is good to have, but don't be too restricted by it. Some super outdoor systems with pumps, water-wheels, pulleys, pipes and streams is available and if your group can afford such an item then great! If you can't, you can improvise with drainpipes, buckets and troughs and enjoy it just as much. Don't forget the paddling pool in summer - on a hot day there is nothing better.

So, it is good to plan for the water tray. There are many interesting things you can do. As with most things, though, you must aim for a balance between offering stimulating opportunities and allowing the children simply to play. Warm water is intensely therapeutic, relaxing and liberating - don't forget to enjoy it!

Vicky Hislop

Scents and additives

These are available from The Body Shop, why not try orange too!
Use mild washing-up liquid for bubbles or hypoallergenic bath liquid.

Learning to count in a variety of play situations helps children to develop an understanding of number values. Popular games such as Snakes and Ladders, Ludo and dominoes are all helpful, but you can also make up your own

Table-top **maths**

A dice can be numbered with digits or spots and with the number on which you wish to concentrate.

If children can confidently count to ten, recognise the numbers, and begin to appreciate their value by the time they are four or five years old, then they will set off on their mathematical journey with confidence. There are many table-top games played with dice or cards which will help to develop a child's concept of number. Here are just a few to try.

When playing all these games the children will be:
■ saying the number names in order and matching the numbers to objects (*Curriculum Guidance for the Foundation Stage*)
■ saying the number names in order; beginning to recognise and use numbers to ten; comparing two given numbers and saying which is more or less; beginning to use the vocabulary of addition and subtraction. (*Framework for Teaching Mathematics*)

Dressing the teddy
A game for four children
Each child needs a card showing the outline of a teddy bear. Number sets of paper clothes, for example 1 for a hat, 2 - shirt, 3 - trousers, 4 - shoes, 5 - gloves, 6 - scarf. The children take turns to shake the dice and win the appropriate article of clothing for their teddy. The first to get all items is the winner.

During the game discuss the numbers they still need and whether the number they get is too big or small. You can make the game harder by insisting that the teddy is dressed in a certain order.

Let's make a garden
A game for up to six children
Give each child a card with five plants drawn on it. Each plant needs stalks and leaves and a circle in place of a flowerhead. Number the circles one to five. Have a selection of flowers cut from a seed catalogue and a dice with the number six blanked out.

The children shake the dice and place a flower in the correctly numbered circle. The first to complete their garden is the winner.

To extend older or more able children, draw ten flowers and use two dice. The children can choose to shake one dice or two, depending on the number required. They then have the opportunity to add two numbers to obtain flowers for plants six to ten. This game gives them experience in the addition of numbers to ten.

Racing rabbits
A game for up to six players
This game gives experience of both addition and subtraction. Each child has a long piece of card on which is drawn a path made of 20 slabs numbered 1 - 20. Place a cut-out cardboard rabbit at one end and a lettuce at the other. The children shake the dice and hop along their path to try to be first to get to their lettuce. During the game, encourage them to compare their progress with their friend. 'Who has got nearest to the lettuce?' 'How many more hops do you need to get there?'

If children are ready, a second dice can be used with four sides marked 'f' and two sides marked 'b'. The children shake the first dice for their number, then the second dice to see whether they go forwards or backwards. Help their understanding by discussing their progress. 'What number are you on?' 'If you go on two more, then what will you be on?'

Battle of the cards
A game for two players
Remove the kings, queens and jacks from a pack of cards (the ace counts as number one). Deal the cards face down and share them out between the two players.

Each child turns over their top card. The one with the higher number wins both cards and places them at the bottom of their own pile. If both cards are the same, the players turn their next card. Then the higher number wins all four cards, or if the numbers again are the same, they carry on until they have a winner - sometimes six or even eight cards are in the pile. The first child to get all the cards is the winner.

This is a good game for helping children to understand the values of numbers one to ten. The rules can be varied, for example the least number can win, or the even number is the winner. The number of cards in the pack can be reduced, just using those on which you wish to concentrate, for example numbers one to five.

Barbara Garrad

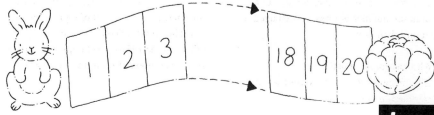

Building a Portfolio Level 2 • • •

Mathematical Development

Take every opportunity to talk mathematically as children play and take part in normal daily activities, says Barbara Garrad. Here she shows how you can help develop an understanding of specific mathematical language using the contents of an average toy box!

Maths from the toy box

The language of position

Make a set of cards, each with a position written on it - up, down, in front, behind, underneath, on top of, next to, and so on. Ask a child to choose a toy from the box and take a card. You can either tell them what to do, according to the card selected, for example:

'Put Teddy **behind** the door.'
'Put the brick **under** the chair.'

or, as they begin to understand the game, the child can tell you what they are going to do with the toy. When all the toys have been placed, ask 'Where is the car?' If they answer correctly, they can put it back in the toy box and the game can start again.

The language of shape, space, and measurement

The children each choose a doll or soft toy from the box then, by holding them upright, compare the height of each.

'The rabbit is **taller/shorter** than the doll.'

'Teddy's head is **higher** than Sooty's.'

Other toys can be compared by length - cars, trucks, trains, and so on: 'This lorry is **longer/shorter** than the truck.'

To help with comparison, give the children strips of paper. By putting their toy on the paper, they can measure and cut off a strip of the correct height or length. These can be mounted to make a simple graph display.

Give each child a shoe box and ask them to pack it with toys - and still be able to put the lid back on! Then let them spread out and count the number of toys they managed to get into their box.

'Who has got the **most**?'
'Who managed to pack in **more than** six? How **many more**?'

'If you tried again, could you pack in **more** toys next time?'
'Why do you think you got **more** in? Did you choose **larger/smaller** toys?'

The language of counting and calculation

Apart from the importance of children learning to count reliably up to and beyond ten, they must also begin to develop their understanding of the language of number.

Encourage the children to search the toy box and to make a collection of their own choosing. It could be toy animals, dominoes, bricks, cars, crayons, - whatever appeals to them. Then get them to lay out their collection in a line and count how many they have. They can then compare their number to others.

'Have you got **more/less** than Sarah?'
'What colour is the **fifth** car in your collection?'
'What comes **before/after** the brick?'
'Who has the **most** in their collection?'
'Is their line the **longest**? No! Why not?'
'**How many more** has Peter than Ahmed?'

Language of data handling

The variety of items to be found in a toy box provide an ideal opportunity for sorting and classifying, and then displaying the data. Ask the children to find a set of toys which are red. Then a set which are green (or any other criteria.) Have two hoops and place a set in each hoop. Count how many are red/green.

'Which is the **larger/smaller** set?'
'**How many more** in the larger set?'
'Can we find **some more** for the **smaller** set so we have the **same number** in each?'

Sort the toys into two or three sets by different criteria. Count, discuss and compare the numbers in each set. Display the findings by means of a simple block graph, or other pictorial ways of displaying the results. Encourage the children to discuss the relationship of items in each set, and the means of display.

When you've done all that, encourage them to put all the toys back in the box and hope you can get the lid on!

Barbara Garrad

The concept of number can be brought into lots of outdoor games. Many physical activities incorporate an understanding of space and mathematical language. All you need is a large outside area for children to move freely around and a variety of play equipment

Maths games **outside**

Warm-up games

■ Tambourine twos
Ask the children to move around carefully, weaving in and out, as they listen to the shaken tambourine. Tap the tambourine and shout 'Twos!'. The children must get into twos as quickly as they can. Try again with threes, fours and fives. Make sure that less confident children are not left out. Reinforce the numbers by counting each pair or group to check that they have found the right number of children.

■ Find the number
Display large number symbols zero to ten around the outside play area. Shout out 'Find the number five!' and ask the children to run to the correct symbol. Most will follow the pack so, after a while, ask individual children to find numbers. Older children can be asked to make simple calculations, for instance, 'Lily, find me the number that is one more than three'.

Number games

These activities will reinforce the use of numbers as labels and for counting. Some can be extended to include calculating.

■ Number target
Using chalk, draw a large circle or concentric circles as a target on the ground. Write numbers in different segments of the circle for children to aim at. Children throw three beanbags onto the target and see how high they can score. Put a small red spot in the centre of the target to be the bullseye or the highest score. Help the children to calculate their score. The target shape can be adapted to fit themes such as a snail shell ('Minibeasts') or a flower ('Growth').

■ Giant number line
Draw a large number line or track on the ground with equal divisions, one to ten. A child stands on number one and counts on two by jumping up the line, or stands on number seven and counts back one.

Using equipment

■ Hoop lotto
Put four different coloured hoops in the four corners of your outside area and a large box of coloured balls in the centre. Divide the children into four colour teams. Ask the red team to find all the red balls and put them inside the red hoop. Which team can find all their coloured balls first?

■ Circuit training
Set up a circuit using a variety of large equipment such as climbing frames, slides, balance beams, tunnels, and so on. Keep a tally of completed circuits and hold a championship to see who can go round safely in the shortest time. The children will enjoy using stopwatches and also gain some understanding of the concept of time.

Shape, space and measuring

■ Shape races
Divide the children into teams of about six. Draw some big shapes on the ground with chalk and give each child a small plastic shape to hold. In the style of a relay, ask each child in the team to run and put a shape in the correct big shape and then return and tag the next child.

■ How many steps?
Ask the children to use steps to measure distances using this rhyme:
Counting steps, as we go
From the fence to the flowerbed,
How many steps, I want to know?
One, two, three, four, five ...
Encourage the children to make estimates.

■ Water games
Put two large clear containers at one end of the area. Divide the children into two teams who have to carry buckets of coloured water along a balance beam, or other obstacles, and pour them into the containers. How far up the container can each team fill in two minutes?

Place five empty plastic bottles on a low wall or box and label them one to five. Invite the children to aim and shoot at the bottles with water pistols. How many can they knock down? Help them to calculate scores.

■ Sliding journeys
Using a stopwatch, help the children to time how long it takes different items to slide down the slide. Which toy travels the fastest? Why?

Judith Harries

Mathematical Development

Cooking is an experience which most children really enjoy. But it's not just enjoyable - it's a very worthwhile experience

Cooking with young children

Children learn through their senses - sight, hearing, smell, taste and touch. Cookery provides experience of all of these:

Sight: the children can look at all the ingredients and the packages they're in. They can see the changes as they mix the ingredients, and as they cook.

Hearing: the children have to listen carefully to your instructions so that they know what to do. You will be talking to them about the changes that are happening, and perhaps about where ingredients have come from, what they like to eat, and so on.

Smell: the children will be able to smell the ingredients as they mix and cook them.

Touch: for some recipes, the children will be able to touch the ingredients, such as the dough when making bread, the vegetables when they chop them.

Taste: this is the best part - when they get to eat what they have made!

It's also good for language. The children will want to talk about what they are doing, and the changes taking place. You should encourage this by asking questions like 'What do you think will happen when...' or 'What's happened to the mixture now?' or 'Why did that happen when we ...?'

When you choose your cooking activity, think about the age and stage of development of the children. They should be as fully involved as possible. If your recipe depends on you to do most of the work, it's not appropriate. You may not have cooking facilities in your setting, but you can still do 'cold cooking'. For example, you could make sandwiches, a fruit salad, or ice some biscuits.

It's really important to be well prepared

before you start. Check with your supervisor when it will be convenient to do the activity, and check whether you can have access to a cooker. Write a list of the ingredients you will need, and write the process. It's best to try out the recipe before you do it with the children, so that you can see if there are any problems and work out how to solve them!

Making bread

Let's choose one activity as an example of what you can do – cooking bread. This is not as difficult as you might think, although you may only be able to do it with one group each session. If you get a one-rise yeast it doesn't take too long to rise. You can do it with children of all ages, and every ability, because every child can have a ball of dough to knead. It's a good activity to do with children for several reasons:

■ Bread is the staple diet in most countries in the world, so it's an excellent opportunity to look at different types of bread and where they come from. You can do this while the dough is rising, or you can make bread a longer topic and in

later sessions get someone to make bread from a variety of cultures – chapattis or pitta bread, for example.

■ It's a real hands-on, tactile activity. The children can mix and knead with their hands, and everyone can have their own piece of dough. They can pummel and squeeze it as much as they like.

■ The children are using several senses during the activity, and language to describe their experiences

■ They're also learning concepts such as how things change when they are mixed together, or when they are heated, and concepts of weight, capacity and size.

■ Most children with a sensory impairment would be able to join in this activity.

■ The children are improving their manipulative skills when they mix and knead the dough.

- They're learning about healthy eating - it's important that you discuss this with them at some point during the cooking activity. You should bear this in mind when choosing recipes.

- You could combine bread-making with growing cress, and even make your own butter by getting the children to shake some cream from the top of the milk (it really works but it has to be full-cream milk). Then you can make sandwiches and eat them together.

- It tastes good!

You do have to wait for the bread to rise, but only once if you use the one-rise yeast, which you can buy in packets in a supermarket. The children can go off and do other things while it's rising, or you might like to have a selection of other sorts of bread to show the children, let them taste and talk about how they are the same and how they are different. Pizzas are good to make with children. You can use your bread dough to make the base, or you can use a pastry base if you prefer. The children can chop different toppings of their own choice. This will need careful supervision, as the knives will have to be reasonably sharp so that they can cut with them - but don't use sharp, pointed knives.

Cooking safely

Hygiene is paramount. You should keep separate tools for cooking, and wash the surfaces you will be using thoroughly. You may want to use a plastic-coated tablecloth, which you keep for cooking only. Keep any fresh food in the fridge until you need it. Make sure you've got all the tools you need. You can't leave a group of children with potentially dangerous tools to go looking for something.

Wash your own hands thoroughly, and supervise the children washing theirs. Work with a small group at a time. For some recipes, and for some age groups, that might be one to one. Never have children sitting waiting for a turn for a long time. It's better to have several small bowls for mixing rather than one big one.

When choosing your recipe, check whether there are any children who are on special diets because of an allergy, a medical condition, or because of a religious belief or a dietary preference such as being a vegetarian. You may have parents who would be willing to come in and cook something from their own culture with the children. If not, many children will have experienced eating in restaurants, or their parents will have tried foods from different countries from the supermarket. There is a good range of fruit and vegetables available from across the world now, so you might like to try these out with the children.

Plan when the children will eat what they have cooked. They may take it home to eat with their parents, or they may eat it at snack time. This will depend on whether everyone has made something. It's not always possible for everyone to cook in one session. You may have to do the activity several times. Make sure you keep a list of who has done the activity, so that no-one misses out.

Food is central to life in all cultures, and usually plays a major part in celebrations, so it's a great way of getting children to appreciate the diversity of the world we live in.

Mary Townsend

Young children are constantly using their hands, but you still need to make detailed plans for the development of manual dexterity or fine motor skills. Jean Evans suggests some suitable activities

Developing fine motor **skills**

Providing appropriate opportunities for children to develop their manual dexterity, or fine motor skills, is an important aspect of the planning of your physical development programme. Children need to develop their manual dexterity in order to cope with their personal needs, such as dressing and keeping themselves clean. Children who have enjoyed activities involving exploration of a wide selection of tools and materials are also more likely to approach directed activities related to drawing and writing with confidence.

Children need time to practise the movements they have already mastered, and the chance to try out and repeat new movements. If you offer a stimulating variety of activities the children will be attracted to them, they will be interested for longer and have fun as well. It is essential, therefore, to produce detailed planning for the development of fine motor skills, which includes opportunities for children to handle a range of equipment, tools, everyday objects, construction equipment and malleable materials.

Planning for every child depends on knowing them really well, being aware of their likes and dislikes, understanding their level of skill and being aware of their ability to concentrate. This knowledge depends on having a successful assessment scheme which is understood by all staff members.

Small equipment

Beads and pegs - children enjoy the challenge of threading beads onto laces. Make patterns using alternate colours or copy sequences from cards. Make number tags to attach to the laces and let them count the beads on. They like to create patterns by arranging coloured pegs on boards.

Tools

Scissors - cut around pictures from catalogues to create a collage; practise cutting lines along the edge of a strip of paper to create a pattern.

Spoons of different sizes - choose from a selection of spoons the best one to fill a container with rice. Include a tiny spoon from an ice cream tub, a set of measuring spoons and a ladle.

Mark making tools - experiment with pencils, crayons, chalk and felt-tip pens to create observational drawings.

Miniature worlds - children love to work with tiny items. Create a miniature beach for small world figures using a shallow plastic dish. Use thimble buckets and mustard spoon spades to create tiny sandcastles.

Objects

Buttons and zips - experiment with different fastenings on children's clothes and dolls' clothes.

Shoes and gloves - sort into pairs. Try putting on gloves of different sizes.

Recycled materials - let the children make their own models with a selection of plastic and card containers and small objects, such as buttons and ribbons. Provide different tools to add glue, such as spreaders, lollipop sticks and twigs.

Construction equipment

Bricks - build a tower of five bricks using as many different types as possible. Which tower is tallest ?

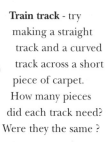

Train track - try making a straight track and a curved track across a short piece of carpet. How many pieces did each track need? Were they the same ?

Malleable materials

Clay - create small pots as presents or divas to celebrate Diwali.

Dough - roll out snakes and compare lengths.

Jean Evans

Differentiation

When planning activities try to think of an easier way and a more complicated way to complete a task as a basis for your extension ideas for younger and more able children. For example, when cutting pictures from a catalogue to create a toy collage younger children could simply tear around a large picture. More able children will be able to cut around the edge of quite small shapes. To glue the picture to paper the youngest children will probably find spreading glue all over the base paper easiest. They can then press the picture onto the glue. More able children will derive great satisfaction from gluing every bit of the back of their picture before sticking it down.

Working with playdough is a relaxing, soothing and sociable activity as well as providing a wide range of cross-curricular learning experiences

Working with playdough

Playdough provides many opportunities for the development of manipulative and creative skills but equally helps develop a range of skills across all areas of the Early Learning Goals, in particular in the extension of language and communication.

It is a valuable activity for introducing and settling children into new environments as well as encouraging shy children to join in. Conversations at dough tables often stimulate a shy child to take part as the experience helps children to relax.

Making and learning

Dough can be made in a variety of ways with recipes producing cooked or uncooked mixtures. Whilst ingredients vary, salt should always be added as a preservative and oil improves texture and pliability. Cooked dough should last well in a sealed plastic container kept in a cool place.

Involve children as much as possible in making the dough, in particular in weighing and measuring, pouring and mixing ingredients.

Achieve differing kinds of elasticity and texture by adding a variety of materials, for example, cornflower, rice, lentils or glitter. Providing more than one kind of dough extends opportunities for the children.

Make sure enough quantities of material are available to encourage children to share and to work alongside each other cooperatively.

Tools to try:
Rolling pins, knives, forks, spoons, garlic presses, pastry cutters, scissors, spatulas, moulds, dough machines.
Good for patterns and imprints:
Cotton reels, pine cones, buttons, shells, coins.

Give them opportunities to explore the dough itself before using tools, then provide a range of tools for children to select from to cut, mould, shape or make imprints.

Encourage children to work effectively in comfortable and appropriate positions such as sitting, kneeling or standing at a table. Support them by questioning and extending thought and language and offering encouragement to try out new ideas, suggesting and demonstrating new techniques.

Developing vocabulary and language

Descriptive language: lumpy, bendy, soft, warm, squidgy, sticky, silky, smooth.
Language of manipulation: squeeze, prod.
Mathematical vocabulary: relating to weight and volume as dough is being made and to size and shape during play.

Questioning and experimentation

Conservation: learning that the same piece of dough can take on many shapes yet remain the same amount. For example, a ball of clay rolled into a snake can become a ball again.

Questioning on cause and effect: for example, what will happen if we add more flour, water, rice?

Experimentation: What will happen if I hold this big stretchy piece up by one end? What will happen if I keep rolling and rolling this ball of clay?

Fine manipulative control

Working with playdough can fulfil the Physical Development Early Learning Goal - 'Handle tools, objects, construction

and malleable materials safely and with increasing control.' Try providing scissors to practice cutting skills on dough.

Occasionally, provide a limited number of tools or none at all and encourage and support the children to achieve a planned effect by using their hands to manipulate the dough.

Balance opportunities for free expression with modelling from observation.

Children need to learn to investigate, experiment and solve their own problems as well as ask questions and learn new language. They should receive positive encouragement to try out new ideas. Even when it is likely these will not work, it is important that children are encouraged to experiment and to take risks. Our role as adults is to support and encourage children to have fun, express themselves creatively and learn from playing with this versatile material.

Sue Fisher

Making children aware of the different textures of materials plays an important role in their learning of science. You can help them to explore materials in a fun way with simple games and experiments

Exploring and investigating materials

Young children explore and work with materials all the time, in nearly everything they do. They find out that some things bend and some stretch, that different materials are hard, shiny, rough or smooth. Your job is to help children focus on the properties of the materials they are working or playing with and to develop their thinking and language by helping them to verbalise their ideas.

Same and different
You'll find it useful to have collections of objects and materials which fall into the following categories:

❑ rough and smooth
❑ rigid and flexible (bendy and not bendy at this stage)
❑ stretchy and not stretchy
❑ shiny and not shiny
❑ transparent and opaque (see-through and not see-through)

Get the children to compare the materials, noting their similarities and differences, and to sort objects in as many ways as they can, using all the appropriate senses. Ask them to tell you what is the same about some of the things in their set, and what is different.

Encourage the children to explore the materials using all the appropriate senses and to tell you about them. How many different ways can they sort them? At first, allow them to use their own criteria and tell you what they are. Then ask the children to sort them using the criteria above.

Always use the correct language, such as 'transparent' and 'opaque' but add a definition every time - 'that means see-through and not see-through'. It is quite acceptable for young children to say 'see-through' and 'not see-through' at this stage.

Some, of course, may remember the correct terminology at once. Others will take a long time to do so.

Make collections of objects made from common materials, both natural and made, such as plastic, wood, metal, stone, ceramic, glass, card, and so on. Ask the children:

❑ Do you know what these things are?
❑ Do you know what each one is made from?
❑ Can you sort them into sets?

Guessing games
Find out which materials disappear in water (dissolve) and which don't. Try sugar, salt, rice, marbles and gravel. You can have fun as well as learn a lot of science through this activity. Use clear plastic glasses and plastic spoons. Get the children to guess (predict) first which things will disappear and which won't.

Language development is a vital part of science learning. Put an object into a feely bag. Ask the children how many words they can think of to describe their object. Is it hard, smooth, rough, soft, squashy? Can they try and describe what is in their bag so well that their friend can guess what it is?

Sand and water
When working with materials such as sand and water, put wet sand, dry sand and water out at the same time. When the children have played with, and experienced, the materials, focus their attention on their properties. How do they behave? What does water feel like? What happens to the water wheel when you pour water on it? Can you catch water in a sieve? Is there any similarity between water, wet sand and dry sand? What is different? Will the wet sand turn the water wheel like the water and dry sand do? Why not? Which sand is best for making sand pies? Why?

Gay Wilson

What would our world be like if there were no electricity? Think of the things we just take for granted - lights, washing machines, mixers, radios, traffic lights, cookers and a whole lot more. Even very young children are masters of the remote control or video game. But what is the basis of all these things?

Batteries, bulbs and wow!

To work, any electrical device must have a complete circuit. Complicated devices obviously have many complex circuits and investigating these is best left to the qualified electrician but simple circuits can be great fun.

Children should be taught never to investigate or play with any equipment that uses mains electricity. They should be warned of the dangers of playing near or climbing on electric pylons or electricity sub-stations which are extremely dangerous. However, working with low energy batteries is quite safe - and exciting!

You will need a small amount of basic kit but once bought this should last a long while except that batteries and the odd bulb will have to be replaced. There are various complete kits on the market, some with easy connections for young children or children with special needs, but these can be expensive.

For a simple basic kit you will need:
- a battery,
- three leads (wires) with crocodile clips,
- a small bulb,

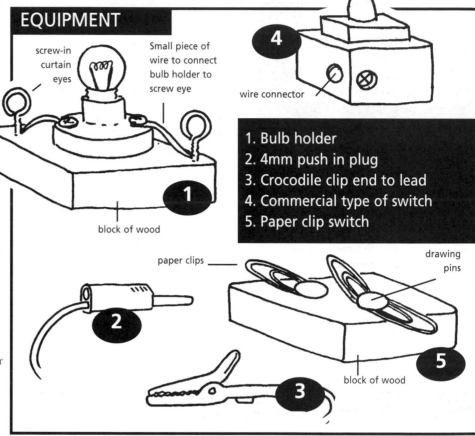

EQUIPMENT

screw-in curtain eyes

Small piece of wire to connect bulb holder to screw eye

wire connector

block of wood

1. Bulb holder
2. 4mm push in plug
3. Crocodile clip end to lead
4. Commercial type of switch
5. Paper clip switch

paper clips

drawing pins

block of wood

- a bulb holder mounted on a piece of wood with screw eye terminals
- and a small switch.

You can make a simple switch from two drawing pins and three paper-clips on a small block of wood instead of buying one. This type also has the advantage of allowing

children to see exactly how the connection is made.

The best type of batteries to use are either the 6 volt power packs or the smaller 4.5 volt flat type of battery with the metal strip connections. If you use ordinary round cells or batteries you will need to put them in a

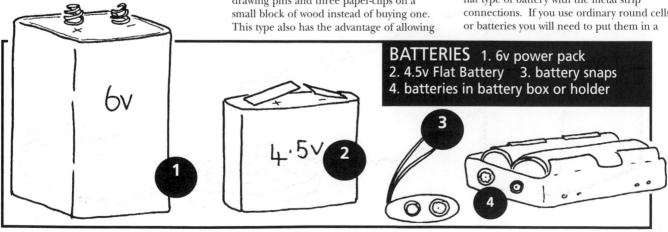

BATTERIES 1. 6v power pack
2. 4.5v Flat Battery   3. battery snaps
4. batteries in battery box or holder

6v

4.5v

suitable battery box that has snap-on connections (rather like large press-studs) to make a good connection.

The important thing to remember is that the bulbs you use should be the same voltage as the battery. If you use a smaller voltage bulb it will shine very brightly for a second or two and then burn out. Never use anything bigger than 6v and avoid rechargeable batteries for this type of activity. They are fine for putting in toys that have special battery compartments but never use them where there is a possibility of children making a short circuit. A freshly charged rechargeable can discharge all its energy in one spurt and become very hot.

Some children find it difficult to manage crocodile clips. You can get bulb holders that have a push-in type of connection into which you push a 4mm plug. These can be less frustrating for younger children or those who are less dextrous.

Children find torches fascinating so start off by looking at a selection of different torches. What do you have to do to make them work? What do you think happens when you operate the switch? You can get a very good torch that has a see-through case that allows you to see exactly how it works when you press the switch. Make up a simple circuit from the bulbs and wires so that the children can press the switch and turn the light on and off.

Compare it with the torch being switched on and off.

Next make the circuit without the switch but leave one of the battery connections undone. Can the children complete the circuit to make the bulb light? If you are feeling very brave, you could replace the bulb with a buzzer. The children love it but make sure you have the headache pills to hand!

Carole Creary

Ideas for parents - or for your setting

Electricity is such an essential part of everyday life that it is often taken for granted. For most children, machines around the home just work and they probably give little thought as to what actually supplies the energy to make them work.

Look around the house or nursery and find all the things that use electricity - don't forget to look in the shed or garage. You could make a list together of all the things or draw pictures. How many things do you have? (Probably more than you realise!) What would happen if there was no electricity? Would it make a difference to the way we cook our food or heat our homes? Would there be any television or radio? How would we see when it was dark? How did people wash their clothes before we had washing machines?

Cut pictures of electrical goods from old mail order catalogues. Sort all the things into two sets - those that use batteries and those we plug into the mains. Stick them on to two sheets of paper to make two sets. Are there any things that could go in either set because they can work from mains electricity or battery?

Remind children that they should never plug anything into the mains unless an adult is there to help, that things like electric kettles, irons and washing machines need to be treated with respect.

SIMPLE CIRCUIT WITH SWITCH

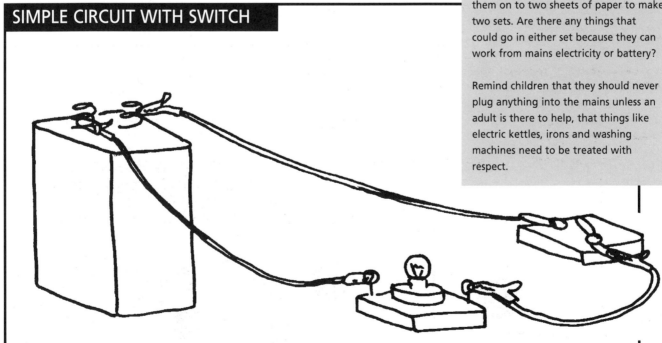

Unit C9: Implement planned activities for the development of language and communication skills

About this unit

Unit C9 is about how you help children to develop their language and communication skills and how you interact with the children when you are carrying out activities. In this unit you will be doing a music session, singing rhymes and telling stories, choosing and displaying books, setting up a role-play activity and working with the children in a talking and listening activity. There is quite a lot to cover, and if you haven't done some of these activities yet, you will need to practise, so discuss how you can do this with your supervisor.

It will also be helpful for you to observe the other adults in your setting. Watch how they talk and listen to the children. Do the children get plenty of opportunity to talk or is it the adults who do most of the talking? Do they ask open questions - that is, questions which encourage children to give more than a one-word answer? Do some activities encourage more talk than others? There is an article on talking and listening later in the chapter. It would be useful to read it before starting this unit. Also, read the section on talking and listening in the *Curriculum Guidance for the Foundation Stage*.

Links with other units

If you have already finished C8 you will be able to use some of the evidence from that unit. For instance, you have done an element on looking at interesting objects with children, which will provide much of the evidence for Element 2, about talking and listening activities. Your assessor may have already cross referenced her observation to this element. If not, write it on your cross referencing sheet so that you don't have to do it again. You may be able to use some of your evidence for C4 because you will be encouraging children to relate to each other (C4.2), helping them to develop self-reliance and self-esteem (C4.3) and encouraging positive behaviour (C4.5). You may also be helping them to deal with their feelings (C4.4).

Values

Find the values grid at the beginning of the unit. As you will see, the **welfare of the child** and **keeping children safe** is important in every element, as it is in everything you do with the children. Together with C8, this unit is centred on **children's learning and development**, but in this unit it will be particularly in relation to language and communication, which is closely linked to sensory and intellectual development. You will see that for every element you need to be a **reflective practitioner**, because you need to reflect on why you do particular activities with children, and what they will gain from them.

There is a lot of emphasis on **equality of opportunity, anti-discrimination** and **celebrating diversity** in this unit. In all of the activities you plan for the unit, think about how you can include songs, music, books and stories from a variety of cultures. How can you make the equipment in the home corner or other role-play area reflect different cultures and avoid stereotyping boys and girls into traditional roles? Think about how you will challenge children if they make discriminatory remarks. Think about how you will make sure that children with additional needs are able to join in the activities. For instance, a child with impaired hearing will enjoy using an instrument like a drum or a cymbal that vibrates, so they will be able to feel the rhythm even if they can't hear it well.

Discriminatory remark - a comment which treats an individual unfairly.

Stereotyping is labelling an individual or group with a particular characteristic, often negative.

By discussing with your colleagues how your activities will fit in with the curriculum plan, you will show that you are **working with other professionals**. You may also come into contact with specialists such as speech therapists if they come in to work with a child. Element 2 has a requirement that children are encouraged to talk to adults. This would be a good opportunity to **work in partnership with parents** by asking if any parents are willing to come in and talk to the children, perhaps about their job or a hobby, or their own culture. You will need to check with your supervisor before speaking to parents.

Getting started

In this unit you are aiming to show that you can:

- plan and carry out music sessions

- plan and carry out talking and listening activities

- choose and use equipment and materials to encourage role play

- choose and display books

- tell stories and rhymes

Read through the elements and use the personal skills profile (page 21) to pick out which activities you are confident to do first, and which you need practice on. Look at the knowledge statements and check which you don't understand, or which you need more information about. Find out from your assessor when the training sessions for this unit will be, or ask her for some suggestions about suitable reading materials. Don't forget to cross reference the appropriate evidence from C8. Then plan with your assessor, using your assessment plan. Your assessor may need to carry out several observations to cover everything. You could do choosing and displaying books and telling stories and rhymes together.

Remember! If you find written work difficult, ask your assessor if she can ask more oral questions, or if you can tape reflective accounts.

Try to show your knowledge and understanding by writing or telling your assessor about what you do and why you do it, what the children gain from it, how you make sure that you cater for individual children's needs. You will need to go on training sessions to make sure that you have the understanding required for the unit. Your assessor may give you some assignments to provide evidence of your knowledge. Try to include examples from your work with the children in your answers.

Element C9.1 Implement music sessions

Key issues

In this element you will need to plan and carry out a music session with the children. Many people find this worrying, but there is no need. Children love singing and playing musical instruments, and you don't have to be an expert musician to enjoy making music with young children. Music-making is often really beneficial for children who have communication difficulties or a sensory impairment, because it's a non-threatening way of communicating and joining in. This is true, too, for children with limited English - music-making doesn't depend on language.

If you think you can't sing, it doesn't matter, because the children won't notice! It is something you need to practise, though, so if you haven't done it before, start by joining in with colleagues, and learn from them. You may have already learned some songs, but it's helpful to write them down to refer to if you're not sure, and try to add to them so that you have a good repertoire. Choose some songs with good rhythm that children can clap or march to, like 'The grand old Duke of York', and action and counting songs like 'Five currant buns' and 'Five little speckled frogs'. Choose songs suitable for different ages, too. Remember that some traditional songs stereotype children of a particular gender or culture, so watch out for these and change the words if you want to use them. We talked about this in C8 so if you need to, refer back to that unit (see page 90).

There are some good song books on the market. Check which are available in your setting and also try the local library. Here are some suggestions:

This Little Puffin Elizabeth Matterson (ed) (Puffin)

Apusskidu: Songs for Children Beatrice Harrop (ed) (A & C Black)

Mango Spice: 44 Caribbean Songs Yvonne Connolly (ed) (A & C Black)

Harlequin: 44 Songs Round the Year David Gadsby (ed) (A & C Black)

Use musical instruments with the children to add to their enjoyment. With younger children untuned percussion instruments - that is, ones you shake, scrape or beat - are best, especially if you are not a musician, because you don't have to worry about getting the notes right! Good instruments do tend to be expensive, but it's better to have a few good ones than a lot of cheap ones which make a nasty sound. Find out from your supervisor what instruments you have in your setting. Your local Early Years Development and Childcare Partnership should have musical instruments which you can borrow, and they may have music-making courses which you can take advantage of. Ask your manager for this information.

You can add to your selection of instruments by making instruments with the children:

- make shakers out of plastic bottles and other containers, filled with seeds, rice, sand and so on;

◆ make scrapers from two blocks of wood with sandpaper stuck on;

◆ cut lengths of dowelling to size to make sticks for beating together;

◆ or use ordinary household objects like saucepan lids, spoons, a cheese grater to scrape, and so on.

When you plan your music session, think about the age of the children. Very young children won't cope with any more than ten minutes, so keep the session short. About 20 minutes is about right for older children in a nursery setting. Children in a school setting may manage half an hour. You could use a format something like this:

Sing a song the children know

Clap to the song

Give out instruments and play them with the song

Do some rhythm games - you clap a rhythm and they copy it (with older children); do some marching or action songs (with younger children)

Collect the instruments in

Teach them a new song

Let them choose a song to finish with

There are lots of other ways you can use instruments. For instance, use particular instruments for different movements - wooden sounds for moving like clockwork toys, triangles for tiptoeing quietly as a mouse, a drum for the big, heavy movement of an elephant, and so on.

The **knowledge evidence** statements for this element are 1, 4, 5, 13, 14 and 17. You need to show that you understand:

◆ development of language and communication (also C9.2, C9.3, C9.4)

◆ the attention span of children of different ages (also C9.5)

◆ how to include talking and listening in activities (also C9.2)

◆ how gender and cultural stereotypes can be expressed in songs and role play, and how to counteract this (also C9.3)

◆ appropriate songs and music for different ages and for the size of the group

Where a statement is relevant for more than one element, we

have put the other elements in brackets, so make sure you include these in your evidence. Number one is the child development question again, so check whether you have covered it already. You should cover some of the others in the evidence for the element. Check with your assessor where there are gaps, and write a paragraph to cover them, or complete any assignments you have been given.

Which type of evidence?

Your assessor will need to **observe** all but two of the PCs and one aspect of each section of the range, so look through and make sure you cover all of these in your activity. Write an **activity plan** to make sure you are well prepared. Remember to fill in the section on children with additional needs, and after you have done the activity write a comment on how it went and what the children gained from it. Include a **photograph** of any instruments you have made. Include your **book of songs**, with examples of songs from different cultures. You can keep adding to this as you learn new songs.

Element C9.2 Implement and participate in talking and listening activities

Key issues

You may have evidence for this element from C8.5, 'Examine objects of interest with children', although the emphasis is slightly different in this element. It emphasises the different ways you can encourage children to join in with conversation, in large and small groups and one to one, and it encourages you to think about the individual needs of children who communicate well and those who have difficulty in communicating.

Find out from your supervisor whether any of the children have a hearing impairment, and sit where they can see your face clearly. If there are children in your group who are not fluent English speakers, they will find it hard to communicate. You will need to reassure them with smiles and hugs, and by showing or demonstrating things to them. Find out from your supervisor what help is available. You may have access to a teacher of English as a second language in your area. Perhaps a member of their family can come in and speak to them in their own language for a few sessions during the week.

It's sometimes too easy to let the children who communicate well do all the talking and the quiet ones not get involved at all. One way of avoiding this is to have an object to pass around, which the children hold when it's their turn to speak. If you have children who are not confident to speak in a big group, make a point of communicating with them in a small group or one to one. Also, listen to yourself and make sure

that you are not the one doing all the talking! Record yourself interacting with the children, and play it back to yourself. It's a good way of telling whether you are communicating and listening properly. It takes a lot of practice to be able to communicate effectively with children, but it is one of the most important things you do.

Many children today live in an environment where there is constant background noise from the television or radio, and many find it difficult to listen properly. Think about activities which encourage listening, such as listening to a sound tape, or to the sounds around, both inside and outside. Get the children to be absolutely quiet for a few seconds, and ask them what they heard. Or play a musical instrument without the children seeing it, and ask them to choose the right instrument.

The **knowledge evidence** statements for this element are 2, 10, 11 and 14. You need to show that you understand:

◆ a variety of communication difficulties children may have

◆ how to communicate with and listen to children

◆ how to fit activities into the curriculum plan (also C9.3, C9.4)

◆ appropriate talking and listening activities for children of different ages

Try to include some of the information in your evidence for the element. Your assessor may give you questions or an assignment to fill any gaps.

Which type of evidence?

Your assessor may **cross reference** this element to her observation in C8.5. If not, she will need to **observe** all but one of the PCs and one aspect of each section of the range. Write a **diary** or **reflective account** of activities you have done with the children which have helped them to develop their talking and listening skills. Think about your interaction one to one, and in small and large groups. You could tape yourself carrying out activities, and include the **tape** as evidence. Ask your supervisor to write a **witness testimony** to say that you are able to interact well with the children.

Element C9.3 Select and use materials to stimulate role play

Key issues

Children learn first by imitation. A very young baby will copy an adult who sticks her tongue out. By about a year old, babies will start to clap and wave in imitation of an adult. Children start to role play from an early age. A toddler will want to copy his parents by sweeping the floor, dusting, ironing, cooking and so on, using child-size toys. If there is a new baby in the house, the older child will love to bath, feed and take out their doll in the pram, to be just like mummy and daddy. Boys will enjoy doing this just as much as girls.

The home corner is always a popular place to play in the early years setting, probably because it is based on the child's home experience and provides a link between home and school. Children act out things they have seen their parents doing. They sometimes also act out things which may be worrying them, like a future stay in hospital. Both boys and girls should be encouraged to take on non-traditional roles. Encourage the boys to do the caring for the baby, cooking and washing up, and the girls to go out to work, as well as the other way round, and challenge the children if they make stereotypical remarks. For instance, if a child says 'You do the washing up because you're the mummy,' you can say, 'But daddies do the washing up as well.'

The home corner provides a great opportunity to widen the children's awareness of different cultures. You should provide play food, utensils and dressing-up clothes to reflect the diversity of cultures and lifestyles. For instance, you might have a chapatti board and rolling pin, chopsticks and bowls. You can buy a lovely range of clothes from different cultures from educational catalogues, but you can make them much more cheaply. It's good to have long pieces of cloth which can be used for cloaks, saris or whatever children's imagination makes them! Have a range of costumes relating to different jobs, too, such as a doctor, nurse, fire fighter, police officer, builder and so on (both male and female).

Children need the opportunity for other types of role play, which may be specific and planned, to fit in with a topic in the curriculum, or it may be child-led free play. Themes linked to the curriculum may be a shop, hospital, post office or café. There is an example of a different type of role-play area - a garden centre - later in the chapter. All these types of role play help the children to play imaginatively, but they also provide opportunities for learning. For example, in the shop, children will learn about shape by handling different containers, they will begin to read labels, count money, weigh and write lists. Play writing is really important in children's play, because they begin to make marks without any pressure about getting it right. You should accept young children's play writing without criticising it.

Children will use all sorts of objects and toys for role play and other imaginative play, both indoors and outside. Cardboard boxes of all sizes are useful, as well as wooden blocks, planks and other large construction, with blankets or other large pieces of material, to make ships, buses or dens. Perhaps you

can think of other ideas. Children need to be able to choose the toys and equipment they want to use. For example, if they have cars and small play people together with building blocks, their play is more likely to develop imaginatively. Some early years settings restrict what the children can have out, and don't let them mix things, but this limits their creativity. The important thing is to teach the children how to tidy up properly and put things back in the right place.

Your role as the adult is crucial in role play, as with other free play. Sometimes it's better to let children develop their own play without any adult intervention. Watch what they are doing, and join in if you think you can help them to develop their play. If you do get involved, follow the children's lead. Don't take over. Of course, if there is a health and safety risk you must intervene.

The **knowledge evidence** statements for this element are 3, 9, 12, 18, 19 and 22. You need to show that you understand:

◆ what role play is and how it changes as a child develops

◆ how role play helps children's creative and other areas of development

◆ how you can support the child's learning and development, but allow them to take the lead

◆ how to set up areas and activities for role play

◆ how to identify equipment which reflects children's own cultural backgrounds and helps then learn about others

◆ health and safety in relation to role play

Try to show your knowledge in your evidence for the element. Your assessor may also give you questions or assignments to complete.

Which type of evidence?

Your assessor will need to **observe** all but two of the PCs and one aspect of each section of the range. Read through these and make sure you cover them when planning your activity. She will also want to ask **questions**. Have a look at your home corner, and make a note of the things in it. Do they reflect different cultures? Do they allow for children to play in non-stereotypical roles? Think about how you might organise it for the observation. Will you keep it as a home corner, or change it into a different role-play area? Or will you provide lots of other materials and let the children play freely? Ask your supervisor what would fit in with the curriculum theme. Write an **activity plan** so that you are well prepared for the activity.

Are the books in good condition and displayed attractively? Can the children reach them easily? Have you taught the children how to use the books carefully and replace them when they have finished? If you think the book corner needs improving, give it a facelift. Check with your supervisor first. Here are some suggestions to help you. You won't be in a position to do all of these things, but do what you can.

◆ Provide a carpet, floor cushions and comfortable chairs.

◆ Position it in a light corner, away from the general traffic so that it is fairly quiet.

◆ Use a display bookcase for the books so that children can choose them easily.

◆ Use posters and pictures on the walls, preferably about some of the stories – you could do a display with the children about a well-loved story.

◆ Make sure that the selection of books has something of interest for every child, so that you encourage those who are not keen to sit and read.

◆ Have a reading time for everyone at some point in the day, when the adults are reading as well.

◆ Spend time in the book corner yourself, as often as possible, to show the children that you value books.

◆ It's better to have a smaller amount of books displayed well and changed regularly, rather than lots of books thrown into a box – as long as there are enough for each child and a few extra.

The **knowledge evidence** statements for this element are 7, 20, 21 and 22. You need to show that you understand:

◆ how to choose appropriate books for different ages, and where to find them

◆ how to review books and stories (also C9.5)

◆ why it is important to provide positive, non-stereotypical images in books

◆ health and safety in relation to display of books

Which type of evidence?

Your assessor will want to **observe** you using books with the children and **inspect** your book display. She will ask some **questions** about the books you have chosen. She will probably combine this observation with C9.5. If possible, give

Element
C9.4 Select and display books

Key issues

In this element you need to show that you can display an appropriate range of books for children, and that you can display them attractively. The notes on this element are helpful in showing examples of the different types of books you should include. You also need to think about the age of the children when choosing books. The article later in the chapter ('Choosing books for young children', page 134-135) gives examples of a range of books and suggestions for different ages, so read it now.

Then look at the books in your setting. Sort the books into categories, and see if you have all the types of books you need. Look especially to see if there are any with negative stereotypes, such as girls doing household chores and boys having all the adventures, or a token black person in the background, or do some books show girls in leading roles, black people in positions of responsibility and people with disabilities in active roles? These types of books are now available from good book suppliers. Use your local library, too. Group settings can borrow a good quantity of books for a period. They can provide books on particular topics. Ask your supervisor if your setting takes advantage of this. It's good to take the children to the library regularly to choose their own books, to get them in the habit of reading.

Now look at your book corner. Is it inviting and comfortable?

your book corner a facelift and display a range of books which you have chosen yourself to cover the criteria for this element. If your book corner didn't need changing, or you weren't allowed to alter it, set up a display of books somewhere else in the setting and supervise a group of children using them. Make a **list** of books you have found under each category of the range. If you want to, take a **photograph** of the book display.

Element C9.5 Relate stories and rhymes

Key issues

Your setting will probably have at least one story and singing session every day. The length of the session will depend on the age of the child - for two-year-olds ten minutes is as long as they will manage to sit still, and you would need to divide this into a very short story followed by some singing and finger rhymes. For three- and four-year-olds, 20 minutes is plenty. If you haven't told stories and rhymes yet, you need to practise before your assessor comes in to observe you. Ask your supervisor to give you the opportunity to do this. Start with a small group if you're not confident.

Try telling stories you know without a book, or if you can, make up your own. You can use props or visual aids to help you. You could make your own story box, with a collection of articles and games which you have collected or made. It's particularly important to use visual or tactile aids (objects to see or touch) if you are telling a story to a child with a hearing or sight impairment. If you have a child with impaired hearing in the group, sit where the light is on your face, and sit the child in front of you so that she can see your face clearly.

Involve the children in the story as much as you can. Some stories have repetitive bits that the children can join in. For other stories you might want to tell the whole story through and then go through it again letting the children talk about it. If you have a disruptive child, try to draw the child in by sitting her next to you or using her name when you're pointing out something interesting in the story, or giving her a visual aid to hold. Try not to lose the continuity of the story with too much interruption. At first, ask if another member of staff can sit in with you, to help you to control the group.

When you're choosing a story, be aware of particular children who might be upset by it. Some stories are quite frightening, or a particular story might give an unwelcome reminder of an upset the child may have had at home. On the other hand, stories can sometimes help children come to terms with a worry or anxiety, like going into hospital or moving on to school. Never read a book to children without having read it yourself first, to check that it's suitable.

It's a good idea to follow the story with some songs and rhymes. Children love to sing, and they don't mind if you're not a good singer! Use taped songs to help you if you need to. The rhythm and pattern of songs, rhymes and poetry is helpful for language development, especially for children whose first language is not English. When you're all singing together there is a lot of eye contact and the children are more actively involved. If you use actions as well the children enjoy it even more because they can do the actions even if they don't know, or can't say, all the words. Make a collection of rhymes and poetry, and add them to your song collection.

The **knowledge evidence** statements for this element are 6, 8, 15 and 16. You need to show that you understand:

◆ how to involve children with hearing or other sensory impairment in storytelling

◆ how children might respond emotionally to stories

◆ why it's important to show different styles and languages in stories

◆ how to choose and use visual aids

Remember that this element links closely with C9.4, choosing and displaying books, so you may have covered some evidence already. There are articles later in the chapter which will give you some more help on choosing books (pages 134-135) and telling stories (pages 136-137). It would also be a good idea to attend a training session and do further reading.

Which type of evidence?

Your assessor will need to **observe** you telling a story and rhymes. In your assessment plan, you might have agreed to do this and C9.4 together. Write an **activity plan** unless you have included this in C9.4. Make sure you have chosen a story and read it through yourself before the observation, and have some songs and rhymes written down if you need to. Have your visual aids ready. Make a **book** of songs and rhymes. You can use this as evidence for C9.1, too.

Music in the pre-school need not be chaotic. Chrys Blanchard gives some ideas which will make it a happy experience

Making music

Music involves:

- listening;
- making sounds;
- choosing, sorting and ordering sounds;
- finding out about instruments, what they look like and sound like;
- reacting to sounds;
- emotional responses, which may then be expressed in a variety of ways - drama, dance, poetry, stories;
- working alone and with others in an interactive way;
- creating new music, sounds and songs, whilst improving motor skills, building confidence and developing language and numeracy.
- Music even involves science, when we look at how sound is made and how size and shape can affect the sound.

If you're not confident about tackling music, always try to start from the familiar. Adapting well-known songs may help and here are just a few ideas you can try with younger children using the instruments from the instrument box. Remember, children don't require us to be wonderful singers, so don't worry about whether you feel you're a good singer or not. It's how you put over the game/song that matters - enthusiasm counts for a lot!

Using instruments one at a time

This game/song allows the children to hear

Useful tips

- Always explain what you want the children to do before handing out the instruments.
- Give out any beaters and sticks *after* all the instruments have been handed out.
- Use a visual sign to signal when you want their attention. I ask the children to put both hands in the air as soon as they see that I have done so. They know that this means 'Be quiet because I have something to say' - it also stops them playing their instruments!

the sound of the instrument chosen and each to have a turn at playing it. Make up a song or adapt a well-known one, to include a child's name and an instrument. 'The wheels on the bus' works well, for example:

All sing   'Jenny can play the tambourine, tambourine, tambourine, Jenny can play the tambourine, all day long'.

Jenny plays the tambourine throughout then at the end of the verse hands it to the next person in the row and the song begins again. Do enough verses for all the children.

Although it might seem a bit daunting to us as adults to do 23 or so verses to let each child have a turn, I've always found it works well with the children - especially as they can each be assured of a go!

Each session you can try a different instrument. (You may have to play around with the words a bit to make them fit your song.)
'Chloe can play the big blue drum, big blue drum...'
'John can play the woody wood block ....'
'Tim can play the shaker shaker shaker, shaker shaker shaker ...'

By using instruments in a controlled and structured way children can get to hear the different sound qualities and can experiment with dynamics.

Other well-known tunes that are easy to adapt are:
'If you're happy and you know it play the drum'
'If you're happy and you know it ting the bell'
'If you're happy and you know it tap the wood'

'The bear went over the mountain' becomes:
Susie plays on the (triangle) (big drum) (xylophone) etc
Susie plays on the (triangle)
Susie plays on the (triangle) to see what she can do
And look what she can do
And look what she can do oh
Susie plays on the triangle
Susie plays on the triangle
Susie plays on the triangle
And that's what she can do

There are plenty of others to adapt. Children don't mind how simple they are, you just need to give them a clear structure and a chance to isolate play on an instrument.

Using instruments all together

'Polly put the kettle on' (or any two-verse or verse/chorus song). When the children sing verse 1, they sing and play loudly; verse 2 (Suki take if off again) play and sing quietly. Repeat over and over and they will soon learn the difference between loud and quiet. If you play, too, they'll learn by copying you.

Playing quietly requires control and, as children develop this, they are able to respond to the dynamic in the game. This game also develops group responsibility and a recognition of structure (verse 1 and verse 2).

Chrys Blanchard

Some children will come into the early years setting already able to talk fluently while others will have limited language skills. As an early years worker, you will need not only to talk to children, but also to listen carefully to what they have to say, and encourage them to develop their language skills

Talking and listening to children

From the day they are born babies begin to communicate, first by crying to tell their parents when they are hungry or uncomfortable, but they will soon begin to make other sounds. They need to interact frequently with their parents and other adults and have a stimulating environment to encourage them to develop their language skills.

Babies learn to talk through imitating the sounds that adults make. Because adults respond with pleasure to their first sounds, this encourages them to keep trying. If you watch a mother or father, or a carer, communicating with a baby, you will see that there is a lot of eye contact, smiling and taking turns to make sounds. This is how the baby is beginning to communicate. He probably won't say his first word until at least a year old, and possibly much longer, but he is taking in and understanding language a lot sooner.

Sometimes, children with older brothers or sisters develop a non-verbal method of communication by pointing, making gestures or using their own way of saying things which only the family will understand. This may be particularly true of children with learning difficulties. Twins may also develop a language of their own, with one sometimes becoming dependent on the other.

Children in the early years setting

When children first come into the early years setting they may be quiet, but they may be real chatterboxes at home. It may take them a while to feel confident enough to talk freely, but there are things

you can do to help. You will need to think about

whether the environment and atmosphere in your setting encourages children to talk, or discourages them. Some studies have found that it's the adults who do all the talking, and the children don't get the chance. Sometimes, adults are so busy organising things that they forget to stop and chat with children.

Ways of encouraging talk are:
- To get involved in children's play, to get down to their level and join in with what they're doing. You will need to watch and listen first to see how they're playing so that you can join in appropriately. If they're making roads and driving cars around the sand, it's no use you going in and saying 'Let's build some sandcastles' because that will spoil their game, not develop it.

- To give children your full attention wherever possible, and encourage them by smiling, nodding or making comments about what they say.

- To know a little about the child's home background, so that you can help them to link what they do at home with what they do in the setting. This is important for all children, but especially for children who belong to a minority ethnic group, who may feel particularly isolated if their home background is ignored.

- To have a relaxed atmosphere without too much noise. A certain amount of noise is inevitable if children are happily engaged, but discourage shouting, and remember that if you and the other adults in the setting shout, the children will shout, too!

- To have quiet areas, or closed-in places, like a den or the book corner, where children will be encouraged to talk with each other

- To have frequent opportunities for free play, where children take the lead.

How we use language
It would be useful to observe the adults and children in your setting, and see whether children have plenty of opportunity and encouragement to talk. It's a good idea to tape yourself while you're doing an activity with the children, to see how much talk is going on, and who is doing most of the talking.

We use language in different ways:
- receptive: language which we hear and understand
- expressive: language which we speak or express
- non-verbal: body language and facial expression.

All of these are important. We need to show children that we are listening to them. You do this by your body language - perhaps by a nod and a smile, stopping what you're doing and getting down to their level. If you need to finish a job and a child really wants to say something, say that you'll come and talk to them when you've finished, and make sure you do. But with younger children, try to make time when they want to tell you, otherwise they will have moved on to something else, and the opportunity is gone.

Here are some ways you might use language during the normal course of the day:

- **talking about what the children are doing during an activity**. Think about the sort of language you want the children to learn. For instance, if you have planned a modelling activity, you may have a list of words relating to properties of shapes – square, circle, curved, straight – or to size – large/small, thick/thin, long/short.

- **recalling events**, such as asking the children to talk about what they did and saw when they have been for a walk or if they have made a model, giving them the opportunity to tell the other children how they made it.

- **conversation**: if your activities are appropriate and relate to the children's own experience, they will be encouraged to talk about something they did at home, or things they are interested in - or anything and everything, just as adults do when they are together. It's important that you don't get so busy doing the activity that you don't listen to children's conversation. You can learn a lot about children's understanding, and help them to gain confidence in using language, by listening to them. If adults don't listen, children are likely to stop speaking to them.

- **information exchange**: you need to be able to give instructions, or explain things clearly to children, and also to give them the opportunity to pass on information to you and other children. This is a good way of checking their understanding.

- **expression of emotion**: very young children express their emotions by smiling or crying, because they don't have the language to express themselves. Two-year-olds have temper tantrums often out of sheer frustration because they can't communicate their feelings in other ways. You need to help children to express their feelings through the language you use with them. You might encourage them to explore their feelings through an activity which makes them think about what makes them happy or angry.

- **questioning**: this is a useful strategy to use, to help children to develop their ideas, but don't over-use it, and think about how you ask questions. Avoid closed questions - that is, questions that need only one word answers, like 'Do you like playing in the sand?' A better, open question, would be 'What do you like doing in the sand?' Open questions tend to start with 'what', 'how', 'why'.

Ask yourself these questions about the activities you provide:

Does your activity give the children the opportunity for talking and listening to each other?

Keep the size of the group small, so that each child gets a chance to talk. The smaller the group, the easier it is to encourage conversation, especially with very young children. Encourage the children to listen to each other. Think about how you communicate with the children. Do you listen enough? Ask some open questions, like 'Why does this ...?' or 'What will happen if..?' 'Tell me how you did ...' Some activities encourage more general conversation, such as playdough, where children are using their hands but not having to concentrate on the activity too hard, and the conversation starts to flow. Let them lead the conversation. Listen to what they're saying, and join in if you think you can help the conversation, but don't take over.

Is your activity interesting, varied and at the right level?

Try to find out what the children are interested in, and follow their lead if you can. Make sure that any activity you plan is at the right level for them and that there is plenty for them to do. Some activities will encourage more language than others. For instance, a child painting a picture may choose not to talk about it, and you must respect that, and not push them. On the other hand, a dressing-up activity is likely to produce a lot of language because it inspires the children's imagination, and often becomes a group activity.

What strategies do you use to overcome stereotyping and discrimination?

You need to be aware of the language you and the children are using, and challenge any negative remarks children (or other adults) make. For instance, make sure that you don't always ask the girls to do the washing or clearing up, or the boys to do all the carrying. If a child says 'only girls play with dolls', discuss with the children why this is not true. Or if a child laughs at the Punjabi writing in a dual language book, talk to the children positively about how many different languages are spoken all over the world.

How would you ensure that the bilingual child is fully involved?

If you have a bilingual child in the group who is not fluent in English, you may need to ask for extra support from a bilingual adult, if it's available, so that the child can converse in her home language too. If this is not possible you will need to use visual aids, body language and gestures to increase her participation in the activity.

How would you ensure that children who have additional needs are fully involved in the activity?

The most important thing is to know your children so that you can make proper provision for individual needs.

For the child who has difficulty in communication: if you keep your groups small, you will be better able to adapt your activity if the need arises, and this will also give every child a chance to talk. You may need to work one-to-one with a child if she has severe communication difficulties. Don't correct wrong pronunciation of words, but repeat what the child has said using the correct form – for instance, if the child says '-low bus' - 'Yes, it's a yellow bus'.

For a child who is visually impaired: give the child a variety of tactile experiences to stimulate her to talk, for instance, large bowls or baskets of fabrics, pan scrubs, brushes; and dough, sand and water play. Have a similar collection of sound objects – bells, rattles and musical instruments – to encourage listening. Draw the child's attention to the sound of things you are doing, like pouring juice.

For a child whose hearing is impaired: tactile objects such as described above, but make sure that she also has bright colours and interesting patterns and shapes. She will enjoy musical instruments which vibrate, like cymbals and gongs, and music with a good rhythm. Sit where the child can see your face, with the light on it – don't sit with your back to the window – so that she can see you speaking.

Now ask yourself these questions about your setting:

How does the organisation of your setting encourage talk?

The way your setting is organised can encourage children to talk. Some examples are:

- interesting and often-changed interest tables and displays

- accessible materials making the children more independent and allowing adults more time to spend with the children

- encouraging cooperative group work

- using opportunities during everyday routines to promote language

- talk in small groups rather than whole-class groups during circle time.

Do some activities encourage more talk?

Most activities in the early years setting have the potential for encouraging talk, but the activities below are particularly beneficial because they stimulate children's imagination:

- role play

- puppets

- sand and water play

- small world toys with construction materials

- books

Do the children have plenty of time for free play?

Sometimes, settings have such a structured session that children are spending too much time on adult-led activities. Children need plenty of time to play freely, to explore and experiment with materials and equipment, and to practise their language. It's important to observe and listen to children as they play, because in this way you can learn a lot about their understanding and language development. This will help you to see what activities the children need to extend their language and learning further. Try not to be too rigid about how the children use the toys during free play - let them mix construction and small world toys, for example. They can tidy them into the right boxes when they've finished playing. This will stimulate more imaginative play, which is a rich opportunity for language.

Talking and listening is one of the most important ways children learn about themselves and the world around them. As an early years practitioner, it's vital that you provide the language-rich environment they need in order to fully develop their language skills.

Mary Townsend

There are times when the quality of play can be increased through adult intervention but, as Margaret Sutherland shows, it's not just a case of bombarding children with questions - you have to know what kind of questions to ask and when to ask them

Asking better questions

Play is a vital part of the learning process and children gain tremendous pleasure from the experience. But sometimes that pleasure is reduced when practitioners, in an effort to make the most of a play situation, keep intervening. Whilst clear questioning will often reveal how much a child understands, and plays a vital role in language development, it must become incredibly tiresome for the child. Asking better questions can contribute significantly to the child's understanding and can also give you an insight into the learning that has taken place, but you have to know when to ask questions and what kind of questions to ask.

When to ask questions

We ask questions for different reasons and it is this which should determine when we ask them.

Some questions will be asked before an activity starts. This allows you to establish:

■ that the child understands what they are being asked to do;

■ that the child knows what equipment is required to undertake the task;

■ that the child knows what they are supposed to achieve by the end of it.

Some will be asked as the activity progresses. These might establish:

■ how much the child understands about what they are doing;

■ why the child is doing certain things;

■ why the activity is going in a different direction from the one you intended!

Some questions will be asked at the end of an activity. These questions might establish:

■ what has been learned as a result of the activity;

■ what interesting things the child found out whilst undertaking the activity;

■ what thought processes the child engaged in whilst undertaking the activity.

You should always be clear about why you are asking a question. If you are clear about why you are asking it, then it will make it easier to ensure that you know when to ask it. If you are not clear, then perhaps you should not be asking the question! You also need to guard against asking a question if you have already decided on the answer you are looking for. If you have preconceived ideas about answers then you may consider an answer wrong when in fact it is not wrong, simply a different perspective on the same situation.

Think about the questions you ask children. Do you:

■ ask too many questions?

■ ask too many of the same kind of question?

■ use questions to take forward learning?

■ use questions to check what learning has taken place?

■ ask questions because it fills the silence and seems the right thing to do?

The 'right answer' trap

You will often observe a child absorbed in solitary play. It is likely that this child will be working alone with little, if any, input from adults. They are likely to have constructed a story line in their head and are happily pursuing it. It is in this situation that adult intervention can actually hamper rather than support the child. If the adult is unaware of what the child is trying to do then inappropriate questioning can frustrate the child or leave them feeling confused. Making sure that you ask open questions which allow you to tune into and follow the child's line of thought can avoid the 'right answer' trap.

I observed the following scenario one day in

nursery. The theme for the week was 'The farm'. David was playing with the toy farm and had some yellow coloured liquid in a plastic bottle. The animals were in the field, tractors, combine harvesters and other bits of machinery were lying about, and the tractor appeared to have broken down. The practitioner arrived at the table and began to talk to the child. The conversation went something like this:

Adult: What's happened here?

Child: It's broken down (pointing to tractor)

Adult: Oh dear. What are you going to do?

Child: Fix it (with a look on his face that said 'obvious answer to a rather silly question'!)

Was it difficult to make? a

That's lovely - how did you make that?

Did you make it all by yourself?

What are you going to do with it now?

How did you get that bit to stick?

Adult: What's that you've got in the bottle?

Child: It's oil.

Adult: Is it? (the adult looks somewhat surprised)

Child: Yes.

Adult: What are you going to do with it?

Child: Use it to help fix the tractor. It's oil, it'll make it better.

Adult: Is that the colour oil usually is?

Child: Yes, I've seen yellow oil.

Adult: That's interesting. Let's look at the book and see what it says.

(A close examination of the book by both child and adult revealed a picture of black oil squirting out of a can.)

Child: (looking at book) That oil's black but mine is yellow and I've seen yellow oil.

Adult: The book shows the farmer using this oil, black oil, to fix his machine.

Child: Well I'm using my yellow oil to fix my tractor.

At this point the adult was distracted by another child and left the table. Later I spoke to David and asked about the yellow oil. He explained that when his mum made chips she used oil and it was yellow!

Having had a chat about black oil and yellow oil and the different uses for oil the child's parting comments to me were: 'I don't think Mrs X has ever seen oil for making chips. She kept going on about black oil - ugh - I wouldn't want chips cooked in black oil!'

Clearly the child had some previous experience of oil. He recognised that there were different kinds of oils. The teacher appeared to be looking for the connection between the picture in the book and the child's own actions. The opportunity to discover what the child already knew was not taken. The child appeared to be questioning the information in the book. Perhaps this was because he had some previous experience of oils. Not allowing for further exploration of this led to a more limiting experience.

In an effort to make links to previous learning experiences (some superb work had been undertaken about the farm in this setting), we can miss wonderful opportunities for developing thought processes that are already taking place inside children's heads. These thought processes can be quite complex and are actually achieving the very aims we wish to pursue through our planning. It's just that the children get there by a different route!

Two kinds of questions

It has been suggested that there are two kinds of questions:

- questions that encourage lower order thinking

- questions that encourage higher order thinking

Lower order thinking questions test recall of knowledge. They are likely to check understanding, revise learning, lead to new learning and diagnose difficulties. Imagine you are reading the story of 'The Three Little Pigs'. Examples of lower order questions would be:

- How many little pigs are there in the story?

- Where do the pigs live?

- Who came to huff and puff and blow their house down?

- What is the first/second/third little pig carrying?

Higher order questions, on the other hand, make children think. They are likely to arouse curiosity, focus attention, elicit views, feelings and experiences and stimulate discussion.

Examples of higher order thinking questions would be:

- How do you think the pigs are feeling?

- The wolf is very hungry. Have you ever been hungry - what did you do?

- What would have happened if the wolf had been a friendly wolf?

- If you were the wolf, what would you have done?

- How can we tell if this story is true?

So next time you go to intervene in a situation by asking questions, stop and think:

- Why am I asking this question?

- Will it allow the child to build on prior knowledge?

- Will it develop the learning experience?

- Will it help the child to think on a deeper level or will it simply check understanding?

So what questions could David have been asked which might have explored his thought processes rather than probing for the right answer?

- You know a lot about oil, how do you know so much?

- What are all the things you can use oil for?

- How do you think it will help the tractor?

- What's the difference between oil and petrol?

- Is oil always yellow?

- Why do you think the book shows the oil as black?

By thinking about asking better questions we will go some way to ensure that adult intervention leaves children feeling more confident, ready to question things and able to take on new challenges.

Margaret Sutherland

Children love to role play - that is, act out the role of another person. This may be in the home corner, when they act out the role of mum or dad, or they may act out a painful or worrying situation, such as going into hospital, a pet dying or the arrival of a new brother or sister

Encouraging role play

Your setting needs to provide a good range of activities and equipment for role play or pretend play. Children need plenty of space, both indoors and out. Dens can be built in little corners with sheets, or bushes if you're lucky enough to have any. You can change the home corner into a hospital, shop, café or hairdresser. Give the children a pile of boxes and they will become cars, aeroplanes, ships, rockets or whatever else takes their imagination. Sandpits can become building sites. The possibilities are endless.

You need to make sure that your equipment encourages children to take non-stereotypical cultural and gender roles. For instance, in your dressing-up clothes you need to include dresses, hats, shawls, cloaks and trousers that can be used for a variety of roles: doctors', nurses' and firefighters' outfits for both boys and girls; clothes from a variety of cultures such as saris, shalwar khamis and African obis. In the home corner, equipment should include play food from countries around the world, and utensils such as a wok and a chapatti board as well as saucepans. Dolls and small world toys should reflect male and female, and different minority ethnic groups. It's also possible to buy dolls and small world toys with disabilities.

Encourage the boys to play a caring role such as feeding the baby or cooking the dinner, and the girls to play roles like going to work or driving the car, to counteract the stereotypical gender roles often expressed in children's play.

Puppets play an important part in pretend play. Children who are less confident about speaking may suddenly come to life once they have a puppet in

wwhoo!!!!

their hand. Dolls and puppets can be used to help children come to terms with difficult situations, or to illustrate particular points you want to make. They have been used in most cultures, so they make a good way of introducing children to different cultures. For instance, shadow puppets are used in some Asian traditions, and Chinese dragon puppets are used in the

Chinese New Year celebrations. Children will enjoy making puppets, too. You can make simple ones, for example a paper plate and a stick, or a sock or glove with a face stuck on, or more complicated ones such as papier mache heads with material bodies.

Your role as an adult

You need to:

■ provide space both indoors and out;

■ provide clothes and equipment to reflect a wide range of cultures and occupations, and to counteract traditional stereotypical roles;

■ allow time for the play to develop freely;

■ add materials to extend the play;

■ observe the children and join in only if you think you can add to their learning and enjoyment;

■ encourage the children;

■ challenge any stereotypical or discriminatory language or behaviour.

Mary Townsend

The value of role play
Role play is valuable because it helps children to:
■ come to terms with the world around them

■ try out new ideas, language and behaviour in a safe situation

■ explore their own feelings and the feelings of others

■ experience being a leader

■ learn to care for others

■ relieve stress and aggression

■ develop their imagination

■ co-operate and communicate with others

And above all, they enjoy it!

Join in the craze for gardening and create your very own garden centre in the home corner or outdoor play area. You'll find it teaches children about far more than just plants and flowers

Role play: garden centres

This project could begin with a walk around the local environment looking at the variety of plants and their effect on the environment, or it could begin with a story about a plant growing, such as *Titch*. Families could get involved by talking to the children about their own gardens, about plants in the park or plants that they find on the way home from nursery.

Although this topic at first appears to be particularly strong in the area of Knowledge and Understanding of the World, it also has strengths in promoting literacy and mathematical development. The garden centre is a wonderful way of introducing young children to the use of factual information found in books. There is a wealth of material available including reference books both for children and for adults, free literature from garden centres, as well as specialist magazines.

The role play can help those who already have a garden to appreciate their own

environment but, perhaps more importantly, this topic will be of particular benefit to children who have no garden and may never have grown any plants of their own. The topic develops in children an awareness of their own environment. Through role play in the garden centre children will be encouraged towards positive behaviour and to care and nurture plants and other living things.

Mathematical Development

■ **Say and use number names in order and in familiar contexts.**
Encourage the children to count plants ready for the trays and give them opportunities to use real coins of small denomination and to count the change.

■ **Count reliably up to ten everyday objects.**
Perhaps one of the most obvious counting opportunities is counting flower pots.

■ **Recognise numerals 1 to 9.**
Encourage the children to do a stock-take of the resources in the garden centre, for example, eight seed trays, three trowels and so on.

■ **Use language such as 'greater', 'smaller', 'heavier' or 'lighter' to compare quantities.**
Fill buckets with dry or wet compost and ask the children to describe the difference when lifting them.

■ **Use language such as 'more' or 'less' to compare two numbers.**
Work with the children in filling a basket or trough with plants and ask them whether the trough needs more plants or less plants. How many plants can we fit in?

■ **In practical activities and discussion begin to use the vocabulary involved in adding and subtracting.**
A child has a tray of ten plants but there is only room to have four plants per pot. Which ones will they choose? Are there enough left for another pot?

■ **Find one more or one less from a number from one to ten.**
Choose six plants for a tub and one more for the middle. How many do you have all together?

■ **Begin to relate addition to combining two groups of objects, and subtraction to 'taking away'.**
Make a pattern using just two sorts of plants, for example, pansies and marigolds. How many plants do we need all together? How many pansies and how many marigolds?

■ **Talk about, recognise and recreate simple patterns.**
Ask the children to design a border and talk about where they would place the plants.

■ **Use language such as 'circle' or 'bigger' to describe the shape and size of solids and flat shapes.**
Have a selection of pots and troughs. Ask one of the children to describe one and see if the others can guess which pot or trough is being described.

■ **Use everyday words to describe position.**
Where would you like me to put this plant?

■ **Use developing mathematical ideas and methods to solve practical problems.**

Resources

Plants (real and made)
Baskets
Trolleys
Displays for plants
Hand-held sprays
Pots, trowels, spades and forks in different sizes
Labels for flowers and plants
Signs:
- Sale
- Cash desk
- Please pay here
Deckchairs
Sunloungers
Parasols
Gravel
Compost
Sand

If the topic is planned in advance, many of the resources can be gathered from families who are willing to lend spare flower pots or give pots of silk/plastic flowers that are no longer used at home. The children can be involved in growing some of the plants from seed.

Building a Portfolio Level 2 • • •

Cross-Curricular

How can I fit all the pots into a tray to take home? Do I need a bigger tray?

Communication, Language and Literacy

■ **Use language to imagine and recreate roles and experiences.**

Work with the children in a role play situation. Be a customer seeking advice from the manager or the shop assistant.

■ **Use talk to organise, sequence and clarify thinking, ideas, feelings and events.**

Every child should have a turn at being a shop manager and leading a team meeting for the rest of the assistants. 'First I would like you to do ……. and then ………..'

■ **Sustain attentive listening, responding to what they have heard by relevant comments, questions or actions.**

Invite a keen parent or grandparent to talk about their own garden and plants and encourage the children to ask them questions. Some children may be quite expert at gardening already. You could use the idea of 'hot-seating' where a child becomes the expert and other children ask questions.

■ **Interact with others negotiating plans and activities and taking turns in conversations.**

Encourage the children to work in pairs or small groups to plan a model garden together.

■ **Extend their vocabulary, exploring the meanings and sounds of new words.**

Explain how plants have Latin names as well as everyday names. Use words such as compost, grit and fertiliser. Children will recognise their meaning when they are used in context.

■ **Retell narratives in the correct sequence drawing on the language pattern of stories.**

Ask the children to tell the story of their imaginary garden. 'Once upon a time there was a girl who planted a seed ......' Show part of the *The Secret Garden* video or read some of the passages in the book to the children as a starter for the session.

■ **Speak clearly and audibly with confidence and control and show awareness of the listener, for example by their use of conventions such as greetings, 'please' and 'thank you'.**

Whether a shop attendant or cashier, children will naturally use phrases such as 'Can I help you?'

■ **Hear and say initial and final sounds in words, and short vowel sounds within words.**

Provide notices around the garden centre and encourage children to find letters and familiar words.

■ **Link sounds to letters, naming and sounding all letters of the alphabet.**

Using the free brochures advertising plants, encourage the children to look at the letters and words as well as the pictures.

■ **Read a range of familiar and common words and simple sentences independently.**

For example, 'ice cream', 'sale'.

■ **Show an understanding of the elements of stories such as main character, sequence of events, and openings and how information can be found in non-fiction texts, to answer questions about where, who, why and how.**

Use plant reference books. Can the children identify any of the plants in the garden centre? There are many attractive reference books now available for children. Also, encourage children to read stories featuring gardens and plants.

■ **Use a pencil correctly and hold it effectively to form recognisable letters, most**

of which are correctly formed.

Encourage children to write receipts for goods which they have sold or bought.

■ **Use their phonic knowledge to write simple regular words and make phonetically plausible attempts at more complex words.**

Encourage the customers to write a shopping list of items they will need, before they go to the garden centre.

■ **Write their own names and labels and form sentences, sometimes using punctuation.**

People in the garden centre will need identifying so the children can write their own name labels. Work with them to provide labels for the garden centre, including some questions such as, 'Would you like a pond in your garden?'

■ **Attempt writing for various purposes, using features of different forms such as lists, stories and instructions.**

Before children visit the garden centre, encourage them to write their own shopping list. Those who work in the garden centre may write instructions on how to care for plants.

Knowledge and Understanding of the World

■ **Investigate objects and materials by using all of their senses as appropriate.**

The garden is a perfect place for children to explore their senses. The sight and smell of flowers, the textures of different leaves, the taste of herbs or vegetables, the sound of feet crunching on gravel.

■ **Find out about and identify some features of living things, objects and events that they observe.**

Children will do this when they take care of plants and should be encouraged to discuss their findings.

■ **Look closely at similarities, differences, patterns and change.**

Encourage the children to talk about what they notice when they are working with the plants, about the similarities and differences and how they change.

■ **Ask questions about why things happen and how things work.**
Reference books may be useful here. Children can find out the different conditions that plants need to enable them to grow and how the weather affects them.

■ **Build and construct with a wide range of objects, selecting appropriate resources and adapting their work when necessary.**
If possible, use a variety of wooden planks and real bricks and let the children work together to create a temporary patio.

■ **Select the tools and techniques they need to shape, assemble and join the materials they are using.**
During their work in the garden centre children will be developing their abilities and skills using tools appropriately. Through experience they will find out when a trowel is more useful than a fork. They will also have an opportunity to assemble materials, for example, constructing a flower trough using either natural or made materials.

■ **Find out about and identify the uses of technology in their everyday lives and use computers and programmed toys to support their learning.**
Talk to the children about the benefits of keeping a list of their stock on the computer.

■ **Find out about past and present events in their own lives and those of their families and other people they know.**
Ask the children to talk to their own families about their gardens and about how they may have changed recently or over longer periods of time.

■ **Observe, find out about and identify features in the place they live and the natural world.**
Take the children on a short walk and encourage them to look at the plants around them in the natural and in the made environment.

■ **Find out about their environment and talk about those features they like and dislike.**
Ask the children to consider the effects of plants on the environment in the different seasons and in different environments.

Creative Development

■ **Explore colour, texture, shape, form and space in two or three dimensions.**
There is a great tradition of garden and flower painting in this country. Give children the opportunity to examine reproductions and then to express their own feelings about flowers using a variety of media - cellophane, paints, pastels and pencils. Children may also wish to make their own pots out of wood or clay.

■ **Recognise and explore how sounds can be changed, sing simple songs from memory, recognise repeated sounds and sound patterns and match movements to music.**
There are many sounds that can be made using garden implements. This work is probably best done outside because of the noise, but try shaking gravel in a tray. Does it make a difference if it is in a metal tray or a plastic tray? Use the metal trowels, the wooden sticks and the plastic pots to scrape and tap!

■ **Respond in a variety of ways to what they see, hear, smell, touch and feel.**
Provide a large bowl of wet compost in which the children can dip their feet. Work with the children in describing the feeling of cold compost squidging through their toes and together, write a shared poem.

■ **Use their imagination in art and design, music, dance, imaginative and role play and stories.**

Be dramatic - go into the garden centre and complain about a plant you bought recently that is now dying. How are the children going to react?

■ **Express and communicate their ideas, thoughts and feelings by using a widening range of materials, suitable tools, imaginative and role play, movement, designing and making and a variety of songs and instruments.**
Encourage the children to work in groups, perhaps to perform a mime.

Physical Development

■ **Move with confidence, imagination and in safety.**
It is important that children learn how to carry things safely. The garden centre needs children to work together in carrying heavy buckets and delicate plants.

■ **Move with control and co-ordination.**
The children will need to devise ways of delivering plants safely and balancing pots.

■ **Show awareness of space, of themselves and of others.**
Working together in a role play situation will encourage children to become more aware of each other and to use phrases such as 'excuse me' when moving past another person.

■ **Recognise the importance of keeping healthy and those things which contribute to this.**
Most of this role play is likely to take place out of doors. Talk to the children about the importance of fresh air. Talk to them about how plants keep healthy and how important it is that we too keep healthy and what is it that keeps us healthy.

■ **Recognise the changes that happen to their bodies when they are active.**
As human beings we all need physical exercise. Children need to have the opportunity to jump and to run and we need to make sure that they are aware of the changes that happen when they do so.

■ **Use a range of small and large equipment.**

Children will be using trowels, big forks and small forks. They will be doing heavy work and delicate work transplanting little seedlings and manipulating dowelling and rods.

■ **Travel around, under, over and through balancing and climbing equipment.**
Take the children on a walk to the park. Talk about the purpose and pleasure derived from parks and let the children exercise on the equipment in the play area.

■ **Handle tools, objects, construction and malleable materials safely and with increasing control.**
Gardening tools need skillful handling. The children need to become aware of the care needed in handling plants and safe ways of using equipment and tools.

Personal, Social and Emotional Development

■ **Be confident to try new activities, initiate ideas and speak in a familiar group.**
Role play is the perfect way to encourage those who are not very confident to take part in speaking, to initiate ideas and to gain confidence.

■ **Maintain attention, concentrate and sit quietly when appropriate.**
Give children the opportunity to report back to talk about their 'day in the life of a garden centre manager', for example.

■ **Continue to be interested, excited and motivated to learn.**
Most children enjoy role play situations. Those children who are confident may like to talk about their new ideas. Perhaps the children could have a shared question/suggestion board which can be shared with the whole group and will motivate learning.

■ **Have a developing awareness of their own needs, views and feelings and be sensitive to the needs, views and feelings of others.**

As a manager, or as a customer, you have to be aware of other people's views and feelings.

■ **Have a developing respect for their own cultures and beliefs and those of other people.**
There are cultural traditions about flowers and plants. Flowers tend to be bought and given on both happy and sad occasions and children can talk about this. When have they seen a lot of flowers? What did they symbolise?

■ **Respond to significant experiences, showing a range of feelings when appropriate.**
The life cycle of the plant engages us in wonder - from when the seed shoots to when the first bud bursts into bloom.

■ **Form good relationships with adults and peers.**
It is not enough to provide role play situations. In order to make it good adults have to be involved in the role play with the children, not to dominate but to take the lead from the children and intervene sensitively.

■ **Work as part of a group or class, taking turns and sharing fairly, understanding that there need to be agreed values and codes of behaviour for groups of people, including adults and children, to work together harmoniously.**

Ask the children what would happen if we did not work together in the garden centre.

■ **Understand what is right, what is wrong, and why.**
Through the practical experience of caring for plants the children will begin to understand why pulling the heads off flowers, or killing plants, is so destructive.

■ **Dress and undress independently and manage their own personal hygiene.**
Gardeners need protective clothing. Talk to children about their wellington boots, gloves, aprons or sun hats to wear in the garden centre. They also need to be aware of the need to wash their hands when they have touched plants or compost.

■ **Select and use activities and resources independently.**
Role play situations give children confidence to carry out activities and use resources independently.

■ **Consider the consequences of their words and actions for themselves and others.**
How does it feel to create a nice environment using plants? How would it feel if that environment was spoilt by vandalism? Why do we give plants and how are they received?

■ **Understand that people have different needs, views, cultures and beliefs that need to be treated with respect.**
Find out about the flowers that represent different things in different traditions. Talk about the allergies that people have to certain plants and the healing benefits of others.

■ **Understand that they can expect others to treat their needs, views, cultures and beliefs with respect.**
If we share in creating a beautiful environment using plants and flowers we need to expect that others will treat that with respect. Flowers and plants are used in times of joy and sorrow. Those times need to be treated with respect.

Naomi Compton

Building a Portfolio Level 2 • • •

The books and other materials we read have a profound effect on the way we look at life. It is, therefore, vital that you choose children's books with great care

Choosing books
for young children

You need to provide children with a wide variety of books which are enjoyable, stimulating and meaningful to them. Don't be tempted to buy cheap, poor quality books. It's better to have a few good quality ones, and supplement them by borrowing from the library while you build up your supply of books.

Most good bookshops provide a wide selection, but there are specialist educational suppliers such as Letterbox, Community Insight and Roving Books who are particularly aware of equal opportunities issues.

Check your books regularly to make sure that they are suitable and also in good repair. You can't expect children to value books if they are torn and tattered.

You will probably have many of the well-loved traditional stories such as 'The Gingerbread Man', 'Red Riding Hood' and 'The Three Little Pigs' on your bookshelves. It's important to keep these, but because they tend to show stereotypical roles and have a white European emphasis, you need to balance them with books which give the children a wider view of the world. Some books, such as 'The Hunchback of Notre Dame', are not suitable at all because they show people with disabilities in a negative way. The check-list below will help you to choose a good selection of books:

■ **Are the illustrations good and in a variety of styles?**
Look for good quality illustrations with the relevant picture next to the text. Some should be clear and bold, others can have more detail. Small books or books with detailed illustrations are fine for use with one or two children, but for larger groups you will need large, clear illustrations. You

---

Why do you need to provide books for children?
■ Firstly, because children of all ages love them!
■ It's a good sharing time between the child(ren) and adult
■ It encourages children to respect books
■ It prepares children for reading and writing
■ It helps language development
■ It extends children's experience of the world they live in
■ It helps intellectual development
■ It encourages imagination and creativity
■ It helps them to come to terms with anxieties and fears

---

can get big book versions from many publishers now, including old favourites like *The Very Hungry Caterpillar* by Eric Carle (Puffin) and *Not Now, Bernard!* by David McKee (Red Fox).

■ **Do they reflect the children's own experience and interests?**
Many older books show a middle class white family living in a detached house with a large garden. Look for stories situated in a town, too, where people live in flats or terraced houses, like *Lucy and Tom Go to School* by Shirley Hughes (Puffin). Choose stories which reflect the children's own experiences, like going swimming, shopping, to the playground, to the doctor.

■ **Do they show people from different cultural and ethnic backgrounds?**
Look for stories which have a black child as the main character, such as *David and the Tooth Fairy* by Wendy Webb (W Webb Books) or *Boxed in* by Ann Sibley O'Brien. Include books which help the children to learn more about different cultures and religions, and ones which include children and adults from different backgrounds as a natural part of

the book, whether fact or fiction.

■ **Do they show girls and boys, women and men in non-traditional roles?**
Some older books show the little girl in the kitchen helping mum with the cooking, and the boy outside with dad, doing DIY or playing football. You need to look for books where dad is in the caring role or doing the washing up, such as *Jamaica's Find* (Houghton Muffin), or mum going out to work or doing interesting things, like in *Alex's Bed*.

■ **Do they show people with disabilities in a positive role?**
There is now a growing number of stories in which a child or an adult with a disability plays a leading role, such as *Are We There Yet?* by Clare Beaton (bsmall) and the Lucy and Letang stories.

■ **Do they include dual language books?**
Many of the well-loved favourites, like *Where's Spot?* by Eric Hill (Puffin) and *Peace at Last* by Jill Murphy (Macmillan), are available in two languages. It's important that children see and hear different languages, so that they accept this as a normal part of life, instead of something to be ridiculed. For bilingual children, it's especially important that they experience books which they can relate to.

■ **Do they include information books, song and rhyme books, funny books, poetry, books without words, books they have made themselves?**
You need to aim for as wide a variety of books as possible, both for children to use by themselves and for you to share with them. Don't forget that children love books they have helped to make – it may be a scrap book with photographs of an outing with captions you or they have

---

written or a story they have produced with a word processor and illustrated.

■ Are they appropriate for the age of the children?

Babies need tough books – board, cloth or plastic – to use on their own, but they will enjoy proper books with an adult. Pictures should be simple, brightly coloured and of things they will recognise.

By the age of two, children will enjoy simple stories, nursery rhymes, and novelty books. Stories should be about families' everyday experiences, with simple text and uncluttered pictures.

By three years old children will be handling books well if they have been taught properly. They will be interested in a wider range of stories which will still be quite short but are becoming more complex. They will enjoy traditional tales like 'The Gingerbread Man' and 'The Little Red Hen', which have repetitive lines for them to join in with, books about special events like birthdays, books about everyday events, and songs and rhymes.

Between four and eight children are enjoying increasingly complex stories on many different themes, both fiction and information. Books will often be used as part of a theme or topic. They will enjoy fantasy and funny stories. From about the age of four, children will be beginning to learn to read, and as this skill progresses they will enjoy reading by themselves, but they will still enjoy listening to an adult reading to them. Seven- and eight-year-olds will enjoy a book with chapters which you can read a little of each day.

Encouraging children to use the books

We must show children that we enjoy and value books. If we give children experience of books from an early age it will help them to develop a positive attitude to books and reading. This means that you should be sharing books with children on a daily basis, both in formal story times and informally, one to one in the book corner when the opportunity arises. Children should also have free access to books during play sessions.

Look at the book corner in your setting. Is it inviting and comfortable? Are the books in good condition and displayed attractively? Can the children reach them easily? If you think it needs improving, give it a facelift.

Telling tales

You should aim to have a story and singing session every day. The length of the session will depend on the age of the child - for two-year-olds ten minutes is as long as they will manage to sit still, and you would need to divide this into a very short story followed by some singing and finger rhymes. For three- and four-year-olds, 20 minutes is plenty. It's better to make it a special time each day, so that the children get used to it – perhaps in the middle or at the end of the session, or straight after mealtimes when you want the children to have a rest.

You don't always need to have a book for storytelling. Try telling stories you know without a book or, if you can, make up your own. You can use props or visual aids to help you – for instance, objects included in the story, toys, puppets, hats, picture cards on a display board, or musical instruments. These props will be invaluable when telling a story to a child with a sensory impairment.

Involve the children in the story as much as you can. How you organise this will depend on the story and the age of the children – you might want to tell the whole story through and then let the children comment, or let them join in as you go. Try not to lose the continuity of the story with too much interruption.

Songs and rhymes

Singing and rhymes have all the benefits that stories have for children and more – the rhythm and pattern of songs, rhymes and poetry is particularly beneficial for language development, especially for children whose first language is not English. There is also a greater mutual involvement of the adult and the children – when you are all singing together there is a lot of eye contact and attention. Using actions increases the enjoyment and concentration for younger children and those who have limited language, because they can do the actions

even if they don't know, or are unable to say, all the words.

There are some good song, rhyme and poetry books available, so if you can, have a selection of these for all of the staff to use. Another lovely idea is to make a collection of your own favourites. You can write or word-process these and collect them into a folder. Illustrate them yourself or look for postcards and pictures to illustrate them. If you protect them with plastic pockets, the children can use them, too.

You can use books and stories in a variety of ways:
- as a starting point for a topic
- as a starting point for music, drama or role play
- to enhance an interest table
- as a learning tool for counting, colour, alphabet and so on
- as a means of finding information

All the time you are developing children's pre-reading and pre-writing skills through the use of books, stories and rhymes. Very young children will be unaware of the difference between pictures and print, but they will gradually become aware that the print is associated with the words you are saying.

You can help them to understand this by following the words with your finger as you say them. You can also use other opportunities like reading labels on food, road names, words on lorries and buses. By writing what children have told you about their pictures or models you will reinforce the link between reading and writing. If you make sure they have access to writing materials, they will begin to do this for themselves, using 'play' writing.

Once children start school they will begin to create their own stories and accounts – at first these may be dictated to the teacher and copied, but they will quickly begin to write for themselves, especially if they have been given the right experiences in the early years setting.

Mary Townsend

Storytelling takes many forms. It can be an active session led by you, drawing upon the children's comments and experiences, or it can be child-led. Use it to teach, to focus attention, to entertain or simply to relax - but use it!

How to tell a good story

Any time is a good time to create or tell a story, although it is best in an informal and comfortable setting, such as circle time. It doesn't matter who is telling the story or which story is being told; it will expand the language and stretch the imaginations of both you and the children. If you've never tried it before and aren't sure how to start, here are a few suggestions.

I spy a story

Try playing 'I spy' then make up a story which connects the spied objects. It doesn't matter if it is nonsensical - should it bother your children, they will be quick to let you know and suggest another word instead. These stories often produce much laughter and are brilliant for enhancing the imagination.

All join in!

In a circle, try creating your own story together by asking the children to contribute a few words in turn. You can add detail and dimension to the story as it goes around. It can be helpful to use an object, for example a hat or a ball, which is passed to the teller in turn. This keeps the attention of the rest of the group and forms a focus on the child telling his or her part of the story.

The interactive story

The interactive story is a lively and exciting form of storytelling. It can be done with one or more adults and/or puppets. The interesting thing about this kind of storytelling is that it is child-led. The story can, for example, be about an adventure into a magic land. Lead the children to key points where their involvement is spontaneous, often physical as well as verbal. Co-operative skills are used as together, they solve clues and achieve goals.

Poems and rhymes

The rhythm and metre of a poem encourages children to remember the words and structure of a story, as they recite and think ahead. This inspires confidence in expression. Another essential part of using poetry in storytelling is the introduction of voice work, such as the importance of diction and pronunciation. Simultaneously, the child is learning to control his or her

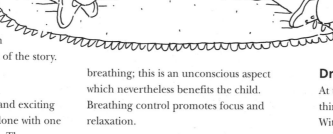

breathing; this is an unconscious aspect which nevertheless benefits the child. Breathing control promotes focus and relaxation.

Actions as well as words

Extended active storytelling is a creative way of letting the children tell the story in an active improvised situation. Taking a simple tale – say 'The Three Little Pigs' – divide your group into three, in this case 'the pigs', 'the market sellers' and 'the wolves'. The groups act out the story with simple actions

and words. A discussion is held after each telling and then the children act out the story again, adding more detail each time. Once they are happy with their story, the final performance can be shown to an audience. This is a good exercise for the more introverted child, as within a group he can express himself more freely, using the support of his fellow actors. It also makes a complete story less daunting to act as it is done in stages.

Statue storytelling

This is the telling of stories without words. One by one, each child takes a posed position, adding to the story tableau. This can be done in a line or in a free shape of any kind. This activity encourages children to think about the story they are telling in a different way – visually. It also promotes physical development as the children learn to balance and hold a pose. It is important to let the children come out one at a time and look at their statue, so they may reflect on its development. It is effective to use music during this activity (make sure it is in keeping with the theme).

Dream stories

At the end of a busy day or activity, to calm things down, try imaginative dream stories. With the children lying down in their own space, ask them to close their eyes and picture the story you tell them. Dream stories can be very real so be constantly aware of each child's reaction. You may find some so absorbed that they are fast asleep - wake them gently!

Explore different ways

As you become more confident in your

storytelling, try to explore different methods to find the language which will engage the children in your group. Think about words which appeal to different senses. Some children are more in tune with one sense than the others. The three main senses to identify in a child are:

- Visual – the visual child sees the world;
- Auditory – the auditory child hears the world;
- Kinaesthetic – the kinaesthetic child feels the world.

It is possible to identify which method of learning is appropriate to which child.

Try to be aware of these various types of learning and include a variety of visual, auditory and kinaesthetic words in your stories. Extra materials such as pictures and music will satisfy the visual and auditory children, and props to touch and pass around will encourage the kinaesthetic children. Using these different techniques together in a group will encourage each child to develop their other senses whilst engaging them in the story.

Emily Cannon and Kathini Cameron

Bringing a story to life

To tell a story - whether it be 'The Three Little Pigs' or a short story off the top of your head - there are a few things to bear in mind if you want to bring it to life.

- When telling active stories, it is often a good idea to have a warm-up, both physical and vocal, to prepare staff and children for the activity. Spend five minutes patting your bodies from head to toe, then stretching out from neck to finger tips, finishing with a shake-out of any sleepy parts (don't forget the face in all of this). Warm up the mouth and voice with repetitions of letters of the alphabet, for example: 'm' 'm' 'm', 'd' 'd' 'd', and 'o' 'o' 'o'. Then encourage them to change the volume and tone. Putting their hands on their chests will enable them to 'feel' their sounds, and will also help them to concentrate on what they are doing.

- Remember your physical position in relation to the children. Don't always sit in front on a chair. Try lying on the floor in a circle, heads together; you can begin or end a story very powerfully in this position.

- Eye contact is important. Your face creates the picture, so try to use as much of it as possible. Raise your eyebrows and open your eyes - or try closing one completely and squinting through the other. A moment in the mirror with an imaginary piece of toffee in your mouth will show you just how much the muscles in your face can move!

- The way we use our voice can invoke vivid pictures in the mind of a child. It can bring a character to life and make a place feel cold, windy and wet. Don't forget:
  Volume – from a whisper to a shout
  Tone – from a high to low
  Variation – try a lisp or a stutter

- Hands, arms and shoulders can also be expressive without moving them much. Experiment.

- Props can be useful, too - a puppet (something simple like a sock with some button eyes and a tongue), or use a hat or a feather for characters in a story.

- To keep the group focused and in control, have a sound or an action which all the children understand when used means 'Keep quiet and keep still'! They may imitate you, by putting hands on top of heads for example - the action in itself often helps resume the focus.

You can sing nursery rhymes every day, every week or even plan a term's activities around a topic on them, and they never lose their appeal or value.

Using nursery rhymes

Nursery rhymes need to be sung and recited regularly so that children can learn the words, rhythms and tunes. You might set aside time to do this at the end of a group session. You can also use them for gaining attention at the start of a session, particularly with new children who may know some of the rhymes from home. This is where the old favourites, such as 'Baa, baa, black sheep' and 'Humpty Dumpty' come in useful. You may prefer to plan a weekly or twice-weekly session where you introduce new rhymes and sing and recite rhymes that the children know well.

When you introduce a new nursery rhyme, start off with an enticing summary to capture children's imagination. For instance, ask them to imagine jumping in a puddle so deep that it goes right up to their tummy ('Doctor Foster'). Sing or recite the rhyme over and over three or four times, encouraging the children to join in when they feel ready. Go on to sing the rhyme daily, slipping it in at the start of a group session such as story time until the children know it well. It can then be added to the repertoire of rhymes that you use regularly.

Nursery rhymes can be used in all sorts of everyday situations. Have as many up your sleeve as possible and aim to respond to different situations with something appropriate. For example, 'Diddle, diddle, dumpling' (one shoe off and one shoe on) when changing into wellies; 'Incy Wincy Spider' when you spot a spider in the sink; 'Doctor Foster' (he stepped in a puddle/right up to his middle) when children are playing outside in the rain.

What to choose

When it comes to deciding what to recite and sing, the most important consideration is the children's enjoyment. Give them plenty of opportunity to make requests. Use a nursery rhyme wheel (see below) or look through a collection of rhymes to remind children of the choice.

Always be aware of cultural considerations and subject matter that might be offensive to some families. You may feel that a few nursery rhymes are inappropriate ('Three blind mice', for example) and you will need to decide whether to boycott these or include them as an accurate portrayal of our past. There is no reason why you should not adapt the original. I have often made use of my grandmother's version of 'Little Miss Muffet' where the spider ends up asking Miss Muffet to play, rather than frightening her away.

Planning how to use rhymes

Communication, Language and Literacy is the area of learning we tend to associate most closely with nursery rhymes and this is the main focus for the activities described below. However, the activities also cover many other areas, in particular Creative and Physical Development through singing, role play, percussion, making up your own rhymes and art work; and Personal, Social and Emotional Development through co-operative activities, sharing resources and developing a group book and shared nursery rhyme corner.

You can use counting rhymes such as 'One, two, buckle my shoe' to promote Mathematical Development or build a topic (Knowledge and Understanding of the World) from one of the nursery rhymes your children have enjoyed such as weather ('Doctor Foster', 'Incy Wincy Spider'); animals ('Little Bo Peep', 'Little Boy Blue'); growing things ('Mary, Mary, Quite Contrary').

Nursery rhyme wheel

A nursery rhyme wheel is a useful resource if you are planning a number of different nursery rhyme activities. Use it whenever you want to choose a rhyme for singing, percussion or role play. Include old favourites as well as new rhymes you want to introduce to the children.

You will need: two circles of card, one slightly larger in diameter than the other; a brass paper-fastener; labelled pictures of different nursery rhymes.

Making the nursery rhyme wheel: prepare pictures of your chosen nursery rhymes, either by drawing, tracing or cutting illustrations from an old nursery rhyme book. Cut a triangular window out of the

larger circle, leaving the rim intact. Divide the smaller wheel into segments and stick a picture onto each segment, making sure that each picture is upright (like the numbers on a clock). Check that the pictures fit into the window and draw a thick black line around each picture so that it is clear where one ends and the next begins. Tape a card tab to the back of the picture circle and join the two circles at the centre with the brass paper-fastener. Check that the join is loose enough for the lower circle to be moved around easily with the tab. Hold the top circle and move the bottom circle so that different pictures appear in the window.

Use the wheel for sorting. Gather items or pictures of items that have some connection with the rhymes on the wheel, for example, an egg and a wall built from plastic bricks ('Humpty Dumpty'); a small bucket of water and a picture of a well ('Jack and Jill'); a posy of flowers and a handkerchief ('Ring a ring o' roses'); a jam tart and a playing card of the queen of hearts ('The Queen of Hearts'). For older children, include labels with the name or first line of the rhymes.

Place the items on a low table. Set out mats for each rhyme with the name of the rhyme at the top of the mat. Ask the children, one at a time, to turn the wheel and identify the nursery rhyme. Sing the rhyme together and then ask the child to choose an item that links with the rhyme and place it on the appropriate mat. Encourage older children to pick the written labels. Continue until all the items have been sorted.

Rhythm activities
Once the children have sung a particular nursery rhyme a few times, you can help them to focus on the rhythm.

You will need: a range of percussion instruments; nursery rhyme cassette tapes or CDs; jingle bells; fabric strips; Velcro.

Beating out the rhythm: help younger ones simply to sing the tune or recite the rhyme in time with you. As their sense of rhythm develops, they can go on to clap out the rhythm and use simple percussion instruments. Choose rhymes with a straightforward rhythm, such as 'Baa, baa, black sheep'.

Older ones can try rhymes with a more complex rhythm, such as 'Hickory, dickory, dock'. Use a range of percussion instruments and include choices that fit in with the content of the rhyme – jingle bells for 'Ride a cock horse', for example. Once older children are familiar with the rhythm of a few rhymes, you can use the nursery rhyme wheel and a book to show two different rhymes and ask the children to guess which rhyme you are clapping.

Dancing to the rhythm: using either a recorded version of a nursery rhyme or a piano, create a dance based on the rhythm of a nursery rhyme. Keep it simple with very young children; choose a circle or line format and plan straightforward movements such as stamping and clapping. If you go for a line, have an adult standing in front of the children and facing the same way, to help demonstrate the movements. Older ones can try hops, jumps, pointing toes, counting the number of steps forwards and backwards

Rhyme activities
Nursery rhymes are a rich source of rhyming words. Try the following activities to help the children develop their own ability to recognise and use rhyme.

You will need: nursery rhyme posters, books or the rhyme written out by hand; sticky notes; Blu-tack; blank cards; a white board and two different coloured pens.

Filling in the rhyming words: as soon as the children know a nursery rhyme, leave out the end words for them to fill in as you sing. With older pre-school children, use the rhyme in its written format and cover over the rhyming words with a sticky note. When the children have said the missing words, peel off the labels so they can see what the words look like.

Making up your own rhymes: for a group of older children, perhaps in preparation for the Literacy Hour, choose a nursery rhyme that yields lots of rhyming words, such as 'Humpty Dumpty'. Write up the first few lines on the white board and make a list of words that have the same rime as 'w-all' and 'f-all': 'all', 'ball', 'call', 'hall', 'tall' and so on. Use a red pen to write each word on a card and try out different rhyming words by sticking a card to the end of the line with Blu-tack: 'Humpty Dumpty sat on the ball'; 'Humpty Dumpty sat on the hall …'

You can also experiment with changing a whole line to accommodate a new word: 'Humpty Dumpty is very tall', 'Humpty Dumpty played with his ball'. When you are all happy with your new version, write out the end results.

Alliteration and phonological awareness
Some nursery rhyme characters have alliterative names, such as Lucy Locket, Peter Piper or Jack and Jill, and this can be used to inspire children to create their own. Sound awareness can also be developed by playing with nonsense words.

You will need: a white board and different coloured pens; plastic letters.

Playing with alliteration: choose a nursery rhyme character with an alliterative name. Emphasise that the initial sound and letter is the same and make up some new alliterative names to fit into the rhyme. To maintain the rhyming pattern, you can keep the rime of the second word – so

'Lucy Locket/Lost her pocket' might become 'Susie Socket /Lost her pocket'; 'Jack and Jill' could become 'Wendy and Will', and so on. Make a note of your new versions.

Playing with nonsense words: the nonsense words in rhymes such as 'Hickory, dickory, dock' or 'Hickety, pickety, my black hen' provide another good opportunity to develop awareness of initial sounds. Write out the original words on the white board and then change the initial letters with a different coloured pen to create new versions such as 'Lickory, tickory, mock'. Those children who are able to associate sounds and symbols can use plastic letters to place at the start of each word. Try out the different words and decide which you and the group like best.

Write out your new nursery rhymes, involving the children as much as possible. Ask them to illustrate the rhymes and make them into a book. Encourage the children to come up with a title for their book and make sure that the authors' names are added to the front cover.

Nursery rhyme boxes

A box of items linked with a specific rhyme appeals to children and is a good way of getting them to explore and play with nursery rhymes independently. Once the children have learned a new rhyme, make up a box for it.

What you will need: sturdy, lidded boxes, preferably in different colours; pictures of the rhymes; an illustrated and laminated version of each rhyme; a cassette tape with a range of recordings; items that link with each rhyme.

Making up the boxes: decide on the rhyme you want to use. Find or draw a picture that relates to the rhyme to stick on the lid – this will tell the children which nursery rhyme the box contains.

Write out or type up the rhyme and mount it onto thin card. Trace or draw illustrations and laminate or cover with clear plastic. If possible, link the box and the rhyme – use

A nursery rhyme box for 'Jack and Jill' could include:

- a dolls' house model of a boy and a girl
- dressing-up clothes
- a small bucket
- ready cut 'well' shapes with paper bricks and pens for decorating the well
- a square of green fabric and cardboard boxes for making a hill
- brown wrapping paper, cotton wool and a bottle labelled 'vinegar'
- a small blanket for making Jack's bed

the same colour for the box and card or the same picture on the lid and the card so that children can put the card back in the correct box. Add a short cassette tape, with a variety of recordings of the rhyme. These could consist of a commercial recording and the children's versions .

Other possible items include a series of laminated pictures to be put in order showing the narrative sequence of the rhyme; your own group version of a rhyme; copies of the rhyme with words missing for older children to write in, or boxes for drawings; small percussion instruments so that children can play along to the rhyme. The remaining items will depend on the rhyme.

Once you have completed a box, compile a laminated list of contents, preferably with the same colour or picture coding as the box.

Using the boxes: the boxes are suitable for all age groups, although you may want to work with younger ones to ensure that they get the most out of them. You may prefer not to keep the writing, drawing or sticking activities in the boxes so that you can monitor their use.

Introduce the children to the items in the box. Show them how to use the tape recorder if necessary. Emphasise the importance of putting everything back in the box once they have finished with it. Show older children the list of contents and help them to read out the name of each item, replace it in the box and tick it off with a felt pen (the laminated surface can be wiped clean once the list is complete.)

A nursery rhyme corner

Think of a nursery rhyme corner as an interactive display. Use it to display a collection of books and other associated activities as a way of encouraging children to explore nursery rhymes.

You will need: several nursery rhyme collections and books that use nursery rhyme characters; a low table for display; floor cushions; posters and pictures of nursery rhyme characters; any other linked activities such as nursery rhyme boxes.

Setting up the corner: gather a range of nursery rhyme books. Try to include books with different formats and styles of illustration: a small paperback, a large hardback treasury of nursery rhymes, books with pictures in a traditional style or genuine historical illustrations, such as Kate Greenaway, books with bright simple pictures, and so on.

Display the books on a low table and add some floor cushions so that the children can sit and read in comfort. Make large collage posters of nursery rhyme characters to help decorate the corner. This is also the place to store your tape recorder and nursery rhyme cassettes, nursery rhyme boxes, your own book of nursery rhyme versions and the nursery rhyme wheel (checking first that it is robust enough for free use – try laminating the circles before assembling).

Using the book collection: encourage the children to explore the book collection and bring in their own examples from home. Whenever possible, sit down with the children and share the books. With younger ones, read and sing the rhymes and talk about the pictures. With older ones, use the nursery rhyme wheel to select a rhyme and see if you can find it in each collection. Discuss different wordings and illustrations. Which do the children prefer? Look at the books that use a nursery rhyme as a basis for a new story or rhyme and see if the child can find the original upon which it is based.

Hilary White

Some children enjoy writing and mark making, others find the physical mastery involved in using a pencil a chore. The key to encouraging children is motivation. Here's a way to get children writing that allows everyone to do as much or as little as they want, and is guaranteed to enthuse even the least interested

Reasons for writing

The Early Learning Goals suggest as a stepping stone to early writing that practitioners 'Make books with children of activities they have been doing, using photographs of the children as illustrations'. Photos are such a sure fire way to engage children that it seems a shame purely to use them as illustrations. Instead why not make the photos central to the activity and the writing a natural by-product of children wanting to communicate something?

Photo cards

Make photo cards with very young children. Take a number of photos of them in the setting and then let them choose which one they think is the best. Mount it on card and ask them to write their name underneath. You can add a line at the bottom for you to write the name or add a computer printed version. Laminate the cards or cover them with sticky-backed plastic and let children play with them, set up galleries or use them to write their friends' names or practise their own.

Photo books

As children get a little older simple concertina books with four pages work really well. Use sturdy card and they will stand up, even under the weight of the photos. Straightforward themes work best: 'My family', 'My favourite things', 'My day'. These books are a great way to bring together children's lives outside

If children are not ready to use a camera by themselves, let them help decide what to take pictures of and to choose the best results for the albums. Even young children can get reasonable results with a simple camera, however. I have used Boots children's cameras, for example, with four-year-olds with remarkable success. Digital cameras are even better because children can instantly see the picture they have taken and re-take it if it is not quite right. Digital cameras also mean no film or developing costs and give children an exciting experience of using ICT.

and inside the setting. A book about 'My day', for example, could start with a photo of the child eating breakfast or end with a picture of the child going to bed. If parents and carers don't have access to a camera and the nursery camera can't be lent out, then pictures of children leaving or arriving at the setting could be used or children could draw pictures.

Photo albums

Albums can be short and themed or long and simply a record of the year as it progresses. Whilst both have merit, themed albums are more unusual and can involve older children more actively in taking the photos. The process is a valuable one, encouraging children to make decisions, discuss their reasoning, problem solve when things go wrong and learn to be creative with a new tool. It's also a great activity to ask a parent helper to work with children on.

Good themes

Whilst children may eventually be able to suggest their own themes for albums some good ideas to begin with include: 'Making soup', 'Our art gallery', 'A trip to the local shops', 'A special visitor', making a new imaginary play setting or playing a favourite game. Children could also be asked to create an album that shows their nursery/playgroup to use with all visitors or more personal albums such as 'My birthday' to take home or 'What I have learned' to take on to their next setting.

Writing the captions

Children will have been aware of the purpose and theme of the album even before the first photo was taken. As they discuss the photos and then talk through the results, possible captions should be easy to agree upon. Try asking children what they wanted to show

with this picture and let them decide on the form of words. The beauty of captions is that they can be short or long and that the value in writing them comes as much from agreeing what to say as it does from physically forming the letters. Ask for a volunteer to write each caption. Let children decide whether or not they want their captions to be in 'proper' writing or whether they can try to spell things for themselves and only give them help in spelling if they ask for it.

Which albums to use

There are advantages and disadvantages to most types of album. A lot depends on how often you think the album will be used. The most durable are the peel-back page albums or using hole-punched laminated card to make your own. These also make adding children's captions straightforward. They are often, however, the most difficult for children to use independently and make moving the photos difficult. Sleeve albums have no obvious place for captions and are likely to fall to pieces. Perhaps the best idea is to use photo corners in a scrap book where captions can be written directly beneath each picture or, if these are not robust enough, consider using smaller pre-made books. If you have a long arm stapler, some thin card for the cover and sugar paper for the pages you could even make your own.

Jo Graham

Chapter 6

Unit E1: Maintain an attractive, stimulating and reassuring environment for children

About this unit

This unit is about how you help to keep the environment in your setting attractive, stimulating and reassuring for the children. You need to think about how you do this both indoors and outdoors. Think, too, about different sorts of areas, such as those used specifically as play areas and those also used as living areas - particularly relevant for childminders who work in their own home.

As an assistant, you will not usually be fully responsible for the environment in your setting, but you need to understand why it's organised the way it is, and take a part in maintaining it. You will be involved in setting out and tidying away, so think about how you do this so that you are encouraging children to become more independent. Can they take things out and put things away easily? Do toys and equipment look attractive, and can children see what they are, so that they are encouraged to use them? Do you encourage children to put things away tidily in the right place? Are they encouraged to display the things they have made?

Links with other units

The unit is closely linked to E2, which is about safety, so you may like to do the two together. For instance, Element E1.1 is 'Maintain the physical environment' and E2.1 is 'Maintain a safe environment'. Your assessor will be able to see evidence for both when she inspects your setting.

If you have finished C8 and C9 you may already have done a display which you could use as part of your evidence for E1.2.

Element 3 is linked to C4.1, 'Help children to adjust to new settings', because for both you need to provide a reassuring environment. Don't forget to make a note of it on your cross referencing sheet. Your assessor will help you with this if necessary.

Values

You must think about the **welfare of the child** for all of the elements. The welfare of the child is paramount in all that you do. As a **reflective practitioner**, think about why the environment is like it is, and see if there are ways you could improve it if you were in a position to do so. There are also references to **keeping children safe** and **children's**

learning and development in each element. When you are setting out activities and displays, you need to ask yourself 'Are the children safe?' and 'What are they learning from this?'

In Element 2 you need to think about **working in partnership with parents** by pointing out displays of their children's work and keeping displays interesting, by changing them frequently. In Element 3, this means agreeing with the parents what comfort objects their child needs and making sure that she has it when she needs it, perhaps at sleep times. You also need to make sure that the equipment used in the setting reflects the different backgrounds of the children.

In terms of **equal opportunities** and **anti-discrimination**, in Element 1 you need to encourage all children to take responsibility for their environment, as appropriate to their abilities, with no gender stereotyping. For instance, encourage both boys and girls to tidy up. In Elements 2 and 3 you need to think about how you **celebrate diversity** through the displays you set up and the equipment and materials you use. Look around your setting and see whether the current displays, materials and equipment reflect a range of cultural groups. Think about this every time you set up a display, not just for religious festivals.

Getting started

In this unit you will need to show how you:

◆ maintain the physical environment

◆ prepare and maintain displays

◆ maintain a reassuring environment

Read through the elements and use your personal skills profile (on page 21) to decide which elements you feel confident about, things you don't understand and need further training in, and things you need to practise or gain more experience in. Discuss this with your assessor and your supervisor if you need to. Then plan with your assessor which evidence you need to gather. She will write an assessment plan, or help you to do it, to make sure that you know what evidence you need to provide.

Element E1.1 Maintain the physical environment

Key issues

You will not have responsibility for the layout of your setting, but you do need to know why things are set out the way they are. Ask if you can read your setting's Ofsted inspection report, so that you know what the requirements are. Your setting should also have a copy of the National Standards for Under Eights Day Care which you will find useful to read. Some early years settings are purpose-built with children in mind, but most have been converted from other use. Many nurseries are in large houses. Playgroups tend to be in church or village halls. Childminders and nannies look after children in the home. All of these areas have to be adapted to suit children's needs.

If your setting is in a church hall or other large space, have the staff divided it up into smaller sections, to create different play areas and make it more homely so that the children feel secure? Do you have adequate heat, ventilation and lighting to keep the children healthy and comfortable? Do you have a safe outdoor play area? If not, how do you make sure that children get outside to play as much as possible? If your setting is in a home, either your own or your employer's, how do you make sure that there is enough space for the children to play in, safe from hazards? Are you able to give children a full range of activities, including sand and water play? If your setting is in a converted house, how do you make space for group games and physical activities? Is the furniture easily moveable?

The layout of the setting can affect the way children play. For instance, if there are big open spaces, children are more likely to run about and become boisterous and noisy. If the room is separated into smaller areas, children are more likely to settle to activities. Some activities can be set out to encourage two children to play or work together, others to accommodate small groups. For older children in school, they all need a table and chair to work at (although in Reception, this is not necessarily true), but in settings for younger children, some tables can be stacked out of the way until needed for mealtimes. If you have children with limited mobility, you need to think about how you can adapt the area to cater for their needs. This would need to be done on an individual basis, because every child's needs will be different, but it's worth thinking about whether you have enough space for a wheelchair between furniture and equipment.

Outdoor space is really important. Many activities can be carried out outside as well as inside. Children can play outside in most weather, as long as they are dressed for it. If you have a covered outside area, that's a real bonus. If you don't have an outdoor space, you need to take advantage of the local playground or park, but you need to be especially careful to check for hazards like broken bottles and animal excrement.

It's important to have a comfortable, homely area where children can be quiet and rest if they're feeling tired or ill, or just need a bit of comfort. It's a long day for some children, and early years settings can seem big and overwhelming. It's also important to reflect different home backgrounds of the children so that the setting doesn't feel totally strange and different. Children need to feel secure if they are to learn and develop.

It's important to keep the environment attractive and tidy, and to encourage the children to help with this. Make sure that toys are put away in the right place - this is good training for the children, too. Allow plenty of time for tidying up. This can become a game in itself, and a beneficial activity - the children are learning to sort things, an important skill for maths. You can make it easier for them by having clear labels on boxes and shelves - pictures for young children to match, then words and pictures, then words on their own.

It's good to change things around regularly, to keep the children interested. You can adapt the home corner to be a hospital, a shop, and so on. The writing and drawing area can have different themes each week to fit in with the curriculum plan. Think about ways your setting has been changed around, or things you could do in particular areas. Check with your supervisor before you change anything!

The **knowledge evidence** statements for this element are 1, 3, 4, 5, 6, 7, 11, 12, 13 and 14. You need to show that you understand:

◆ how the physical layout helps children to have control over their activities

◆ how the layout affects the type of activities

◆ how to organise the layout to encourage pair and group activities

◆ how to modify the layout to include children with additional needs

◆ your responsibility to enable children to explore safely and securely

◆ ways to encourage children to take part in making decisions and taking responsibility for their actions

◆ why children need to feel secure and the effects when this is increased or decreased

◆ health and safety in relation to heating, lighting and ventilation

This seems like a lot but some of the points overlap. Your assessor will be able to use some of the evidence from her observation, inspection and questioning, and the other evidence for the element. You may need to complete any questions or assignments she has given you. You should have had some training to help you with this.

Which type of evidence?

Your assessor will need to **inspect the setting** and ask you **questions** about how you help to keep the setting attractive and stimulating for the children. She may ask you about health and safety, for E2.1, at the same time. She may want to **observe** you working generally with the children during activity time, and see how you involve the children in setting out and clearing away. You could ask your supervisor to let you be responsible for setting out the activities on the day your assessor will observe you. Draw a **plan** of your setting, including the outside area, showing where different activities take place, or take some **photographs**. If possible, include an example of a **curriculum plan** to show the range of activities the children do during the week. Highlight the activities you have been involved in.

Element E1.2 Prepare and maintain displays

Key issues

In this element you need to show evidence that you can set up interesting and attractive displays for children. You need to have some practice in setting up displays, so take note of the techniques other staff use, and ask if you can help them, before you are ready to be assessed. If you have already done Unit C8.5, 'Examine objects of interest with children', that will provide some evidence for this element.

Displays can include:

- wall displays of the children's own work, which might be paintings and other art work carefully and attractively displayed on the wall. Avoid using templates and pre-drawn pictures. The children's own art work looks great when it's well displayed. It doesn't have to be perfect.

- other wall displays such as pictures and posters. These should reflect positive images of people from diverse cultures, men and women in non-stereotypical roles and people with disabilities in positive roles.

- table-top displays of children's models made from recyclable materials, clay, or construction materials. When tidying away, try to let children save their models to show their parents, rather than having to break them up, at least for the rest of the day. It's frustrating to have spent a long time making a model, only to be told 'Put it all away, it's time to tidy up'.

- displays based on a theme, such as 'Colour', 'Shape', 'Sound', wooden, metal and plastic things, and so on, linked to the curriculum plan.

- displays based on a festival, such as Christmas, Divali, Chinese New Year

- book displays. These should show a range of different styles and illustrations, some dual language books, books with themes, and so on.

- displays of natural materials such as plants, animals, rocks and leaves

- all equipment should be attractively displayed, to make it inviting for the children. For instance, the dressing-up clothes are much better hung on a rail than thrown in a box. Art materials should be displayed where children can reach them, so that they can choose their materials.

When you're planning to set up a display, you should involve the children. When making table-top displays, try as far as possible to make them things which children can handle. Ask them to bring things in from home, and let them help set up the display, as far as health and safety will allow. Think about the range of senses the display will stimulate - sight, touch, smell and hearing. This is particularly important if you have children with impaired sight or hearing, or other additional needs. Avoid things to taste - this would be a health risk.

You need to change displays regularly, to keep the children interested. The children quickly stop noticing a display. You can keep their interest longer if you talk about it, add things to it, or if they can handle the objects. It's important to point displays out to parents, so that they take a pride in their children's achievements. It's also a good way of keeping parents informed about the activities you do. Some settings display photos of the children doing activities, with captions about how the activities help the children's learning and development.

Displays should always be clearly labelled, in a form that is appropriate for the children. This will normally be in small or lower case letters, in the form that the children will learn to write in. Check with your supervisor that you are using the correct lettering. Schools will have an approved form which they use. It takes practice to write lettering well. You may have had some practical sessions on this during your training. Many settings use letter templates, so you only have to draw round them and cut them out. You should have examples of writing from different languages around the setting. Many settings have welcome posters in different languages.

The **knowledge evidence** statements for this element are 9, 15, 16 and 17. You need to show that you understand:

◆ how important it is to display positive images of people from different social, cultural and racial backgrounds, genders, and people with disabilities or additional needs (also E1.3)

◆ how to choose appropriate items from children's homes which reflect the cultural and social backgrounds of the children

◆ how to display children's creative work attractively and enable children and adults to talk about it

◆ how to care for plants and natural materials in the setting

Your assessor should be able to gain most of this evidence from your evidence below. Hopefully you will have had some practical training sessions on techniques for display.

Which type of evidence?

You may be able to **cross reference** some evidence from C8.5 - or if you're doing this unit first, remember to make a note of it on your C8 cross referencing sheet. Your assessor will need to **inspect the setting** to see what displays you have set up, so you need to arrange with your supervisor which display she would like you to do. You assessor may also want to **observe** how you have involved the children in setting up and maintaining the display, or she may ask you **questions** about it. Take **photographs** of displays as you do them, with a brief explanation of why you did them and how you used them with the children.

Element E1.3 Maintain a reassuring environment

Key issues

This element is about making sure that children feel happy and secure. The other two elements will have contributed to this, because by providing equipment and displays and an environment which reflect a range of home backgrounds, you have already helped the children to feel secure. This element is about how you constantly reassure children and give them a sense of belonging. It is closely linked to C4.

When children start at the setting, it can be an anxious time for both children and parents. You need to be sensitive to this, and always be warm and welcoming to children and parents. Children will often bring with them a comfort object - something from home which they need, to maintain that link when parents are away. You should allow children access to these objects whenever they need them. Another way you make children feel a sense of belonging is to give them a space

that is theirs - a coat peg and a drawer with their name and picture on it - somewhere to keep their things, and to put pictures they have drawn for mummy and daddy.

Children don't always cope well with change, so if you know there are going to be changes to the normal routine or environment, prepare the children for it by explaining what will happen, if they are old enough to understand. If not, be there with them, cuddle and reassure them. If the change is unexpected, again, be positive and reassuring. You can plan for some changes, like moving up to big school, by talking positively about it and reading appropriate stories. Children will normally be invited to visit their school with their parents before they start.

There will be times when individual children who are usually happy and secure suddenly become insecure and upset. This may be due to a death in the family, a marriage break-up, or some other life-changing event such as the birth of a new baby. This may make a child withdrawn, or they may become aggressive. It's important to find out why their behaviour has changed. This will normally be the responsibility of your supervisor. You will need to be particularly reassuring with the child while they come to terms with the situation.

The **knowledge evidence** statements for this element are 1, 2, 8 and 10. You need to show that you understand:

◆ how to recognise fear and anxiety in children

◆ how children are affected by separation from their main carer

◆ how to deal with anxieties and reassure children, and the use of comfort objects

◆ why the setting should reflect the home environment

You should have done some training on this element to make sure that you understand the issues, such as how to recognise children's anxiety and how to deal with it. Your diary and reflective accounts may be all the evidence you need. Check with your assessor.

Which type of evidence?

Your assessor will have evidence from her **inspection of the setting** for the other two elements for the three PCs she needs to observe. It may be difficult for her to observe the other PCs unless she is a work-based assessor, working with you. You need to keep a **diary** of how you have dealt with situations as they arise, like a planned change and how you prepared the children, or how you helped them to cope with an unexpected change either in the nursery or in their home life. Write a short **reflective account** of how you are generally reassuring to the children and help them to feel happy and secure.

Some early years staff work in accommodation that is far from ideal, but it is still possible to enhance and improve the environment for young children

Providing a quality environment

A good quality environment allows children to feel confident and secure. It gives parents faith in the competence of the carers and educators. It can even influence people's perceptions of the quality of their own work. Are you happy that you are making the most of your setting?

Always bear in mind some of the key principles of good early years practice:

- Children learn most effectively by doing rather than by being told;
- Children learn most effectively when they are actively involved and interested;
- Children need time and space to produce work of quality and depth; and
- Playing and talking are the main ways through which young children learn about themselves and the world around them.

The way in which the physical environment is organised can help you to uphold principles or it can create a barrier to them being fulfilled.

When you review your learning environment you should consider:

1 Are children and parents valued? Displays - photographs - ownership

2 Can children freely access and select resources and materials? Storage - use of furniture - labelling

3 Can children move between the different curriculum areas? Use of space - designated areas - indoor/outdoor provision

Show that children and parents are valued

Your setting should be inviting and welcoming to all children and adults. Photographs of children and adults working together are a good way of showing the range of curriculum activities which you provide. Notices for parents should be carefully printed and mounted and be written in positive language rather than as instructions. Dual language notices and signs help to welcome all races and religions, and some are available commercially.

Involve the children in helping you decide how to organise the rooms. They can have particularly strong views about which areas work best. Parents should be encouraged to enter the setting with their child to help them start work and you need to think carefully about how this can best be organised.

Displays of children's work help to develop self-esteem and self-worth and offer a stimulus. The work needs to be carefully mounted and labelled to reflect its value and, where possible, the displays should be at children's height.

Everyone needs a safe place to store their personal belongings.

Children need a place for their coat, shoes/boots and bag. (Bags are now the bane of early years workers' lives but are needed to transport lunches, spare clothing and comfort toys.) This storage space has to be easily reached by the children and be within their sight to give them confidence that their possessions are safe. Adults - whether it be fellow staff or parents who come in to help - need these facilities as well.

The environment for young children often reflects the home in that there are curtains, carpets, plants, photographs and easy chairs. This is important because it allows children to make that move from home to an early years setting more easily. However, the setting must reflect the variety of cultures and backgrounds that children come from. It is usual to mix fabrics, furniture, pictures, and artefacts so that all cultures are represented regardless of the area the setting serves.

The environment should be maintained to a high standard for health and safety reasons. With young children this task is demanding but essential. The mandatory requirements of the Children Act must be met.

Making it easy for children to choose and reach resources

Storing resources and materials properly is the key to ensuring that children can reach and choose for themselves. Young children cannot manage large, floppy board boxes; they need rigid containers, preferably plastic. Because they are small, they also need furniture of the correct size in which to store their resources.

Word and picture labels help young children who cannot read to determine what is inside the boxes. This is made easier if the containers don't have lids. You may be able to stick one of the objects onto the outside of the boxes along with the label. You can also use photographs or pictures cut from commercial resource catalogues.

You can buy plastic containers at competitive prices in most supermarkets, DIY stores and garages. They come in a variety of sizes and colours. Another helpful strategy to help young children choose resources and put them back in the right place is to use silhouettes of the shapes of objects. This is particularly useful for large objects, for example equipment in the sand area.

When storing bricks and construction materials then it is better to store different items separately. For example, when children are working with Mobilo they want to be able to find a connecting joint or a pair of wheels quickly rather than rummaging in the bottom of the box. The speed of access allows the children to create and construct without interruptions. It also teaches them about how things work because they can see the component parts clearly.

Help children use the different curriculum areas freely

Your furniture should be arranged to let children use the resources in the space provided or to carry them in their play to another area. It is important that all the resources and materials needed for a particular activity are stored within the same area or nearby. Other resources may have to be carried by children in their activities, for example role-play clothes. Continuity and consistency in the storage of resources is vital to let children know exactly where to find things.

It is particularly important to provide materials for literacy and numeracy development. Writing materials and books are required in every single area of play to support children's learning. You can do this by providing a clip-board and pencil, for example, in the construction area, along with some simple plans and relevant books.

Temporary displays

Some settings are not allowed to put up permanent displays but many playgroups cleverly overcome these restrictions. Here are some of their ideas:

i) Buy rolls of corrugated card (approximately four feet in height and six feet in length) to pin work on. These rolls are usually best propped around adult upright chairs, and can be re-used time and time again (see diagram).

ii) Buy pieces of pinboard (size 1m x 2m) to use around the room propped up behind low cupboards for displays.

iii) Display children's work three-dimensionally by sticking it onto cardboard and zig-zagging this on cupboard tops or on the floor.

iv) Pin work onto curtains if available (using nappy pins for safety).

v) Use the reverse of low furniture to display work.

vi) Buy perspex clip frames for children's work which may be more acceptable to the other users of rented premises.

To support children's literacy and numeracy you will need to consider the quality and amount of relevant print and numeracy in the environment at children's level. This print will provide children with a stimulus and a starting point for their own reading and writing.

Try to organise the furniture so that the available spaces can be divided up into areas of work. This will help staff to fit out areas for particular curriculum activities and create secure spaces for children to work in. However, the furniture should not stop children from making connections between other areas. For example, children playing in the home area may not have realised that there is a role-play shop at the other end of the room. This may restrict their play and language use. Through their interactions and participation with children adults will be encouraging them to make full use of all the available spaces and resources by modelling and role playing themselves.

As a general rule the furniture should be away from the wall and placed at angles to create distinct areas. Before starting to arrange the furniture you should first consider which areas you want to provide. These should include the following:

- **reading and listening centre**
- **writing centre**
- **construction areas**
- **role-play areas**
- **floor-play area, eg train set**
- **sand and water area**
- **creative area, eg paint, collage**
- **mathematics centre**
- **music area**
- **snack area/food preparation**
- **interest displays of artefacts for investigation**

In addition, staff should also consider where the computer can go (if you have one), and what will be provided outside.

The amount of space available is often regarded by staff as being limited. Often, the space is only limited by the large number of tables and chairs, which are not all necessary and restrict the room available.

You should name the areas which staff create, with the children's help. This naming is important to give children a sense of belonging, to help them understand what adults are referring to and to distinguish between the different spaces. Very occasionally in early years settings one particular area becomes a place where harassment or bullying can occur. Be vigilant about this. Talking to children about the environment will highlight potential problems. In some settings areas are labelled for reinforcement and to help parents, helpers and students. The names given to areas will reflect the resources and activities within them.

The design and location of the areas should take account of the needs of the children. These needs include opportunities for being quiet or resting; lying down to play; splashing or spilling materials like sand and water; being physically active; talking and singing; working in groups, in pairs or alone; and leaving and returning to unfinished activities. After successfully considering all of these needs the result should be an environment which is truly child-centred.

Finally, a good quality environment for young children is dynamic, challenging, inviting and interesting. To ensure that this is true for all settings, staff need to monitor and review their organisation and accommodation regularly.

Ruth M Baldwin

Colour lends itself to bright interactive displays which will motivate and inspire children. Set up an interest table using this sheet as a handy reference guide and feature a different colour on the table each week

Colour displays

Find a table which is the right height for the children and position it where they can go up to it easily at any time during a session. Collect the following items: bright coloured material, three hoops, a 'Colour' frieze, cardboard, thick markers of a variety of colours, shoe box, attractive wrapping paper, pot, crayons (colour of the week), a wooden or cardboard easel that you can clip a large piece of paper to, box of cards with children's names on.

Cover the table with attractive material and fix the relevant sheet of the frieze up on the wall behind it. On a piece of card write 'Colour of the week'. Cut out a large arrow and stick it to the sheet to highlight the colour.

Put the three hoops on the table (make them out of card if you don't have any plastic hoops). In one hoop, near the front where they can reach, put all the red objects that you have collected (with a red sign). Add little cards that say the name of the object to create a print rich environment.

In the next hoop, place objects that are not red. Encourage the children to go to the table and sort the objects by colour. Older

children can sort by other categories.

Ask children to bring in something from home that is the colour of the week and place these in a hoop near the back. Again, add labels. Attach to your easel a large piece of paper and a sign that says

'Come and draw something that is our colour of the week'. Encourage children to go to the paper and draw, using the pen provided, something that they know is red. Each week replace the sheet with a clean piece of paper. When you have worked through all the colours, collect all the papers together and your children will have created their very own 'Big Book of Colours'.

Cover the shoe box with bright paper and cut a slit in the top to make a posting box. Place next to it a box which has individual cards with children's names on. Also add a pot of crayons that are the week's colour. Encourage children to vote for their

favourite colour. If red is their favourite, they need to choose their name, colour a red dot next to it and then post it in the box. As the weeks pass, you can post up the results , such as 'Ten people liked the colour red,' 'Five people liked the colour blue.'

Make sure that you and other adults join in with the activities on your display as well as your children.

Use the lists below to help you think of new items to put on display.

Ideas supplied by Rebecca Taylor

Red: a tomato, soft ladybird, shiny red apple, red shoe, toy fire engine, crayon, hair bow, traffic light, bucket

Blue: socks, jeans, t-shirt, bluebird, picture of sky, toy car

Yellow: a flower (buttercup, daffodil - in winter a chrysanthemum or pansy), rain hat or raincoat, picture of sun, bananas, sand, lemon

Green: a plant, green vegetables such as a cabbage, beans, peas, plastic frog, watering can, grass, traffic light

Pink: plastic pig, tissue, soap, flower - eg carnation

Orange: an orange, carrot, pumpkin, life jacket, traffic cone, traffic light, goldfish

Purple: some grapes, a party hat, wool, candle, plums, a pansy/violet

Brown: soil, wood, teddy bear, brown bread, suitcase, monkey

Black: cat/cow (models), umbrella, spider, panda bear, picture of blackbird

White: chalk, newspaper, milk, picture of ice-cream, domino

Caroline Jones suggests some ideas for seasonal displays related to the weather, changing seasons and food

Autumn displays

Weather

Observing and recording changes in the weather should be an ongoing part of the pre-school routine. However, fog is something that most children have forgotten by the time it appears each year. *Postman Pat's Foggy Day* story is a good introduction to the idea of fog and can give rise to some display ideas.

Talk about the idea of not being able to see clearly. If they put greaseproof paper in front of their eyes children will get the idea of what it feels like. Carry on observing the clouds and notice the colours in the autumn sky. Talk about autumn colours and allow children to paint fog pictures. Encourage them to explore colour, making shades of grey by mixing black and white.

Autumn words

Introduce the children to the new vocabulary associated with autumn and ensure displays are labelled with the words:

- harvest
- fir cone
- hibernate
- autumn
- brown
- golden
- grain
- cereal

Changing seasons wall display

Scrunch up brown paper or let the children paint some paper brown and scrunch it up to make the bark of a tree. Staple it to the wall to represent a tree trunk. Add some branches – you could use real ones. Then add the children's individual leaf prints in autumn colours.

Each day choose a child to take a few leaves off and let them fall to the ground until the branches are bare. Then use the same tree as a basis for a winter display by adding snow using cotton wool or children's home-made snowballs. The background sky can be cloudy and change colour as the seasons change.

Display children's paintings of shades of autumn and leaf prints or seasonal collages .

Ideas for interest tables include:

- a selection of fir cones
- seeds
- nuts
- conkers
- cereals
- leaves
- vegetables cut in half

Alternatively, create a harvest display with an array of vegetables, fruit and canned produce.

Table display

Create a table display using different types of bread, cereals, seeds, grains and nuts. Encourage children to touch, taste (but check first for children who may have allergies) and compare various samples of medium, thick and thin sliced and unsliced bread such as:

- white/brown/wholemeal
- baguettes/rolls

- crusty/soft
- pitta/naan/chapatti

How long does it take for the bread to turn mouldy? Which bread lasts the longest? Which ingredients are used to make bread?

Display cereals in raw form and as samples of breakfast cereals in bowls for children to nibble. You could include cereal boxes and a large bar chart showing the children's favourite cereals.

Caroline Jones and Lisa Collins

Building a Portfolio Level 2 • • •

The crucial handover period when children arrive at playgroup or nursery is not always given the thought and planning it deserves. Sarah Stocks sets out some strategies

Arrival time: making families welcome

Imagine arriving at a party that you didn't really want to go to, being dropped off by someone you would rather stay with, entering a loud and busy room and being left to find your way around or pluck up courage to join in established conversations. If your host is ignoring you into the bargain you would be forgiven for turning tail and leaving straightaway!

No matter how often you have done it and no matter how confident you and your child are, arriving at nursery or playgroup represents a break away from the parent or daytime carer and the more challenging atmosphere of an early years environment. Unfortunately, this crucial handover period is not always given the thought and planning it deserves. Getting this aspect of your day wrong will jeopardise your ability to win the trust and attention of both the child in your care and his or her parent.

Situations to avoid

Before we look at some suggestions for arrival time, let's first look at the problems that might occur if the child and his or her family are not welcomed and integrated into the group. If a parent has to leave her child standing forlornly in the middle of a room, unspoken to by an adult and excluded from ongoing activities by other children then you may assume that:

■ The child will be upset, gaining little positive value from her time in the group.

■ The parent will leave feeling that they have abandoned their child. These bad feelings will affect the way they deal with the handover period the next time and you will have clingy children and parents who do not feel able to leave - a vicious circle!

■ Your relationship with the parent will suffer.

■ The stressful atmosphere in the room will affect all the children's responses to you and the activities you have planned for them.

Be ready

Be ready to greet the children as they arrive. The first activities should be set up, your hands should be free and all staff should be available. The activities on offer should be chosen to allow inclusion of arriving children easily. Keep the atmosphere as calm as possible.

Say hello!

Smile and say hello to every parent and child. Yes! Every child, every morning! Ensure that parents know the routine, where to put coats, who to hand the child over to etc. Larger groups may find it useful to have a leaflet to hand out to new parents - 'How to drop your child off' - they will appreciate it. Don't stand in a huddle - spread yourselves out around the room, it makes you more accessible.

Make eye contact

Touch the child. Take his or her hand and lead them to an activity, get low enough to establish eye contact and make sure they are happy before you move away. Let the parent see that you are caring for their child, he is happy and safe and that you are going to settle him in properly. A backward smile or nod and a reassuring word as you lead the child away will reassure the parent that all is well. Encourage parent and child to say goodbye to each other. A parent who sneaks away when the child is not looking is storing up problems for the next time!

Settling-in policy

Have a coherent, enforced settling-in policy which allows the new child and parent time to be at the group together. A rough guide would be a whole session to begin with, then half a session, then the first hour and then to be dropped off like all the other children.

A child should not move to the next stage until he is happy with the stage he is on. Allow for individuals and their differing needs.

Message system

Have a system for parents to leave messages - a book to write in is ideal. It is too easy to forget one of the six important messages you were given in a five-minute period at the busiest time of the day! Do not let the written message system replace your availability, however, some things need to be said. Remember, too, that not all parents find writing as easy as you - be sensitive to parents who may not be able to write.

Firm handling

Be prepared to be firm with parents who want to spend too long chatting. A polite 'May we continue this later, Mary? I can see that Sophie needs a hand!' will usually do the trick. More persistent parents may need firmer handling; it may be that they have problems of their own that they need help with. You may be able to help but arrival time is not the right time to do

it. Make a note to speak to her at a more convenient time.

Children who cry

If you are having difficulties with a child who is often disruptive on arrival, ask the parent to bring her in a little later. This will reduce the stress in the room as other children arrive. Remember that it is as hard for the parent as it is for the child! Leaving your child crying is the hardest thing to do and serves no purpose. It is fair to say, however, that individual children who are always upset may well have problems other than ones

> 'A good relationship with parents is the key to effective pre-school education - identify parents who are slipping through your net and find another way to make contact with them.'

caused by your arrivals policy! Knowing your children and being confident that you are providing a welcoming environment will help you decide if a persistent crier has other problems.

Late arrivals

Children who arrive late still need to settle in and you should make time to greet them properly. It is rarely the child's fault that he or she is late! If you have a persistently late arriver a quiet word to the parent may suffice. Explain that it makes it hard for you to concentrate on your job if you have to keep stopping.

Carers

If the child is being dropped off by a carer other than the parent you should afford them all the same respect, attention and support you would to the child's parent. They are acting on the parent's behalf and will welcome your support and inclusion. The child has the same rights as one dropped off by a home-based mother and will benefit from this understanding approach.

Regular contact

A key worker system should ensure that all parents are spoken to regularly, otherwise the group leader might keep an eye on those who do not seem to be speaking to anyone. Some parents are intimidated by people they see as officials and will not approach you. A good relationship with parents is the key to effective pre-school education - identify parents who are slipping through your net and find another way to make contact with them. If the family does not speak English then consider using an interpreter, certainly for the first few sessions and thereafter at parents' evenings or social events.

Finally, a good honest look around you is always a valuable exercise. Don't be afraid to stand back and watch. If the atmosphere is relaxed, happy and productive then you must be doing something right! Remember new problems are inevitable, treat each one as an opportunity to improve and give yourself praise where praise is due!

Sara Stocks

Chapter 7

Unit E2: Maintain the safety and security of children

In this unit you will look at how you keep the environment safe for children. We have already looked at how to make the environment attractive and reassuring for children in Unit E1, and safety is very much part of that. Young children are full of curiosity and don't understand danger, so you need to make sure that you keep the environment safe, both indoors and outdoors, and that you supervise the children at all times.

The unit is also about dealing with accidents and emergencies. Your setting will have a fire procedure which you will practise regularly. We strongly recommend that you do a recognised first aid course so that you are able to deal with accidents competently. Most centres give candidates the opportunity to do this. You also look at how to recognise signs of abuse, and how you can protect children from abuse. Finally, you look at how to keep children safe when you organise outings.

Links with other units
We have already suggested that it would be helpful to do E1 and E2 together, because there is a lot of overlap. There are links with C1.1, 'Help children to toilet and wash hands', and C1.2, 'Help children when eating and drinking'. It links with all other units, because in every unit you need to consider the health and safety aspects of what you are doing with the children.

Values
Throughout the elements, the **welfare of the child** and **keeping children safe** are paramount, of course, because that is what the whole unit is about. As always, you as a **reflective practitioner** need to think about whether you're doing your best to keep the children safe, and whether things could be changed for the better. If you see something that is unsafe, it's your duty to do something about it, or report it to your supervisor if it's beyond your responsibility. In Element 2, you will be promoting **children's learning and development** through explaining safety rules to the children, and making them more aware of how to keep themselves safe.

There are aspects of **working with parents** and **working with other professionals** in most elements. As an assistant, you will need to be constantly aware of what is within your role and what you need to report on to your supervisor, such as damaged equipment, incidents that happen with children,

recording and reporting accidents. Element 2 stresses how important it is to follow the setting's procedure for collection of children at home time. Make sure you know what it is, and stick to it. Never let a child go with an adult unless you're sure it's the right person. In Element 3, the emphasis is on having contact numbers for use in emergencies. You won't be directly responsible for collecting this information or notifying parents, but you need to know the procedure. In Element 4 you need to be able to give parents information about an accident calmly and accurately if you're asked.

Element 5 is about protection of children from abuse. Your training centre should give you some basic training on child protection. You need to be aware of your setting's policies and procedures. You need to note and report to your supervisor any explanations from children or parents about injuries and bruises on a child. If you have any concerns, report them to your supervisor. You must maintain **confidentiality** about any information you receive about parents and children.

In Element 6, about outings, parents' permission must be given, and parents should be given all relevant information about clothing, food and so on. Contact information must be taken with you if you leave your setting. Again, all this is not going to be your responsibility, but you need to be aware of it. As an assistant you should never take the children out alone.

Getting started
In this unit you will need to show how you:

◆ maintain a safe environment for children

◆ maintain the supervision of children

◆ carry out emergency procedures

◆ cope with accidents and injuries to children

◆ help protect children from abuse

◆ maintain the safety of children on outings

Go through the elements, with your assessor's help if you need to, and use the personal skills checklist (page 21) to help you decide which elements you are confident about, which you need more experience or practice in, and where you need some training. Check with your assessor when you will be doing the training for this unit. You should have done the training before starting the unit, especially in first aid and child protection. If you have done E1 and C2 you may have evidence you can cross reference. You may also have done an induction assignment on safety, which you can use as evidence. If you're ready to be assessed, plan with your assessor which evidence you will collect. Use the following pages to help you plan.

Element E2.1 Maintain a safe environment for children

Key issues

You need to be constantly aware of the safety of the children in your care. Your setting will have an annual inspection to ensure that the premises are safe. The setting should also carry out regular safety checks on the premises and equipment. In addition to this, on a day-to-day basis you and the other staff have a responsibility to watch for hazards and supervise the children properly.

In this element, you need to show how you can clean surfaces properly so that they are safe and hygienic to use. Your supervisor should have explained to you all the health and safety procedures when you started. If not, ask to see the health and safety policy, and discuss it with your supervisor. You will probably be responsible for things like cleaning tables before and after meals, cleaning toilets and disposing of waste materials safely. Make sure you follow the procedures properly, especially in relation to storage of cleaning materials. They should be in a locked cupboard where the children can't get at them.

Be aware of what toys and activities are available for each age group of children. If you work with children of mixed ages, don't let very young children have toys with very small pieces. If older children are using these things, you need to keep younger ones away from them. Follow manufacturers' instructions for use of equipment and toys. Only use toys with recognised safety kite marks on them. As you put out and clear away equipment, look for broken and damaged bits. If you can repair them, do it. If not, remove them and report the damage to your supervisor. Make sure that safety gates, door fastenings and outside gates are properly fastened.

If your outside play area is prone to being damaged by vandals or fouled by animals, you need to check it carefully before allowing the children out. You need to be especially careful about this in public play areas.

The **knowledge evidence** statements for this element are 1,

8, 9, 10, 11 and 15. You need to show that you understand:

- the importance of stages of development when considering safety

- health, safety and hygiene requirements in the care of children, including on outings (also E2.6)

- health and safety requirements of the setting and the importance of these being displayed and discussed with all adults in the setting (also E2.2)

- procedures for identifying and dealing with hazards, indoors or out, without undermining children's confidence

- why and how to carry out routine safety checks on premises and equipment

- importance of following manufacturers' recommendations and relevant safety standards

You should have covered all this information in your induction and in training sessions, but if there are any gaps in your knowledge, discuss this with your assessor and supervisor.

Which type of evidence?

Your assessor will need to **inspect the setting** and **observe** you carrying out routine procedures for seven of the PCs. She will want to ask **questions** to make sure that you understand the requirements. You may be able to **cross reference** some evidence from C1.1, 'Help children to toilet and wash hands' and E1, 'Maintain the physical environment'. You may have made a note of these on your cross referencing sheet, with your assessor's help. If you're doing this unit first, note any evidence you can use for E1 and C1 on the cross referencing sheets for those units.

> **Try** to get into the habit of making a note of evidence you can cross reference on your cross referencing sheet. You will need your assessor's help at first.

If you did a health and safety **assignment** as part of your induction include this as evidence. Include any of your setting's **health and safety procedures**, making a note of how you have used them in your work, or discuss this with your assessor. Ask your supervisor to write a **witness testimony** that you are fully aware of health and safety when working in the setting. This statement could include a comment on your supervision of the children, for Element 2.

Element E2.2 Maintain the supervision of children

Key issues

It's crucial that children are supervised at all times; never leave children alone for a moment. There should always be a qualified person supervising the group. As an unqualified assistant you should not be left alone with the children. Your setting will be required to have a specific ratio of staff to children in each age group, as laid down in the National Standards for Under Eights Day Care (this does not apply to schools):

1:3	children under two years
1:4	children aged two years
1:8	children aged three to seven years

If you're employed, you will be part of the ratio. If you're a trainee, you will be an extra member of staff. All supervisors must be qualified to Level 3. Half of the other staff must hold at least a Level 2 qualification.

Be calm and relaxed with the children so that they feel secure - we have discussed this in E1.3, 'Maintain a reassuring environment'. Keep a watchful eye for hazards, but do give the children enough freedom to explore the equipment and environment. Don't be over-protective. If you're over-anxious, this will be transmitted to the children and they won't be confident to try new things. If you've prepared the setting well and there is good supervision, the children should be able to play safely without too many restrictions. You need to explain the rules to them in such a way that they understand why rules are important for their own and other children's safety. In this way they will learn to control their own actions. Outside, there are potentially more hazards, because the larger and moveable equipment is often outside. There is more space, so children tend to be more active and boisterous. So some basic rules for safety and close supervision is even more important.

Very young children - from the time they start to roll, crawl and walk - need careful supervision, because they see no danger, and they are too young to understand why things are dangerous. Never leave a young baby on a changing table or on a chair. You may think they can't roll, but one day they will. Once babies start crawling you need a stair gate, because they will climb the stairs and possibly fall down them, so be one step ahead all the time.

When you first start working in your setting, you will probably be given activities to do with a small group, which is easier to supervise, but you need to be aware of what is going on around you as well. Try to get into the habit of looking around, and keeping your ears open, while doing an activity with one group. It's a well-known saying that you need eyes in the back of your head when you're working with children!

Your setting will have a procedure for collection of children. It's essential that you stick to it. In many settings, you wouldn't be given that responsibility. If you are given the task of handing children over to their parents, be absolutely sure that you are handing over to the right person. Check if you're not sure.

The **knowledge evidence** statements for this element are 12, 13 and 23. You need to show that you understand:

◆ the registration requirements for adult/child ratios

◆ the importance of policies and procedures for collecting children, taking account of special circumstances

◆ the importance of maintaining records to enable parents to be contacted (also E2.3)

◆ why adults sometimes over-protect children, and how adult reactions can prevent a child developing self-confidence

You may cover these in your evidence for the element. Your assessor may check your understanding through oral questions, or she may ask you to do an **assignment**. You should have attended training to make sure that you have the necessary knowledge and understanding.

Which type of evidence?

Your assessor will need to **observe** the whole of this element. You will have planned with her whether she will do a general observation of you supervising the children, either inside or outside, or a specific activity. She may have included this element while she observed E1.1. While your assessor is observing you, explain your setting's rules to the children if you can. She will want to ask you **questions** to check your understanding. Your **witness testimony** from Element 1 will hopefully include a comment on your supervision of the children. Include any relevant **procedures** of your setting, such as the collection procedure.

Element E2.3 Carry out emergency procedures

Key issues

You will need to know where all the safety equipment for use in emergencies is kept, and where the emergency exits are. You should have had this explained to you during your induction, but check again so that you're sure where things are. Your setting will also have a fire/emergency procedure, which should be on display, and all contact details of the children's parents, for use in an emergency. If you haven't yet been involved in a fire drill, ask your supervisor when the next one will be, and make sure you're there for it. Read a copy of the procedure, so that you're prepared. Ask to see where emergency contact information is kept. If an incident does occur, report it calmly and quickly.

When practising a fire drill, be calm and reassuring, because children can be frightened by the sound of a loud alarm. With very young children, you should explain beforehand that it's only a practice, and nothing to be afraid of. Older children will get used to having practices, because they will have done it regularly in the time they have been in early years settings and in school.

The **knowledge evidence** statements for this element are 14 and 16. You need to show that you understand:

◆ routine emergency procedures and how to respond promptly in a calm and reassuring manner

◆ your individual responsibilities in relation to safety including requirements for reporting emergencies

You should have covered the knowledge during your induction. Your assessor will probably have the evidence she needs from the questions she asked you and your induction assignment.

Which type of evidence?
You may be able to **cross reference** some evidence from your induction and from E1. Your assessor will need to observe four of the seven PCs if she hasn't already, and ask **questions**. Sometimes it's difficult to arrange a visit at the time of an emergency practice. If so, ask your supervisor to write a **witness testimony** to say that you have been involved in a practice. Include a copy of the **fire drill** with a **reflective account** of how successful the practice was, and whether you needed to reassure any children.

Element E2.4 Cope with accidents and injuries to children

Key issues
You need to have had some basic first aid training for this element. You may be able to take a course leading to a recognised qualification. If you haven't had the opportunity yet, find out if there is a course available through your training centre or through the nursery. You probably won't be responsible for dealing with first aid - there is at least one named first aider with a qualification in your setting at any

time - but you still need some knowledge of how to deal with minor accidents, and what the reporting and recording procedures are. All accidents must be recorded and reported to your supervisor, who will then report it to the child's parents. Minor accidents would be reported when the parents collect the child, but obviously for more serious ones, the parents would be contacted immediately.

Check where the first aid box is, and what materials are in it. This will vary from one part of the country to another. Ask whether you are allowed to deal with minor accidents such as cuts and grazes, and what the procedure is, such as wearing protective gloves and disposing of waste safely. You must protect yourself and the child from infection when dealing with any body fluids and open wounds. Your setting will have a policy on the handling and disposal of body fluids and waste, to make sure that children and adults are protected from HIV/Aids and hepatitis. Make sure you follow it.

If you're dealing with a serious accident you must call a qualified first aider, but don't leave the child. You should never be alone with a group of children, so there should always be one of you who can stay with the child, and the other children, to reassure them, and someone else to fetch help. Any child who has had an accident will be upset by it, so be reassuring and comforting. Keep the child near you, and give her a cuddle if she needs it.

Remember!
You must call a qualified first aider to deal with accidents unless you have permission to deal with something minor.

The **knowledge evidence** statements for this element are 2, 14, 16, 17, 18, 19 and 24. You need to show that you understand:

◆ how to recognise and cope with a child being upset after an accident or emergency

◆ how to respond promptly in a calm and reassuring way

◆ your individual responsibility for recording and reporting accidents

◆ policies and procedures for handling and disposing of body fluids in the light of HIV/Aids and hepatitis

◆ basic first aid and how to apply it

◆ what should be in the first aid box, who should replenish contents and why

◆ how to pass information to parents without causing undue alarm

You should have had some training for this element to ensure that you have the necessary understanding of these important issues. Try to cover the knowledge requirements in your other evidence. Your assessor may give you further questions to check your understanding.

Which type of evidence?

Your assessor will need to **inspect** the first aid box and its contents, and ask you **questions** about first aid procedures, but she is unlikely to be able to observe you dealing with an accident unless she works with you all the time. So you need to get a **witness testimony** from your supervisor to say that you are able to deal with minor accidents competently and that you know how to record and report accidents. If you have dealt with accidents, keep a record in your **diary** or write a **reflective account**. Write a **list** of the contents of your first aid box, how often it's checked and by whom, and say why certain things are not included. For instance, in some places, you are not allowed to use plasters because some children are allergic to them. Include an example of your setting's **accident record book**, with names removed for confidentiality. Also include a copy of your first aid **policies and procedures**.

Element E2.5 Help protect children from abuse

Key issues

You need to have some basic training in child protection and be fully familiar with your setting's policies and procedures. If your supervisor or manager hasn't discussed these with you, ask them if they can as soon as possible. This is a difficult and sensitive area, and it needs to be handled carefully. It will not be your responsibility to deal with it, but if a child discloses something to you, you need to know what to do. You also need to know what signs of abuse to look for. If your centre hasn't provided any training yet, find out from your assessor when it will be available. The EYDCP will also hold regular training for early years settings, so ask your manager if you can attend. There is a useful article later in the chapter (see pages 163-164), but this is not as good as attending a course and exploring the issues in a group.

Abuse may be physical, emotional, sexual or neglect. You need to be observant of any signs of physical abuse such as bruising and physical injuries, neglect, such as an under-nourished and unwashed child, changes in a child's behaviour, such as becoming withdrawn or aggressive, or showing sexual behaviour inappropriate to their age. If you have any concerns, report them immediately to your supervisor. If a child discloses anything to you, listen, but **don't** question the child. Report it immediately to your supervisor, as accurately as you can.

The **knowledge evidence** statements for this element are 3, 4, 5, 25, 26, 27 and 28. They will be covered in the assignment. You need to show that you understand:

◆ the signs of physical, emotional or sexual abuse or neglect, including bruises on different skin colours

◆ how to observe children for signs of injuries or abuse during care routines

◆ the significance of negative changes in a child's behaviour and why it is important to observe, record and report incidents

◆ parts of the body where bruising is not usually caused by accident

◆ the importance of following rules laid down by the setting

◆ the boundaries of your work role

◆ how important it is to inform the manager of explanations given by parents

◆ the importance of involving parents from the early stages of enquiries

◆ the importance of confidentiality

Which type of evidence?

Evidence for this element will normally be through a written **assignment** following a training session. There is no requirement for observation, but your assessor may ask you **questions**. Include a copy of your setting's **procedures**.

Element E2.6 Maintain the safety of children on outings

Key issues

Outings are an important part of the experience you offer to children, because it gives them an opportunity to discover more about the world around them. The type of outing you decide on will depend on the age of the children. You need to take distance into account. Very young children will not be able to cope with long journeys. Even with older children, you need to keep the journey fairly short, so that they can enjoy as much time as possible at the venue. Also, think about the sort of experience when they get there and the safety implications. Try to choose a venue where there is something of interest to see and do, perhaps linked to your curriculum plan, such as a farm. You also need to allow time and space for running about and letting off steam, or having some games, at some stage during the day. Ideally, choose somewhere you can eat in the dry if it turns out to be a rainy day.

You may go out of the setting quite frequently on little outings to the park or shops, or a local place of interest, which don't need too much preparation. As an unqualified assistant, you must be accompanied. Bigger outings take careful planning. You will not be responsible for planning an outing, but hopefully you will be involved in the planning meetings. You need to think carefully about what you need to take. You will need a first aid kit, a 'sick bucket', possibly some changes of clothes, food and drinks, wet weather clothes and/or sunhats and sun cream.

It's important to keep parents fully informed. They will need to know, for instance, whether a packed lunch is needed, what clothes and footwear will be suitable, how much money children need to take, if any, and what time children will be setting off and arriving back. It's good to invite parents to join in if they can. It's essential to get parents' permission for any outing, however small. Some settings get permission for the year, for small outings to the shops or park during the normal routine. Check whether your setting has written guidelines for outings.

Safety is a major consideration when taking children out. The early years setting is geared to the children's needs, but not the world outside. There are many hazards, so it's crucial that children are supervised closely. Babies and toddlers should either be in buggies or on restraints. It will normally be necessary to have extra adults to accompany you. Each adult should be responsible

for specific children. You should carry a list of the children with you, and check regularly that they are all there. Put badges on the children with the name of the setting and a telephone number in case a child gets lost, but **don't** put the child's name on the badge. If a stranger approaches a child and calls him by name, the child might think it's all right to go with them. If you're using private transport, you need to check that the insurance of the drivers adequately covers what is required. Use reputable companies if you're hiring a coach. You must take contact details of parents with you in case of an accident or emergency.

The **knowledge evidence** statements for this element are 6, 7, 8, 20, 21, 22, 29. You need to show that you understand:

- appropriate outings for the age of the child and how outings can help learning

- health and safety and hygiene for outings

- how to plan and prepare for an outing with regard to safety, transport, appropriate clothing, food and equipment

- regulations covering insurance and safe transport of children in private cars

- how important it is to keep a list of children and check them regularly

- the need to gain permission from the manager to take children off the premises, and when you need parents' permission

You will never be solely responsible for all of these issues, and many are beyond your responsibility, but you need to know what the issues are so that you can play your part in ensuring that children are completely safe.

Which type of evidence?

There is no requirement for your assessor to observe this element, as it would be difficult for her to give up a day for an outing - although it's fine if she can spare the time! You need to write a **reflective account** of the outing, from planning to going out and returning. Note what safety measures were taken. Ask your supervisor to write a **witness testimony** that you carried out your tasks competently during planning and going on the outing. Include any examples of **information to parents**.

Use this check-list when you carry out your daily inspection before children arrive

20 tips for a safer pre-school

Tick box when checked

Comings and goings

- Corridors and doorways are free from prams and buggies ☐

- Main entrance door handles let adults in but stop children getting out ☐

- Tasks are allocated to staff:

  - greeting children, parents and carers ☐

  - taking and passing on messages about collecting children, their health etc ☐

  - keeping an eye on siblings not staying for the session ☐

  - checking that children leave with an appropriate adult ☐

  - making arrangements for children left late after the session ☐

Premises

- activities are set up away from doorways and fire exits ☐

- fire exit doors are unlocked ☐

- doors don't slam on children's fingers ☐

- fire extinguishers are fixed securely to the walls ☐

- the toilet area is kept mopped and dried ☐

Equipment

- climbing equipment is placed away from walls/staging/other equipment ☐

- climbing frames are not more than two metres high and have safety mats below ☐

- painting easels and book cases stand secure ☐

- floor toys eg small cars/building bricks, are placed away from doorways and climbing equipment ☐

- dressing-up clothes don't have trailing pieces eg elastic, ribbons, cords ☐

- broken play equipment is removed for mending or disposal ☐

- large unused equipment and containers are stored securely ☐

- carpet pieces are flat and have no frayed edges ☐

Activities

- spills of sand, water and paint are swept up or mopped and dried ☐

- scattered floor toys and small pieces like Lego are returned to designated play area ☐

- ride-on toys are kept away from floor activities ☐

- hot drinks are kept away from children's activities ☐

All information supplied by Child Accident Prevention Trust

Building a Portfolio Level 2 • • •

Use this check-list as a useful guide on how to make your home a safer place for the whole family and the other children in your care

20 top home safety tips

Tick box when checked

1   The floor and stairs are clear of junk or spills in case the family trip or slip. ☐

2   Medicines and chemicals are stored high up and out of reach in case a child drinks something harmful. ☐

3   Safety catches are fitted to prevent a child falling out of the window. ☐

4   Babies or toddlers are never alone in the bath as they can quickly drown in just a little water. ☐

5   The hot water thermostat is turned down to 54°C (130°F) or less in case a child turns the hot tap on and is scalded. ☐

6   Rear hobs on the cooker are used and pan handles turned away from the edge. ☐

7   The smoke alarm is working in case of fire and the family need time to escape. ☐

8   The baby never uses a babywalker - they may fall over or reach for something dangerous. ☐

9   The front door is shut and can't be opened by small children in case they run into traffic. ☐

10 Someone in the family has taken a first aid course to help cope if an accident does happen. ☐

All information supplied by Child Accident Prevention Trust

Use this as a guide for a monthly review of your fire precautions

Fire precautions check-list

Name of setting

Date of inspection

Name of person carrying out inspection

Fire alarm

	Yes	No
Is there an effective means of raising the alarm in the event of a fire?	☐	☐
Do all staff and helpers know how to raise the alarm and what the alarm sounds like?	☐	☐
Do they know the drill for fire practice?	☐	☐
Can the alarm be heard throughout the building?	☐	☐
Has the electric fire alarm (if installed) been activated weekly from a different call point or zone and a record kept?	☐	☐
Are records of tests being entered into the fire precautions log book?	☐	☐
Is the electric fire alarm being electrically inspected every six months and the inspections recorded? Check your records.	☐	☐
When was the last practice drill? (They should be quarterly.) Date	☐	

Fire fighting equipment

	Yes	No
Is the fire fighting equipment being serviced annually and records kept?	☐	☐
Check all fire extinguishers to see whether they have been damaged, discharged or stolen and record your findings.	☐	☐
Are fire extinguishers, hose reels and fire blankets readily accessible and unobstructed?	☐	☐
Is there enough fire fighting equipment and is it in the appropriate places?	☐	☐
Are all fire extinguishers marked with standard identification signs?	☐	☐

Fire prevention

	Yes	No
Is there any accumulation of rubbish, waste paper or other combustible materials?	☐	☐
Are corridors and exits which are part of a fire escape route kept clear at all times?	☐	☐
Are fire doors kept closed and never propped open?	☐	☐

First aid and resuscitation

It is important that you know the basics of first aid. Ideally, everyone on your staff should receive basic training to enable them to give the best possible first aid treatment in an emergency. This is for your own peace of mind as well as to reassure the parents of the children in your care. Information about first aid training in your area may be obtained from:

St John's Ambulance,
27 St John's Lane
Clerkenwell
London EC1M 4BU
Tel: 0207 324 4000

St Andrew's Ambulance,
St Andrew's House,
48 Milton Street,
Glasgow G4 0HR
Tel: 0141 332 4031

British Red Cross Society - You will find local numbers in your telephone directory.

ABC check

You may have to deal with an emergency at any time, so familiarise yourself with the most important principle of first aid - the ABC check:

Airway - is it clear?
Breathing - is the child breathing?
Circulation - is there a heart beat?

There is no legal requirement for there to be a qualified first aider in a nursery. However, the Health Education Guide recommends that a school has one nominated qualified first aider who has undergone approved training for 18 hours. This is renewable every three years. The principles and practice of first aid are included as part of the curriculum for NNEB students and most colleges offer a separate first aid certificate. However, this would need updating regularly.

Airway - Lift the chin with two fingers and tilt the head back. If the child is breathing, place him in the recovery position.

Breathing - If the child is not breathing, start artificial ventilation.

Circulation - Check the child's pulse by pressing on the groove of the neck, in front of the large muscle at each side. If you cannot feel a pulse, then start cardio pulmonary resuscitation (CPR).

If the child is unconscious, ask someone to call an ambulance. While you wait the child should be put in the recovery position as follows:

The child lies on his side almost on the tummy with the arm underneath preventing him rolling forward. The head should be tilted back to keep the airway open.

In an unconscious baby tilt the head back slightly whilst holding the baby securely in your arms. This prevents them from inhaling their own vomit.

Dr Shabde, consultant paediatrician, Northumbria NHS Trust.

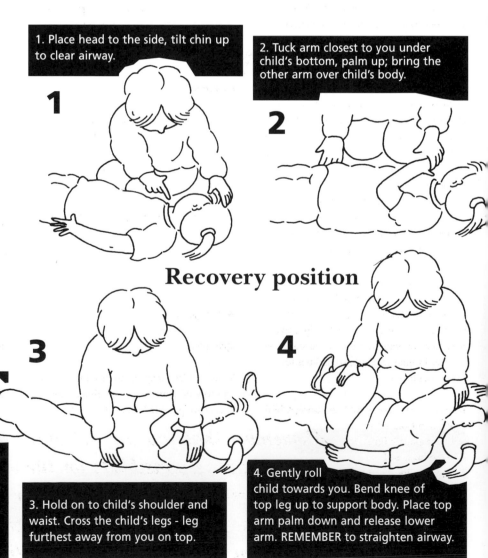

1. Place head to the side, tilt chin up to clear airway.

2. Tuck arm closest to you under child's bottom, palm up; bring the other arm over child's body.

Recovery position

3. Hold on to child's shoulder and waist. Cross the child's legs - leg furthest away from you on top.

4. Gently roll child towards you. Bend knee of top leg up to support body. Place top arm palm down and release lower arm. REMEMBER to straighten airway.

You have a duty to help to protect all children within your care and are well placed to observe and report any causes for concern. But what does this mean in practice?

Child protection: what you need to know

It is a sad fact that child abuse has been happening for many, many years with research showing that it can be found in all socio/economic groups and in all cultures. It is when a child abuse case hits the media headlines that most people become aware of the problems. No-one ever feels comfortable discussing child protection issues and everyone dealing with child abuse will have come to terms with their own feelings and emotions, which can range from concern, shame and fear to anger and revulsion.

One of the underlying principles of the Children Act 1989 is that the welfare of the child is paramount at all times. As a childcare worker you have a duty to help to protect all children within your care and are well placed to observe and report any causes for concern. Often it is the fact that a childcare worker has been able to listen to and observe a child that has helped to ensure that a child at risk receives the protection he or she needs and that their family gains help and support.

Remember that you are not alone and that many people share responsibility for the welfare of children. All agencies, whether voluntary or statutory, and all childcarers have to co-operate with the police and social services in their legal responsibilities to protect children.

In every area there should be an area Child Protection Committee whose responsibility it is to establish and operate the local child protection procedures. All childcare facilities should have their own policies and procedures in place,

with which you must be familiar. These will have been based on the handbook/guidance issued by the local Child Protection Committee. Ask to see a copy of the handbook/guidance.

If your facility needs help in compiling a policy of its own contact your local social services under-eights advisers who will be able to refer you to appropriate guidance. If you are a childminder, discuss with your under-eights officer how you should act if you suspect any form of abuse.

In simple terms:

■ Some types of abuse occur because of the deliberate actions of an adult.

■ Other types of abuse occur because an adult fails to take action.

There are four main categories of abuse:

■ Physical

■ Sexual

■ Emotional

■ Neglect

Some children may experience more than one type of abuse at any one time. (More details are provided overleaf.)

In many areas the child protection co-ordinator will run courses on child protection which will give you an in-depth knowledge and understanding of what child abuse is and the local procedures and routes of referral to follow if you have any concerns. We strongly recommend that you ask at your local social services or contact the NSPCC about courses.

'Remember that you are not alone and that many people share responsibility for the welfare of children. All agencies, whether voluntary or statutory, and all childcarers have to co-operate with the police and social services in their legal responsibilities to protect children.'

The areas of abuse cannot easily be separated from one another. It is likely that if a child is being, for example, physically or sexually abused, the child will also be showing signs of emotional abuse and neglect.

What is child abuse?

Physical abuse

Non-accidental injury - deliberately inflicted. Examples - hitting, shaking, squeezing, burns, bruises, broken limbs, scalds, weals, bites, cuts, gripping. Giving a child inappropriate drugs or alcohol. Attempting to poison, suffocate or drown.

Physical abuse can cause long-term problems. Examples - scars, internal injuries, brain damage, even death.

Neglect

Persistent or severe failure to meet a child's basic needs. Examples - lack of adequate food, inappropriate diet, exposing a child to cold, leaving a child unattended, inappropriate clothing, failing to attend to personal hygiene. Failing to seek medical attention.

Neglect can lead to a child having health problems. The child may be failing to thrive.

Sexual abuse

Taking advantage of a child for the sexual gratification of an adult. Examples - inappropriate fondling, masturbation, oral sex, anal sex, full intercourse, use of foreign objects, exhibitionism, exposing a child to pornography, making pornographic materials, sex rings, ritualistic abuse.

Sexual abuse can have long lasting effects. This will include having difficulties in later life in forming trusting and stable personal relationships.

Emotional abuse

Persistent lack of affection and physical interaction with a child. Examples - continuously failing to show love and affection, persistent rejection, criticism, belittling, bullying, frightening, harassment, taunting, threatening, ridiculing, 'scapegoating', ignoring.

Emotional abuse can cause a child to become nervous, withdrawn, lacking in confidence and self-esteem.

Young children need special care when they are in the sun. They are not aware of how the sun can damage their skin, so it is important that you take precautions for them as well as educate them about the dangers of the sun and sunburn

Caring for **children in the sun**

Over-exposure to the sun's harmful ultra-violet (UV) rays causes sunburn. Redness of the skin, however slight, is a sign that it has been damaged. Getting sunburnt as a child leads to a greater risk of skin cancer later in life, but the sun damage can be avoided. Experts believe that in four out of every five cases skin cancer is a preventable disease.

Skin cancer

More than 40,000 people in the UK are diagnosed with skin cancer every year and around 2,000 people die because of it. It is the second most common cancer in the country.

Doctors have identified several different types of skin cancer. The most important distinction is between malignant melanoma and non-melanoma skin cancer.

■ Malignant melanoma

Malignant melanoma is the least common and most dangerous type of skin cancer. It is thought to be linked to occasional exposure to short periods of intense burning sunlight - such as at weekends or on holiday - and is more common in indoor than outdoor workers.

Melanoma is more prevalent in women than men and is one of the most common cancers among 20- to 35-year-olds.

Malignant melanomas can develop unpredictably and may spread rapidly to other parts of the body, but if recognised

and treated early, chances of survival are good.

■ Non-melanoma

Non-melanoma skin cancers are not usually fatal but may be disfiguring. They are most often found on the face, neck, ears, forearms and hands - all parts of the body that are commonly exposed to the sun. They are found most often in outdoor workers and in the over-fifties. Most cases are caused by a lifetime of over-exposure to the sun.

Sun protection and sunscreens

Sunscreens offer some protection from the sun but should only be used in combination with other methods. They may contain physical barriers, chemical absorbers or

both. Physical barriers reflect the sun's harmful ultraviolet (UV) radiation away from the body. Chemical absorbers soak up UV radiation, reducing the amount of UV that reaches the skin. A sunscreen's SPF (sun protection factor) is a measure of how much radiation it allows through. The higher the SPF the greater the protection.

Two bands of ultraviolet or UV radiation

reach the earth's surface - UVA and UVB. It is important for sunscreens to block out both. The SPF tells you how well a sunscreen blocks out UVB. Different companies use different ways of measuring ability to protect against UVA - the most common is a star system. Always use a sunscreen with an SPF of 15 or above. It should also have three stars (***) or more. But don't rely on sunscreen alone - you should still limit the length of time children spend in the sun.

When using sunscreen, remember:
■ apply it thickly and evenly over all exposed areas;

■ those parts of the body which are not usually exposed to the sun will tend to burn more easily;

■ pay particular attention to ears, neck, bald patches, hands and feet;

■ re-apply regularly, especially after swimming or playing in water.

Based on information supplied by the Department of Health. More information is on their website: www.doh.gov.uk/sunknowhow

---

Remember
■ Avoid burning. You can still get burnt on a day with light cloud or a cool breeze.

■ Keep out of the midday sun. The sun is strongest between 11am and 3pm. Make use of natural shade such as trees.

■ When it's hot, ask parents to send their children dressed in a close woven material, such as a T-shirt, a wide-brimmed hat and sunglasses.

■ Use a high factor sunscreen with an SPF of at least 15.

■ Provide plenty of water to avoid dehydration.

■ Keep babies less than 12 months old out of the sun.

Using sun cream
It is good practice for parents to provide their own sun cream for you to use on their child. This is to ensure that the child suffers no adverse reaction. Sun cream is classed as protection not medication, so there is no need for parents to sign a permission form.

Have you ever thought about the wealth of potential learning experiences available from the world on your doorstep? Angela Milner looks at the value of visits and offers some practical advice on how to go about organising them

Using your **community** as a **resource**

The Foundation Stage *Curriculum Guidance* requires early years practitioners to extend and develop children's knowledge and understanding of the world. Where better to start than with the world on your own doorstep, which is already familiar to the children. It is easily accessible and relates to the day-to-day life of all members of your setting.

Your local area is unique. It provides a resource for your teaching, allowing you to model behaviour, teach specific skills and knowledge, such as developing a child's sense of time or place, and use carefully framed questions to develop the children's understanding and enable you to assess what they know. This questioning approach will enable the children to learn to ask their own questions and not to take their world for granted.

Children need to explore and investigate their world by using all their senses to identify features and objects, look closely at similarities and differences, patterns and change and ask questions about why things are as they are. You will need to link your environment as a resource to your children's learning needs and the stepping stone stages in the Foundation Stage *Curriculum Guidance* moving through a three-stage approach:

■ **Identification**
Involves the children in:
Observing – handling – listening – naming – describing – labelling – interpreting - similarities and differences

Involves adults in:
Facilitating and questioning - encouraging the children to communicate orally about their findings.
■ **Analysis**

Our Walk

Involves the children in:
Making relationships – sorting – matching – ordering – sequencing – comparing – classification – making sense of the world

Involves adults in:
Encouraging children to search for patterns and explanations; continuing to encourage children to communicate orally and to develop other ways of recording/ communicating their findings.

■ **Evaluation**
Involves the children in:
Investigational skills - using their findings – formulating their own predictions – developing

What resources do we mean?
There are bound to be some of these features nearby whether your setting is in the town, city, countryside or suburbs: street, road; building - the doctors, the clinic, the post office, the school, shops; a park, fields, woodland; water features; vehicles; emergency services; viewing points where you can look down on an area; industrial estates; places of employment; homes; building sites; offices; services, for example the hairdressers.

their sense of reasoning – explaining – interpreting – judging

Involves adults in:
Promoting critical thinking skills and encouraging children to ask their own questions and look for their own solutions as well as record their finding using an appropriate medium of communication.

First-hand explorations

The local environment provides a meaningful way of approaching many traditional themes covered in the early years, for example, 'The environment', 'Shops', 'Roads and traffic', 'Journeys', 'Our street/town', 'Buildings', 'Weather', 'Rocks and soil', 'The seasons'.

Using the world on your doorstep means that children can learn:

■ *about* their environment by acquiring knowledge and understanding about their world;

■ *through* the environment using it as a first-hand resource for learning;

■ *for* the environment considering issues, values and attitudes that affect themselves and their environment.

Children learn best through sensory exploration, but remember that some young children's senses are far more sophisticated in certain areas than others. Some children will not be able to see or hear as well as others and this needs to be taken into account when planning your activities. You may need to provide supplementary or alternative experiences for children with any sensory impairment.

Organising trips

You motto should always be 'Safety first!' Follow these three rules and you shouldn't go far wrong:

■ **Background preparation:**

All settings must follow their own policies in relation to health and safety and their LEA's fieldwork guidelines. You must seek the children's parents' or carers' permission and make sure that you have permission from the manager of your own setting. You should also check children's medical forms for useful information such as allergies. You must leave lists in school to indicate who has gone where with whom.

■ **Planning and preparing other adults:**

Going out of school needs to be planned like a military campaign. You should always explore the venue and route yourself to make sure you have planned for every possible eventuality and conduct a risk assessment of the area you intend to use. This way you can identify any hazards such as narrow pavements, busy roads and consider the necessary precautions. This will not only help with your planning for children's learning but also help you to brief the other adults involved.

■ **Prepare the children:**

Prepare the children for the activities they will be engaged in before you go out. Check that they have appropriate clothing to match your activity and that you have all the

equipment with you, that you will need to explore your environment. This includes a first aid kit.

With young children you should try to visit the locality a little and often for short periods of no more than ten to thirty minutes (even though it might take longer than this to get all the children ready). Remember to use as many trained adults and helpers as you can. You should be working with very small groups of two to three children, in accordance with your own setting's and LEA guidance. Providing a dedicated adult in a controlled learning context is the key to your success. Always ensure that the children know where you are going and why. Discussion before and after

such visits with the children is essential if you are to make the most of learning opportunities. Similarly, all adults need to be well prepared and briefed about risk factors and health and safety issues as well as be able to get the most out of planned and spontaneous learning opportunities which arise whilst you are out and about. Adults need to take with them everything they might need and need to be able to return with their group to your setting if someone falls over or if the children have gained all they can from the activity.

Below are some things to try when you take children out and about to explore their locality for the first time (see boxes).

Angela Milner

The advantages of using the world on your doorstep

■ It is within easy walking distance so you can transport children to different learning environments relatively quickly and easily.

■ You can work on a small and meaningful scale with young children in a context with which they are already familiar and in which they and you feel safe.

■ You can make short visits repeatedly to look at different aspects of the real world.

■ You can provide a range of learning experiences such as: providing first-hand learning experiences, independent learning opportunities and the opportunity to work in groups and co-operate with others

These experiences could lead into activities undertaken outside such as observational drawings or can enhance subsequent learning experiences back inside such as model making and simple map making.

Which way shall we go?

Directional games can be played as you walk along. Ask the children what they can see when they look up, down, straight ahead, behind, to their right or left. Children may need some prompts to help them with 'left' and 'right'. Large arrow cards turned to point in the direction you want them to look work well. Children can draw what they see or rub with paper and a large wax crayon surfaces they find. Adults can show children maps of journeys made. Take photographs while you are out and about and use them to make a large picture map to describe your journey or to jog children's memories about their visit and enable them to write about their walk. Photographs of previous journeys can be used to compare how things have changed.

Maths everywhere

Collecting, counting and simple measuring can all be done outside. Which is the longest road by pacing it out? How many lamp-posts can they find? Where do they find numbers? (front doors, hydrant signs, phone numbers on notices) Children can collect things that are safe and appropriate to collect - linked to a colour, shape or association, for example.

Children's views

As you walk along, ask children whether or not they like the area. Why or why not? What doesn't it have? What would make it a better place to visit?

Sensory walks

Go on a journey to practise observational skills and develop children's vocabulary. Have you walked around your locality in the different seasons? Do you use this opportunity to really develop the children's senses – looking, listening, feeling and touching?

As you walk around, constantly talk to the children and ask them questions - What can you see? What do we call things? Which of these words do children know - doors, windows, drainpipes, grates, steps, flagstones, pavement? Do they use them accurately?

Look at and feel textures; look at and describe patterns, sizes, shapes and materials. Can the children describe the environment – Is it natural? green? built? Can they spot any creatures/people that live there?

Print everywhere

Go on a word or letter hunt. Where do the children see print in the environment? Can the children record it with a camera? What does it say? Why do the children think there is so much print in our environment? How does it help them and us?

If you have found that the children have gained from this first-hand experience then try taking them further afield physically or by using secondary sources such as television, music, costume, role play, visitors, parents, photographs and ICT.

Chapter 8

Unit M3: Contribute to the achievement of organisational requirements

About this unit

This unit is about how you work with others. You need to be clear about your role, and how it fits in with the organisation of your setting. As an assistant, you will have to carry out instructions, and give feedback on the work you have done. You will need to respond positively to other staff's suggestions for your own development and improvement. Be aware of your limited responsibility and be careful not to undermine other members of staff when making suggestions for change. However, you do have a contribution to make to the development of good practice. You will be involved in evaluating existing practice and making suggestions for improvement. You need to have a good knowledge of the setting's policies and procedures, and work within them. Make sure you have read and understood them before continuing with this unit. Discuss them with your supervisor.

This unit really pulls together much of what you have achieved during your training. It's about your attitude to your job, and to your colleagues, as well as to the children and the parents. It's crucial that you are able to interact in a positive, professional and friendly manner. Your assessor will almost certainly have picked up some of the evidence, possibly all of it, as she has observed you working on other units. It will be important for her to get feedback from your supervisor and manager, because they work with you every day, and will have a good picture of how you have developed in the time you have been in training. The very fact that you are doing an NVQ and constantly reflecting on your own practice is good evidence for this unit.

Values

The **welfare of the child** and **the reflective practitioner** are key values in this unit. In everything you do, you need to reflect on how it will affect the child. The other two values important in this unit are **working with other professionals** - the whole unit is centred on this - and confidentiality. It's as important to maintain **confidentiality** about colleagues as it is for the children and their families.

This list of ten golden rules has been adapted from a list drawn up a number of years ago by the Professional Association of Nursery Nurses. It sums up the values you need to believe in as a childcare worker:

1. Value and respect every child as an individual and meet her or his needs to the best of your ability.

2. Always try to be motivated and enthusiastic. Only the best is good enough for children.

3. Make sure you know and understand the policies and practices of your workplace, and that you follow them.

4. Recognise your own strengths, and use them to contribute to the work of the team.

5. Recognise your own weaknesses, find ways of improving them and accept support when you need it.

6. Respect the strengths and weaknesses of your colleagues, value their contribution and give them the support they need.

7. Be reliable and punctual. The rest of the team are depending on you.

8. Respect the child's parents or carers, and work with them for the benefit of the child.

9. Recognise the skills of other agencies and professionals and cooperate with them.

10. Be aware of the need for confidentiality and a professional approach at all times

Getting started

In this unit you need to show how you :

◆ carry out instructions and provide feedback

◆ contribute to the development of good practice

Your assessor should be able to cross reference some of it from previous units. Discuss this with your assessor and agree an **assessment plan**.

Element M3.1 Carry out instructions and provide feedback

Key issues

To work successfully with children, you also need to work well as a member of a team. You will have to follow instructions, you will be accountable to other members of the team for what you do, and you also need to take the initiative to do things when they are needed as part of the normal routine. You must respect the opinions of others even when they are different from your own, and discuss differences in a professional manner. You need to be aware of what you are good at and where you need to develop and improve.

When being given instructions, it's a good idea to have a little notebook and write them down, unless you're sure you can remember them accurately. If you don't understand an instruction, or don't know how to do what you've been asked, don't be afraid to say so. If you think you need help, ask for it. Carry out the task to the best of your ability, and in the appropriate time.

If you've been asked to give feedback about the task you've done, make sure you do it. Again, make notes if you need to, so that your feedback is accurate and you don't forget anything. For instance, you might have been asked to mix the paints, and make a note of which colours are running low and need replacing. Or you may have been asked to play a colour game with a group of children, and to note which colours individual children can recognise. You would certainly need to write this down, as it's unlikely that you'll remember otherwise. If anything unexpected happens, such as an accident, or a child has hurt another child, again you will need to report this accurately.

Sometimes a job which seemed simple turns out to be more serious than you thought, and outside of your responsibility. For instance, you have been asked to give out the children's paintings to the parents as they come in to collect the children, and one parent comes and tells you about a worry she has about her child being picked on by another child in the nursery. You must refer this on, and not try to answer it yourself. Treat anything you are told by parents with strict confidentiality. Even within the nursery, only the staff who need to know should be informed.

There are often times, when working with children, when other staff will be too busy to tell you what to do, and you need to show initiative and get on with the job. If you're on a rota for carrying out certain routine tasks, make sure you do them without having to be reminded. Learn how to prioritise your jobs, and manage your time effectively. When you're not

carrying out a specific task set for you, check with your supervisor whether there is anything she wants you to do, and if not, get involved in the children's play. Never stand doing nothing. Always be aware of what's going on around you, and where you see a need, do something about it or refer it to a colleague if necessary.

The **knowledge evidence** statements for this element are 2, 3, 4, 8 and 15. You need to show that you understand the importance of:

◆ prioritising and managing your time efficiently

◆ listening and recording information accurately

◆ carrying out instructions as specified

◆ confidentiality

You should by now have had some training on how to work well with others in the team. Your assessor is likely to check your understanding through your other evidence and questioning.

Which type of evidence?

Your assessor will have seen you many times carrying out activities with the children, and carrying out instructions, so she should be able to **cross reference** the evidence for this element. She may want to ask you some **questions** to make sure you understand the issues involved. If you have kept a notebook or **diary**, you can use this as additional evidence. Some of your **reflective accounts** will also show how you have fulfilled some of the evidence. It would be helpful to have a **witness testimon**y from your supervisor to say that you have carried out instructions and given feedback competently over a period of time. She could write one statement for the two elements of the unit.

Element M3.2 Contribute to the development of good practice

Key issues

You will hopefully be given the chance to take part in staff discussions and staff meetings. These are an invaluable way of extending your understanding of the policies and practices of the setting, and an opportunity for you to contribute suggestions for changing practices within your responsibility. Staff at nurseries have often said that they like having people in the setting who are training because they bring new ideas with them, so don't be afraid to speak up if you think you have a good idea.

As you will be working closely with the children, you will have a responsibility, along with the other staff, to report back on how the activities you have carried out have helped (or hindered) the children's learning and development, and to join in discussions about how practice might be improved. If you have been given suggestions about how to change your practice for the better, accept it positively and put it into practice. Take advantage of courses on offer through the local EYDCP. Your nursery manager will discuss these with you if you're employed. If not, you can still ask about them. Many nursery managers will include trainees when applying for courses.

Some staff development will take place in the nursery. Sometimes members of staff with particular expertise will give guidance and support to the rest of the staff. The nursery may also invite outside professionals in to talk to the staff, or people with knowledge of a specialist area. Take part in these if you can. Also watch how other members of staff do things. You will learn a lot in this way.

You may have a regular staff appraisal or review, where the manager discusses your work, and highlights your strengths and areas in your work that you need to develop. This should be a positive experience, which helps you and your setting to continuously develop good practice. Some settings are also members of a quality assurance scheme, which aims to raise the quality of childcare and education.

Sometimes you will see things you would do differently. If you have serious concerns about the practice of a member of staff you may feel you can discuss with her why she is doing it. Or you may be able to bring it up as a general question in a staff

meeting. If you don't feel able to do this, have a quiet word with your line manager or the nursery manager. You will have to handle this carefully, but if you are concerned that it may be affecting the well-being of the children, you do need to do something about it.

The **knowledge evidence** statements for this element are 1, 5, 6, 7, 9, 10, 11, 12, 13 and 14. You need to show that you understand:

◆ the value of developing the setting through training, consultation and support of individuals

◆ the value of your own contribution to developing and evaluating good practice

◆ the current practice and objectives of the setting, and how information is shared

◆ why and when to bring in or use outside experts

◆ how to share ideas with others in your setting

◆ your own responsibility to follow through ideas and how you will do it

◆ how to act appropriately when you have identified unsatisfactory practice being used

Many of these issues will be covered in the witness testimony, or cross referenced from other units.

Which type of evidence?

Your assessor doesn't need to do any observation for this element, but if she has had the opportunity to see evidence through other observations, so much the better. She may want to ask you **questions** about how you have contributed to developing good practice, or you could write a **reflective account** about ways you have contributed.

You may already have some examples, so **cross reference** where you can. For example, some of your evaluations on your activity plans in other units may have led to changes in your practice.

You do need a **witness testimony** from your supervisor or the nursery manager to say that you have contributed to the development of good practice. One statement for the two elements would be best. If there are any policies and documents which you have been involved in developing, put a copy in as evidence, saying how you were involved. You need to ask permission first.

A successful team depends on members supporting each other. Where staff work together as a team, they do their jobs better, they enjoy their jobs more – and the children benefit as a result

How to be a good team member

As an early years worker, you will inevitably be working with other adults, whether as a nanny with the parents or in a larger setting such as a nursery or school, within a multi-professional team. Each team will be different, because it's made up of individuals with their unique set of characteristics, strengths and needs. There may be people you find difficult to work with, and you will have to work out for yourself how to deal with this. The children's welfare is of paramount importance, and very much depends on a good atmosphere where adults are seen to be cooperative and friendly.

Your role

The nature of your role will depend on the setting, and your position within the team. Most jobs have a job description so that you are aware of what is required of you. As a member of the team, you will have to carry out tasks which you have been given. Listen carefully to instructions and don't be afraid to ask if you haven't fully understood. If you don't feel able to carry out the task on your own, ask for support. But do show initiative to work on your own. If you have been asked to report back on what you have done, or if you have been asked to keep a record of children's development, do it promptly and accurately. If you have a number of tasks, organise your time and carry them out methodically.

Your training will have given you a good foundation for your work with young children, but don't think that you know it all. If you can, go on to achieve your Level 3 qualification. Take the opportunity whenever you can to increase your knowledge and experience. Your local Early Years Development and Childcare Partnership will have many courses on offer throughout the year, and national organisations such as Early Education and the National Children's Bureau organise conferences regularly. Magazines such as *Practical Pre-school* keep you up-to-date with the most recent news, research and events, as well as many practical ideas.

Shared aims

Each member of the team comes with his or her own philosophies and ideas, and inevitably there will be differences which need to be worked through. Everyone needs to feel that they have contributed to the overall philosophy and aims of the setting. The manager will need to have a clear vision of what she or he hopes to achieve, but it's essential to involve the whole team. If the whole team has been involved in developing policies, every member of staff will have had the opportunity to discuss the issues fully. Once a decision is made, all members of the team need to work towards putting it into practice, even if there is some personal disagreement about certain aspects. You must stand by team decisions, even if you disagree. It's essential that all members of the team are giving the same message, both to the children and to the parents.

Managing relationships

An important aspect of the work of the early years team is to develop relationships - not only with the children but with each other. The early years worker is a role model for the children, so personal relationships within the team will affect them. Conflicts will probably arise from time to time, but it's vital to deal with them in a way which does not jeopardise the children's well-being.

There are other things which affect relationships in the workplace - issues about equality in relation to gender, race, religion, sexual orientation, additional needs or disability. Children have few role models who are men, black or disabled in the early years environment. We need to find ways of encouraging people from these groups into early years care and education and we need to examine our own attitudes to these issues. Are we as professionals open enough to equality for all groups? How can we as a team work towards encouraging people other than able-bodied, white women into the profession? There has traditionally been a stigma attached to men who want to work with young children. They have been refused jobs, or treated with suspicion in some settings, and yet they are tremendously important as role models, especially for children who have no father living with them.

Team meetings

Most settings hold regular team meetings. Some meetings will be informal, others will be more organised, with an agenda. But however informal the meeting, it's important to record the outcomes and follow-up needed, otherwise things will not get done. Meetings will be held for a variety of reasons - a full or part staff meeting, a case conference, a management meeting, a meeting with parents, or to deal with a specific issue such as a behaviour difficulty, or the next parents' evening.

You need to know what's expected of you at the meeting. A good manager will let you know beforehand. If you feel you can make a valid contribution but you're unsure whether it's appropriate for you to comment, write down your comment and hand it to your manager. She will ask you to speak if she wishes.

Liaising with other professionals and the community

It's important for you as a staff to establish good links with external professionals and the local community. You may be asked to contribute to case conferences about children who are having difficulties. You may be asked to observe these children on a day-to-day basis. You will need to be confident to record and report your findings accurately.

You can also extend children's experience of the world around them through inviting men and women in from a wide range of walks of life, and those doing non-traditional jobs. Invite parents, grandparents and other adults from the local community.

'Working with young children is both rewarding and demanding. Early years workers need to support each other. They need time to reflect and share concerns with colleagues.''

Supporting each other

A successful team depends upon members supporting each other. Each member of the team should be prepared to offer help, contribute ideas and information, and also to listen. You may feel that as an assistant you are not able to contribute, but you may have more up-to-date ideas because you have recently trained. You may have a particular talent or skill which will enhance the work of the team. Don't be afraid to put forward your own ideas, but do it in a positive and friendly way, without being over-assertive.

Working with young children is both rewarding and demanding. Early years workers need to support each other. They need time to reflect and share concerns with colleagues. One important source of support is feedback and praise. We know that children thrive on praise and encouragement, and this is equally true of adults. Adults are not good at saying well done to each other, and yet most of us can quickly become discouraged and disheartened if the good things we do are ignored, or if we are criticised unduly.

Staff will come from a diversity of backgrounds. This can bring in a richness of experiences, talent and ideas to the setting,

but it can also bring misunderstandings. It's important for the team to listen to each other, to be open to learning from each other and to make the best possible use of individual skills and experiences.

Communication

Good communication at all levels is essential in order to ensure that the setting runs smoothly, and to show all members of the team that they are valued. Individual members of the team need to listen to each other. There should be opportunities for frequent discussions with a senior member of staff to deal with any concerns as they arise. It's helpful for staff to join local support groups, so that they don't become isolated, and they can share good practice. Staff should have the opportunity for staff appraisal or review on a regular basis.

Conflict

Conflicts will arise from time to time. They are part of everyday life. But if they are not dealt with quickly and effectively, this can have serious consequences. It will result in a very poor environment for the children. Therefore, any conflicts must be dealt with sensitively, and away from the children.

You can minimise conflicts by following a few simple rules. Deal with small issues before they become big ones. If there is a misunderstanding, stay calm and listen to the person involved. Put your case firmly, but not aggressively. Be professional, and try to reach an outcome that you can both live with. You need to be able to admit if you're in the wrong, or compromise if you are in disagreement about an issue. Don't gossip to other members of the team about it. If you cannot solve the problem yourself, you will need to take it to your supervisor or manager. Accept the decision made by your manager with good grace.

You never stop learning - even after many years of experience the professional worker is still looking for ways to improve his or her practice.

Mary Townsend

Chapter 9

Unit P1: Relate to parents

About this unit

In this unit you will show how you get on with parents, and how you share the care and education of the children with their parents. Parents know their children better than anyone, and it's vital that you recognise and take account of that in everything that you do.

The Children Act of 1989 states that children should be cared for in ways consistent with family values and practices, and expressed wishes. This includes taking account of religion, origin, cultural and linguistic background. Before a child starts at the nursery, the manager will have found out all sorts of information about the child. You may not have access to the records, because they are confidential, but your supervisor will make sure you know what you need to know in order to care for the child in line with the parents' wishes. For instance, whether the child has any medical conditions or allergies, her sleep routines, whether she needs a comfort object and so on.

Remember!
Parents know their own children better than anyone. They are their children's first educators. You must respect that.

As an assistant, you may not have any chance to speak to parents, especially if you work in a school setting. You may be more likely to be able to talk to them regularly in a nursery or playgroup. Your assessor will discuss with your supervisor whether there will be opportunities for you to talk to parents. No observation is required for this unit, because of the difficulties for some candidates. However, it's better if there are some opportunities to observe how you relate to parents.

Links with other units

There are close links with Unit C5, where we looked at settling children into the setting. You may have had contact with parents if you went on an outing (E2.6). Check whether you have any evidence you can cross reference.

Values

As you would expect, the emphasis in both elements is on the **welfare of the child** and **working in partnership with parents**. The whole unit is about how you work with parents to provide the best care and education possible for their child. The initial contact is the most important time for establishing a good relationship with parents. If you get that right, the parent and children will be happy and confident in the setting. This is a two-way partnership, so you must listen to parents. You may be the professional, but parents know their children better than anyone, and have a right to say what they want for them.

As a **reflective practitioner**, you need to reflect on how well you communicate with parents and take account of their wishes. **Children's learning and development** is important in Element 2, which is about taking account of parents' wishes in relation to the care of their children, so that there is continuity between what happens at home and in the care/education setting.

You need to be aware of **equal opportunities** and **anti-discrimination** through taking account of the different family and cultural practices, such as dietary requirements. You need to respect the fact that families may have different values and practices than your own. And you must maintain **confidentiality** about all information you receive from or about parents. As we have said, you may have little or no contact with parents, but you do need to be aware of the setting's policies on working with parents, so that you know what is expected of you.

Getting started

In this unit you will need to show how you:

◆ interact and share information with parents about their children

◆ share the care of children with their parents

Read through the two elements and make sure you understand them. Fill in your personal skills checklist (see page 21) to help you identify which areas you feel confident about and which you need training, practice or further experience in. You will need training in this important area, so find out from your assessor when the relevant training will take place, if you haven't done it already.

Element P1.1 Interact and share information with parents about their children

Key issues

It's a very anxious time for parents when their child starts attending a care or education setting for the first time. Every parent needs to feel confident in the care and education their child is receiving. The way you communicate with parents and their children will affect how confident they feel. Children will feel more secure if they see that the staff and their parents are friendly towards each other. So when a parent walks in with their child, always greet them with a word and a smile. If it's your responsibility, go up to them and welcome the child. Ask the parent if there is anything you need to know. If that is not your responsibility, at least smile and say hello.

These tips will help you to develop a good relationship with parents:

◆ Look relaxed - smile!

◆ Use the parent's preferred name

◆ Listen to what the parent is saying

◆ Make eye contact

◆ Avoid using jargon

◆ Don't talk down to parents

◆ Treat all parents equally

Your manager will have gathered a lot of information about each child from the parents when they started. Your setting will have registration forms which include all the information they are required to keep. Ask if you can see a copy of this. You may not have access to individual children's records, but at least you will know what information is collected. Make sure in your day-to-day work that you take account of any information passed on to you by your supervisor.

Some nurseries write a daily report on each child, especially for very young children, so that parents are clear about how many feeds, sleeps and so on the child has had, and any milestones in their development. Some nurseries have a diary which they encourage parents to write in as well, so that there is two-way communication and information exchange. This is good practice, because it shows the parents that you value their opinion. If you get the opportunity, at the end of the day show parents what their child has done - perhaps a painting or a model, or it could be that they've been very helpful or kind to another child. Children will feel a great sense of achievement if their parents have praised them for work you have shown them or something good you have told them about. You must not, however, pass on any information beyond your responsibility to report. If a parent asks you anything outside your responsibility, refer them on to your supervisor.

Some settings have a display board with photographs and captions telling parents what activities the children do and what they gain from them. This is a really good way of showing parents the benefit of learning through play. Many settings also have a newsletter to keep parents informed. Find out all the things your setting does and make a note of them.

The **knowledge evidence** statements for this element are 1, 2, 3, 5, 6, 7, 8 and 9. You need to show that you understand:

◆ why it is better for the child's care and education to develop good relationships with the parents

◆ which information you can pass on to parents and which is beyond your responsibility

◆ the policy of the setting on confidentiality (also P1.2)

◆ some parents' apprehension and lack of confidence when talking to staff